Francis Young is a Fellow of the Royal Historical Society and gained a PhD in history from the University of Cambridge. He is the author and editor of seven previous books. These include *English Catholics and the Supernatural, 1553–1829* (2013), *The Gages of Hengrave and Suffolk Catholicism, 1640–1767* (2015), *The Abbey of Bury St Edmunds: History, Legacy and Discovery* (2016) and *A History of Exorcism in Catholic Christianity* (2016). He broadcasts regularly for the BBC on historical topics and is centrally involved in efforts to locate the coffin of St Edmund, Martyred Monarch of the East Angles. His new book, *Edmund: In Search of England's Lost King*, will be published by I.B.Tauris in 2018.

'The study of magic in medieval and early modern England has been dominated by its having been located within the study of witchcraft, to the detriment of its study outside the history of witchcraft accusations. Legal histories of treason have similarly marginalised the role of magic. This has led to the virtual ignoring of the relationship between elite magic's significant role in political crime and in accusations of treason against its practitioners. The first book devoted to the study of magic and political crime, Francis Young's new volume substantially redresses this situation. Taking us on a fascinating journey through the terrain of treasonous magic, it illuminates how, from the fourteenth to the seventeenth century, treasonous activities against both the monarch and the government were often driven by magical practices – whether by means of astrological calculations, the stabbing or melting of effigies or occult knowledge of poisons. It makes an original and significant addition both to modern studies of the European magical tradition and to the political history of medieval and early modern England, while

serving too as a salutary reminder that that history cannot be fully understood without recognition of the intimate relation between the magical and the monarchical.'
– Philip C. Almond, Emeritus Professor of Religion, University of Queensland

'While most histories of medieval and early modern magic have focused either on the theories and practices of magic, or on its troubled relationship with religious authority, Francis Young's impressively argued and richly documented study offers a new area of investigation: the close links between moments of political instability, fears of sedition and treason and accusations of harmful magic. Young's book will be warmly welcomed by all those who work on the social and cultural history of European magic and the history of ideas.'
– Stephen Clucas, Reader in Early Modern Intellectual History, Birkbeck, University of London

'Francis Young's new book is an accessible and wide-ranging narrative history of a fascinating subject: magical treason, its methods, practitioners and – supposedly – its "victims". Atmospheric and engaging, it is notably well written.'
– Marion Gibson, Professor of Renaissance and Magical Literatures, University of Exeter

'This volume makes an important contribution to the field and is a welcome counterbalance to the literature on witchcraft, which tends to view the history of magic simply as a road leading to the witch trials. It brings together the scattered literature on treasonous magic and convincingly demonstrates that magical threats interwoven with courtly politics and political intrigue were key elements in the shifting approaches to magic in early modern England.'
– Frank Klaassen, Associate Professor of History, University of Saskatchewan, author of *The Transformations of Magic: Illicit Learned Magic in the Later Middle Ages and Renaissance*

FRANCIS YOUNG

MAGIC AS A POLITICAL CRIME
IN MEDIEVAL AND EARLY MODERN ENGLAND

A History of Sorcery and Treason

I.B. TAURIS
LONDON • NEW YORK • OXFORD • NEW DELHI • SYDNEY

For Rachel

I.B. TAURIS
Bloomsbury Publishing Plc
50 Bedford Square, London, WC1B 3DP, UK
1385 Broadway, New York, NY 10018, USA

BLOOMSBURY, I.B. TAURIS and the I.B. Tauris logo
are trademarks of Bloomsbury Publishing Plc

First published in Great Britain 2018
Paperback edition first published 2020

Copyright © Francis Young, 2018

Francis Young has asserted her right under the Copyright,
Designs and Patents Act, 1988, to be identified as Author of this work.

All rights reserved. No part of this publication may be reproduced or transmitted in any form or by any means, electronic or mechanical, including photocopying, recording, or any information storage or retrieval system, without prior permission in writing from the publishers.

Bloomsbury Publishing Plc does not have any control over, or responsibility for, any third-party websites referred to or in this book. All internet addresses given in this book were correct at the time of going to press. The author and publisher regret any inconvenience caused if addresses have changed or sites have ceased to exist, but can accept no responsibility for any such changes.

A catalogue record for this book is available from the British Library.

A catalog record for this book is available from the Library of Congress.

ISBN: HB: 978-1-7883-1021-5
PB: 978-0-7556-0275-9
ePDF: 978-1-7867-3291-0
eBook: 978-1-7867-2291-1

Series: International Library of Historical Studies, 107

Typeset in Stone Serif by OKS Prepress Services, Chennai, India

To find out more about our authors and books visit
www.bloomsbury.com and sign up for our newsletters.

Contents

Preface ix
Abbreviations xiii
Chronology xv

Introduction 1
   Histories of Magic as Political Crime 4
   Studying Magic as Political Crime 7
   Defining Magic 8
   Magic and Witchcraft 12
   Magic and Treason 16
   Structure of the Book 20

1. **'Compassing and Imagining': Magic as a Political Crime in Medieval England** 23
   John of Nottingham and the Plot Against Edward II 27
   Magic and the Statute of Treason 31
   Application of the Statute of Treason 32
   The Case of Eleanor Cobham 35
   Magic in the Wars of the Roses 46
   The Reign of Henry VII 51
   Conclusion 53

2. **Treason, Sorcery and Prophecy in The Early English Reformation, 1534–58** 55
   The Tudors and the English Reformation 57
   Prophecy and Treason 61
   Magic and Treason at Court 70

	The Reigns of Edward VI and Mary	78
	Conclusion	84
3.	**Elizabeth versus The 'Popish Conjurers', 1558–77**	87
	The Elizabethan Reformation	87
	The Accession of Elizabeth	89
	The Fortescue Conspiracy	91
	The 1559 Bill against Sorcery, Witchcraft and Buggery	93
	The Waldegrave and Pole Conspiracies	95
	The Burning of St Paul's	105
	The 1563 Act Against Conjuration and Witchcraft	108
	The Abduction and Trial of John Story	111
	The Case of Rowland Jenks	116
	Conclusion	118
4.	**'A Traitorous Heart to the Queen': Effigies and Witch-Hunts, 1578–1603**	119
	Effigy Magic	121
	John Dee and the Wax Effigies	123
	Leicester's Witch-Hunt	129
	Vincent Murphyn's Conspiracy	139
	The 1580 Act for Suppressing Seditious Words and Rumours	140
	'Anabaptistical Wizards'	141
	Elizabeth's Last Years	144
	Magical Treason in Shakespeare's *Henry VI Part Two*	147
	Conclusion	150
5.	**'A Breach in Nature': Magic as a Political Crime in Early Stuart England, 1603–42**	153
	James VI and Magical Treason	154
	James's English Reign	161
	The Case of Sir Thomas Lake	167
	Magical Treason in the Plays of Shakespeare	170
	The Poisoning of James I	172
	Towards Civil War	176
6.	**The Decline of Magic as a Political Crime, 1642–1700**	179
	Political Magic in the English Civil Wars	180
	Interregnum and Restoration: The Decline of Magical Treason	182
	Witchcraft and Treason	186
	England and the 'Affair of the Poisons'	188

Treason without Magic: The Popish Plot	193
Magic and Politics Part Company	195
Echoes	197
Conclusion	202
Notes	205
Bibliography	231
Index	243

Preface

Between the fourteenth and seventeenth centuries treasonous plots and other forms of subversion directed against the monarch and government often contained a magical element – whether in the form of illicit astrological calculation, the stabbing or melting of effigies, or occult knowledge of poisoning. A number of such cases played a pivotal role in well-known political events: the 1441 trial of Eleanor Cobham, duchess of Gloucester, discredited her husband and led ultimately to the Wars of the Roses; George, duke of Clarence's attempt to defend a servant accused of magical treason led to his drowning in a butt of wine in 1478; and Richard III's accusations of magic against Edward IV's queen, Elizabeth Woodville, were key to his rise to power. However, other less well-known magical plots were of equal concern to medieval, Tudor and Stuart governments at the time, such as the panic that surrounded a supposed plot to kill Queen Elizabeth and her advisors using wax effigies uncovered in 1578, which lasted over two years. Even James I was widely rumoured to have been murdered by magical poisoning in 1625. Although magic as a form of political crime never gained the prominence in England that it enjoyed in early modern Scotland or France, it remained a significant source of concern to governments that has largely been overlooked by historians.

The idea for this book emerged from the process of writing my earlier monograph *English Catholics and the Supernatural, 1553–1829* (2013), which examined the attitudes of post-Reformation English

Catholics towards ghosts, witchcraft, magic and exorcism of demons. There I addressed early modern Catholic attitudes towards magic, but restrictions of time and space did not permit me to explore thoroughly the accusations of magic levelled against Catholics, who from 1534 onwards (apart from the interlude of Mary I's reign in 1553–8) often found themselves politically at odds with English governments. Accusations of treasonous magic were by no means exclusively aimed against Catholics, but the anti-Catholic trope of Catholic obsession with superstitious ritual, combined with the real existence of Catholic plots involving Mary, Queen of Scots and Yorkist pretenders in the reign of Elizabeth, meant that Catholics were often the focus of post-Reformation accusations of treasonous magic. Having previously undertaken the first study of the relationship between English Catholics and supernatural belief, it seemed appropriate for me to attempt this first study of an overlooked aspect of treason accusations as well.

A history of magic as a political crime in England must transgress the customary periodisation of medieval and early modern history, since most of the evidence suggests that the practices used (or alleged to have been used) by magical traitors in the sixteenth and seventeenth centuries were essentially survivals or revivals of medieval techniques. Furthermore, memory of famous medieval treasons involving magic was kept alive in the sixteenth century in popular chronicles as well as in dramas such as Shakespeare's *Henry VI Part Two*, which reinterpreted Eleanor Cobham's conjurations for an early modern theatre audience. Early modern plots frequently echoed their medieval antecedents, and although the political and religious motivations behind accusations may have changed over time, early modern magical treasons cannot be truly understood apart from their medieval origins.

Many people have provided inspiration, encouragement and guidance for this book. I am grateful to James Noyes for directing me to I.B.Tauris and to Alex Wright for being an immensely supportive editor and guiding this project smoothly towards publication. I am indebted to Richard Kieckhefer, Claire Fanger and Frank Klaassen for their early encouragement, to Christina Cameron for kindly proof-reading the text, and to Inga Jones for pointing me in the direction of some important material on the English Civil War. I thank the staff of the British Library manuscripts and rare books rooms, and of the manuscripts and rare books rooms at Cambridge University Library, the National Archives at Kew and everywhere else that I have conducted research over the past three years. My wife Rachel has, as always, earned my greatest debt of gratitude by patiently supporting my scholarship and recondite preoccupations, and this book is dedicated to her.

All translations from Latin, French, Scots and Spanish are my own unless otherwise stated, and naturally I take responsibility for all errors in any translation or transcription. I am grateful to Esmeralda Salgado for reviewing my translations from the original Spanish. The transcription of magical texts presents particular difficulties, as it is sometimes a challenge to distinguish between magical *nomina ignota* (exotic-sounding names without obvious meaning, deliberately inserted into texts) and abbreviated Latin or English. In transcriptions I have expanded abbreviated words in square brackets [thus] and indicated later insertions by the original scribe \thus/. In quoted extracts from medieval and early modern texts I have modernised the spelling, but have made no attempt to modernise grammar or substitute contemporary equivalents for obsolete vocabulary.

All dates given in the text are Old Style (following the old Julian Calendar), although I have taken the year to begin on 1 January. All line numbers of quotations from Shakespeare's plays are taken from *William Shakespeare: The Complete Works*, ed. S. Wells, G. Taylor, J. Jowett, and W. Montgomery (1986).

Abbreviations

Acts of the Privy Council	Acts of the Privy Council of England (London HMSO, 1890–1974), 45 vols
BL	British Library
CSPD	Calendar of State Papers: Domestic Series, of the reigns of Edward VI, Mary, Elizabeth and James I, 1547–[1625], ed. R. Lemon and M. A. E. Green (London: HMSO, 1856–72), 12 vols
HMSO	His/Her Majesty's Stationery Office
Letters and Papers	Letters and Papers, Foreign and Domestic, of the Reign of Henry VIII, ed. J. Brewer, J. Gairdner and R. Brodie (1892–1932), 21 vols
Life and Letters	The Life and Letters of Thomas Cromwell (Oxford: Oxford University Press, 1902), 2 vols
MS(S)	manuscript(s)
ODNB	The Oxford Dictionary of National Biography (Oxford: Oxford University Press, 2004), 60 vols
Salisbury MSS	Calendar of the Manuscripts of the Most Hon. the Marquis of Salisbury (London: HMSO, 1883–1973), 24 vols
Simancas	Calendar of Letters and State Papers relating to English Affairs: preserved principally in the Archives of Simancas, ed. M. A. S. Hume (London: HMSO, 1892–99), 4 vols

Chronology

1324	John of Nottingham tries to kill King Edward II and others by magic
1351	Parliament defines treason as 'compassing and imagining' the death of the king
1376	A friar in the service of Edward III's mistress is accused of trying to affect the king's judgement by magic
1399	Rumours circulate that King Richard II was under the influence of magicians
1419	King Henry V accuses his stepmother Joan of Navarre of plotting with a friar to kill him by magic
1430	Seven witches accused of trying to kill King Henry VI
1441	Eleanor Cobham, duchess of Gloucester, and others are accused of trying to kill King Henry VI by magic
1470	Thomas Wake accuses the queen, Elizabeth Woodville, and her mother Jacquette of Luxembourg of bewitching King Edward IV
1478	George, duke of Clarence, executed for treason after trying to defend a retainer against a charge of magical treason
1483	Richard III accuses Elizabeth Woodville of trying to kill him by magic
1497	The archdeacon of London and prior of the Knights of St John plot to kill Henry VII by magic
1533	First version of an act against conjuration drafted by Parliament

1534	Execution of Elizabeth Barton, the 'Holy Maid of Kent', for prophesying against Henry VIII
1535	A friar claims to know by magic that Henry VIII's religious policies will fail
1536	Anne Boleyn is accused of bewitching Henry VIII
1537	Mabel Brigge fasts to kill Henry VIII
1538	A wax baby found in a London churchyard is identified as an attempt to kill Edward, prince of Wales
1540	Lord Hungerford executed for buggery and magical treason
1542	An act of Parliament imposes the death penalty for virtually every kind of magic
1547	Repeal of the 1542 act
1551	A revision of canon law retains magic as an offence
1555	John Dee imprisoned on suspicion of calculating Mary I's death
1559	Parliament proposes a new act against conjuration
1561	A magical plot to kill Elizabeth I is uncovered in Essex; a fire at St Paul's Cathedral is rumoured to have been a magical attack on the queen
1562	Arthur and Edmund Pole conspire with John Prestall and others to overthrow Elizabeth
1563	Parliament passes a new act against conjuration and witchcraft
1566	The first trials under the new act target witches in Essex
1567	John Prestall pardoned for conjuration and treason
1569	Prestall flees to Scotland, then to the Netherlands where he plots with John Story
1570	John Story is kidnapped, brought to England, tried and executed
1572	Prestall is allowed to return to England, but placed under arrest
1574	Prestall is released from prison
1577	Rowland Jenkes supposedly uses magic to kill the judges at his trial
1578	Three wax figures resembling Elizabeth and her councillors, discovered in a barn at Islington, provoke a widespread treason panic
1579	Thomas Elkes reveals the Islington effigies were intended as a love charm; Vincent Murphyn claims he was involved in a plot with Sir George Hastings to overthrow the queen

Chronology

1580	'An act for suppressing seditious words and rumours' makes it an offence to calculate the monarch's death by astrology
1583	A woman at York is accused of 'witchcraft and treason'
1584	Sir George Hastings is accused of employing wizards and witches to kill Elizabeth
1589	The North Berwick witches attempt to kill King James VI of Scotland
1591	Puritan William Hacket found guilty of treason for piercing an image of the queen
1592	William Kinnevsley denounces John Prestall for magical treason
1594	Shakespeare's *Henry VI Part Two* first performed, telling the story of Eleanor Cobham
1597	James VI publishes his *Daemonologie*, which is reprinted in England
1602	Probable first performance of Shakespeare's *Hamlet*, featuring the murder of Hamlet's father by *veneficium*
1604	A new act of Parliament outlaws 'entertaining' an evil spirit
1607	The leader of the Midland Revolt, 'Captain Pouch', carries a magic pouch to guarantee success
1611	Shakespeare's play *The Tempest* performed before James I
1612	Trials of the Lancashire Witches
1619	A schoolmaster is tortured for trying to manipulate James I's judgement by magic
1625	The duke of Buckingham and his mother are suspected of killing James I by *veneficium*
1639	John Hammond claims to have the power to take away the kingdom from Charles I at any moment
1645	John Lowes, vicar of Brandeston, is executed for sinking ships by witchcraft
1648	Oliver Cromwell supposedly takes the advice of a 'witch' to put Charles I on trial
1655	First publication in England of *The Fourth Book of Occult Philosophy*, containing effigy magic attributed to Cornelius Agrippa
1660	A witch at Kidderminster threatens the life of King Charles II

1672	A witch at Looe, Cornwall claims to have hindered the navy in the Battle of Sole Bay and made Queen Catherine of Braganza barren
1675/6	An unnamed English nobleman is involved in sacrilegious rites aimed against Louis XIV in France
1685	The duke of Monmouth is found in possession of magical charms at his execution for high treason
1735	A new act of Parliament repeals the 1604 act against conjuration and witchcraft

Introduction

The desire to kill, injure or control another person remotely, by the power of projected thought, is probably as old as humanity itself. It is well attested in the gruesome language of lead curse tablets recovered from the sacred spring at Bath, deposited by visitors during the Roman occupation of Britain.[1] When it came to magical attack, a ruler, however well protected by material walls and guards, was as vulnerable as any other human being, and magic represented a unique class of threat to political stability for as long as people contemplated the possibility of its effectiveness. Magic was, in theory, the perfect method of treason. It could be performed remotely and secretly, and required the involvement of few (if any) other people, invoking instead the assistance of powerful non-human forces against the supreme earthly power of the monarch.

Most private magical operations that were performed against the monarch in medieval and early modern England, by their very nature, would never have been discovered. When they were discovered, this was often because they were one component of broader plots involving more conventional methods of rebellion. The failure of magical plots rarely seems to have deterred such attempts. When magic did not work, practitioners were far more likely to think that they had performed the procedure incorrectly than to conclude that magic was an ineffective instrument. The persistence of magical plots would suggest that, at the very least, the working of magic against the government provided some degree of psychological relief for the powerless and politically excluded.

The connection between harmful magic and treason is a deeply rooted one in Christian culture. According to the Geneva Bible of 1560 and the Authorised Version of 1611 'rebellion is as the sin of witchcraft' (I Samuel 15:23), and this verse was much exploited in early modern England to blacken all critics of official policy. The verse had a double effect: on the one hand, it allowed an *analogy* to be drawn between treasonous activity and the supreme treason to God (idolatrous magic or witchcraft); and on the other hand, it served as a reminder of the tendency of traitors to commit magical crimes. The connection between magic and treason was reinforced at the linguistic level by the fact that the same Latin word – *coniuratio* – could mean both a conspiracy and the summoning of demons. However, rhetorical accusations levelled against traitors that they were *like* witches did not amount to formal accusations of supernatural crime, and it is important not to confuse the two separate discourses that flowed out from I Samuel 15:23.

This book is not concerned, except tangentially, with the rich political metaphor of treason as the sin of witchcraft – which is certainly worthy of a study in its own right. Instead, it focusses on real or suspected magical plots. On one level, every illicit magical act after 1563 (when 'conjuration' and 'witchcraft' became felonies) was in some way a threat to good order and therefore to the government. However, the definition of 'political crime' adopted in this book, whilst a broad one, is not so broad as to treat all magic as political. The primary focus of this study is magical acts that were perceived by the authorities as a direct and specific threat to the life, health or judgement of the monarch and regime rather than a generalised threat to society. Many magical plots came within the ambit of the law of treason because they aimed to harm or kill the monarch, and many that were not technically treasonous could be classed as other crimes of political dissent, such as sedition and *lèse majesté*. Christina Larner, in a study of witchcraft in Scotland, found the connection between magic and treason so close that she coined the term 'treason-cum-sorcery' to describe many charges of treason.[2] Larner's model of treason-cum-sorcery does not hold up quite as well in England as it does in Scotland, but the tendency to pile supernatural accusations on suspected traitors operated on both sides of the border.

Magical acts could also become political crimes when they were associated with activities proscribed by government policy at a particular time. In the 1530s any kind of prognostication or prophecy that hinted at comeuppance for Henry VIII's religious changes was treated as a political crime. P. G. Maxwell-Stuart states well how easy it was for someone to become the target of a charge of treasonous magic:

> Inquisitiveness might lead someone to ask when the ruler would die and who was likely to be his or her successor; or to find out whether such and such an uprising, rebellion, or war stood a chance of being successful; or to discover a person's career prospects in royal or imperial service. Should the individual's prospects look favourable or grim, they could always be assisted by magic. So, too, a rebellion or the succession to the throne. Consequently both divination and magic could be seen as fraught with danger to the authority and stability of the state.[3]

In most cases, we must accept that the original intentions of people accused of magical crimes are no longer recoverable. Some may have intended to perform magic, some may have been innocent victims, and some may have been magicians whose practices were mistaken for treason. Ultimately, as Maxwell-Stuart suggests, it was what 'magic could be seen as' by the authorities that mattered. Any attempt to assess the guilt or innocence of the accused parties is almost impossible, primarily because the historical sources are almost always the product of an official investigation or a report on it. However, basing this study solely on official sources would mean ignoring the question of whether government suspicions accurately reflected what magicians themselves thought they could do. It is crucial, therefore, for the historian to engage with the history of magic, since even if the truth of the magical practices of particular accused traitors is lost to us in official accounts, we can study comparable magical practices preserved in other texts. A significant gap often existed between official fears of what magicians might do and what magicians themselves tried to do.

HISTORIES OF MAGIC AS POLITICAL CRIME

Accusations of magic as a political crime have received surprisingly little attention from historians; the present book is the first dedicated to the subject. One reason for this neglect is that cases in which magic was entangled with treasonous acts do not fit comfortably within the historiography of 'witchcraft studies' as it has developed in the last forty years. Because he wrote so long ago, George Lyman Kittredge (1860–1941) made no distinction between witchcraft and magic in his *Witchcraft in Old and New England* (1928), a book that is still a good starting point for cases of magic as political crime. However, the cases cited by Kittredge received little subsequent attention because they were not clearly instances of 'witchcraft', and the dominance of 'witchcraft studies' historiographically marginalised ritual magic. Even the title of Kittredge's book gives the impression that the history of magic is a footnote to the history of witchcraft.

Historians of early modern England have tended to treat ritual magic as a sideshow to the persecution of accused witches between 1563 and 1717. Criminal trials of people accused of witchcraft vastly outnumbered those of people accused of magic under the same statutes, and because 'witchcraft studies' often approaches witchcraft as a social phenomenon rather than one defined by the law, many historians have set aside trials for magic. No case of magic in English history has acquired the same level of notoriety as the great East Anglian witch-hunt of 1645–7, but there is no shortage of evidence that treasonous activities involving magic were of much more direct concern to governments than witchcraft ever was. There can be no doubt that witchcraft was a more *socially* significant phenomenon than magic at all levels of English society, but the elite nature of magic – and the elite status of those involved – added to, rather than detracted from, its *political* significance.

As early as 1933 Cecil L'Estrange Ewen (1877–1949) realised, on the basis of trial records and contemporary pamphlets, that English witches (in contrast to their Scottish counterparts) were never portrayed as being involved in treason; rather, they were almost always portrayed as being motivated by personal revenge or financial gain.[4] In only two English cases can it be argued that a conventional victim of a witchcraft charge was also executed for treason. The charge on which Margery Jourdemayne was burnt to death in 1443 may have been treason (although this remains unclear, as Chapter 1 will demonstrate), and another witch was condemned on a charge of high treason at York in the spring of 1584. Mary Lakeland was burnt to death for treason in 1645, but this was 'petty treason' (killing her husband).[5] Yet the tiny number of *witches* accused of treason has no direct bearing on the significance of *magic* to treason, because the vast majority of those accused of magical treason cannot be classed as witches. The historical categories adopted by Ewen created the appearance that cases of treasonous magic were rare and marginal. In reality, such cases were not uncommon, but cases of treasonous *witchcraft* were almost non-existent.

Keith Thomas's *Religion and the Decline of Magic* (1971), perhaps the most influential book on the supernatural in English social history in the last fifty years, followed Ewen's lead by treating magical treason as a marginal activity.[6] Geoffrey Elton's *Policy and Police* (1972) did something to redress the balance, since Elton was the first to uncover the full extent of government concern about magic in Henry VIII's state letters and papers. Elton's work was followed by important articles on magic as treason by William Jones, Henry Ansgar Kelly and Jonathan Van Patten.[7] The case of Eleanor Cobham also attracted some interest,[8] while John Leland has made a detailed study of Richard III's claims of magical treason against him.[9] Retha Warnicke has investigated suspicions and accusations of magic at the court of Henry VIII.[10] Kelly argued that, whilst medieval English monarchs were worried about magical treason, early modern monarchs were not. Prophecy became more important than magic as a threat to the state, and the greater faith in providence that prevailed in England had the effect of controlling witch-hunting.[11] The latter claim may or may not be true, but the evidence presented in this book tends to undermine Kelly's view that early modern monarchs (or at least their councillors) stopped worrying about magic; if anything, they became more anxious than their medieval predecessors.

Historians specifically concerned with the law of treason have also neglected the subject of treasonous magic. Lacey Baldwin Smith's *Treason in Tudor England* (1986) examined the unrealistic schemes of sixteenth-century traitors, but strangely omitted a discussion of magical treason. Nevertheless, Baldwin Smith's argument that a 'conspiracy theory of politics' dominated Tudor thinking, in which there was always a more sinister and larger plot behind outward dissent,[12] provides a useful framework for understanding why accusations of treasonous magic arose. Accusations of magic were one way of showing that a traitor was implicated in the most diabolical and unnatural activity of all. Baldwin Smith also noted the tendency of paranoid figures of authority to see their enemies as almost infinitely evil,[13] which made it much easier to imagine that traitors were also dabbling in necromancy.

David Cressy's *Dangerous Talk* (2010) considered the early modern development of the law of treason to cover treason by speech from the reign of Henry VIII onwards, but stopped short of treating treasonous magic (in spite of the fact that it is explicitly mentioned in the 1580 act against seditious words).[14] An important 1998 article by Norman Jones dealt with the subject of magical conspiracies against Elizabeth I, recently complemented by an equally valuable study by Michael Devine.[15] Glyn Parry, in his biography of John Dee *The Arch-Conjurer of England* (2011), has probably done more than any other historian to unearth the lost history of magical plots against Elizabeth I. Accusations of magical treason from the reigns of James I and Charles I are touched upon in the work of David Underdown and Nathan Johnstone,[16] and the conspiracy theories surrounding the death of King James I are considered in Alastair Bellany and Thomas Cogswell's *The Murder of King James I* (2015).[17] The theme of magic as political crime after the English Civil Wars has never been studied.

Perhaps the most significant historical work on magical treason to date has been accomplished by P. G. Maxwell-Stuart, first in his book on Scottish witchcraft, *Satan's Conspiracy* (2001), and latterly in *The British Witch* (2014), which departs from previous studies by stressing the treasonous component in accusations of witchcraft in the late Middle Ages and early sixteenth century. The growing literature on magic as treason means that it can no longer be marginalised in English history and regarded as a Scottish phenomenon that barely existed south of the border. The governmental energy expended on investigating a single suspected magical conspiracy to kill Elizabeth I between 1578 and 1581 is astonishing. Parry has shown that official concern about magic was not just a feature of the early Reformation in the 1530s, as Elton and Van Patten supposed; rather, it extended well into Elizabeth's reign. Prophecy, which was very significant in the 1530s, receded in importance after the 1560s while magical treason retained its vitality. This book will demonstrate that the utility of accusations of magical acts directed against the government as a political instrument lasted well into the seventeenth century.

STUDYING MAGIC AS POLITICAL CRIME

The study of magic as a political crime poses the same historiographical challenges as the study of any kind of magic, owing to the difficulty of defining what 'magic' is and the proscribed and secretive nature of magical activities in past societies. The material and literary evidence of magic, such as books and ritual paraphernalia, was customarily destroyed as part of judicial proceedings, and this was especially true if suspicions of treason were involved. By definition, such items do not survive as evidence, although some surviving texts by other magical practitioners may contain comparable rites. It is the aim of this book, as far as possible, to set individual accusations of magic in the context of known varieties of magical practice in order to enable some basic assessment of the plausibility of accusations.

All too often, historians dealing with magic make little effort to recover the content of the rites and practices that were used and fail to engage with textual traditions of magic. Brian Copenhaver has argued that this shortcoming derives from prevalent academic assumptions rooted in the anthropology of Sir James Frazer. By arguing that magic precedes religion as a more 'primitive' category of human behaviour, Frazer created an enduring idea that magic is intrinsically 'primitive', a visceral and universal category of human experience almost beyond rational analysis. Although Frazer's methodology has been comprehensively challenged, his view of magic remains influential, and the idea of magic as an intellectual tradition (or at the very least a textual tradition) is marginalised in comparison with anthropological approaches. However, Copenhaver argues that attempting to understand western magic by analogy with sub-Saharan practices ignores the literary tradition of western magic rooted in the Classical world.[18]

Just as historians before the publication of Eamon Duffy's *The Stripping of the Altars* (1992) may have written off the devotional practices of the pre-Reformation church as 'superstition', so some historians continue to be dismissive of magic. Some historians functionalise magic since they are interested only in the non-magical motivations of those who used magic, and are content with the knowledge that magic was a forbidden act without enquiring into its content. Alternatively, historians may take accusations against magicians seriously while little or no attempt is made to understand the probable practices of those magicians. Richard Kieckhefer, Owen Davies, Frank Klaassen, Claire Fanger and others have made important contributions to the study of the textual tradition of magic,[19] but attention to the inner workings of magic remains rare amongst historians who are not specialists in the field.

Accused witches rarely speak for themselves, and we hear their voices only through court records. Magicians, by contrast, were a literate group who produced their own literature, however meagre its surviving instances. The study of magic is therefore both richer in source material and can potentially achieve a greater balance between the voices of the accused and their accusers than the study of witchcraft. Accounts of magical practice were also preserved by those keen to attack or discredit practitioners. The care taken by Duffy to reconstruct the details of pre-Reformation and Reformation-era liturgies is now seen as essential to early modern religious history, and the same attention to the details of rite and ceremony should also be seen as essential to the history of magic.

DEFINING MAGIC

Many attempts have been made to define magic by anthropologists, archaeologists and historians, most of which are unsatisfactory in one way or another. The archaeologist Ralph Merrifield defined magic as 'the use of supernatural power vested in the operator or in the ritual he employs, without the intervention of a supernatural being'.[20] Although this definition might cover some forms of magic, it does not apply to necromancy or ritual magic, which is based almost entirely on the intervention of invoked supernatural beings. Merrifield's definition sprang from a desire to distinguish 'religion' and 'magic' as categories, a task that is probably impossible and, arguably, misconceived in the first place. As Klaassen has shown in his study of the fourteenth-century Benedictine monk John of Morigny, ritual magic was regarded by many in the Middle Ages as one spiritual path among many, and as an expression of religion and piety rather than something opposed to it.[21] Just because magic was regarded as illicit by inquisitors and church officials, we cannot assume that its practitioners acted as if *they* considered it illicit and forbidden.

However, whilst magic had religious significance for some practitioners, this does not justify subsuming magic entirely within the realm of religion, given that people in the past often made their own distinctions between religion and magic and perceived a difference between unacceptable religious opinions (heresy) and magic. As David J. Collins notes, 'the premise that magic had (and has) coherent, rational significance in relation to discourses of religion has so far proven itself more elucidative of the historical phenomena than has the alternative premise that magic and religion cannot be distinguished at all'.[22] In other words, there may be no solid theoretical justification for considering 'magic' a meaningful historical category, but it remains extremely useful to the historian to separate 'magic' from 'religion'. The anthropologist E. E. Evans-Pritchard (1902–73) used the terms 'magic' and 'witchcraft' but declined to define them, describing them as 'only labels which help us sort out the facts'. Such labels could be discarded if they proved unhelpful, and 'The facts will be the same without their labels'.[23] Copenhaver defends Evans-Pritchard's nominalist approach, noting that 'since no essences are available, no definitions will be possible'.[24] The 'terminological slipperiness across cultures and through time' associated with magic must be acknowledged,[25] yet at the same time the adoption of some working conceptual distinctions is crucial to understanding people's beliefs.

The classic approach to magic and religion within the historiography of medieval and early modern Europe, advocated by

Bronislaw Malinowski in his essay 'Magic, Science and Religion' (1948),[26] has involved distinguishing magic from religion as an individualistic attempt to compel supernatural powers for short-term ends; religion, by contrast, involves ritual performed for more abstract and less immediate ends, often with community participation.[27] It is not difficult to find examples of 'religion' that fit this definition of magic and examples of 'magic' that fit this definition of religion, and Stuart Clark observed that 'only something entirely contingent – legitimacy' separates magic from religion.[28] In other words, one person's (or one faction's) religion is another's magic, which is vividly shown in Reformation writers' redefinition of Catholic practices as superstitious magic.[29] The fact that almost any ritual practice might be seen or defined as magic by others enabled the coercive use of accusations of magic by governments and made magic the perfect material for a case of constructive treason.

Distinctions between different kinds of magic *within* the history of magic are perhaps less controversial than the definition of magic itself, and the categories of ritual magic (conjuration, demonic magic or necromancy), natural magic and astral (or astrological) magic are broadly accepted. In addition, Kieckhefer identified a 'common tradition' of unlearned magic,[30] which Catherine Rider defines by purpose rather than form. Common magic 'responded to widespread and fundamental concerns, such as curing illness, seeking prosperity or love and explaining or averting misfortune'.[31] Although the rise of printed translations of works such as Heinrich Cornelius Agrippa's *Of Occult Philosophy* led to a convergence between common magic and learned magic in the seventeenth century, learned magic was defined by its faithfulness to Classical sources, philosophical interests and what Collins describes as 'The struggle to carve out an intellectually and morally legitimate field of magic'.[32]

Practices considered magical today were not always classed as magical in medieval and early modern England, while practices no longer considered magical were regarded as magic. Alchemy and astrological prognostication were learned pursuits rarely condemned by religious authorities. Knowledge of poisons (*veneficium*), on the other hand, was considered a branch of magic from antiquity because it gave the power to kill remotely, without warning, and without physical strength. The Latin word *venefica* was often used to render the English word 'witch', meaning that *veneficium* could also function as a synonym for 'witchcraft' (or at least heavily imply it). *Veneficium* was an important category of magic that could be used to kill,[33] and it was not until the seventeenth century that learned commentators in England began to accept that poisons were entirely natural substances. Elsewhere in Europe the conceptual separation of poisoning and witchcraft took much longer, and Owen Davies has shown that the last woman in Europe to be executed on the basis of accusations of witchcraft, Anna Göldi of Glarus, Switzerland, was beheaded in 1782 on a formal charge of poisoning.[34] Any study of medieval and early modern magic must strike a balance in the scope of what it considers 'magic' between what seems 'magical' to the modern reader and what was considered 'magical' in those eras. Activities usually considered non-magical also sometimes led to accusations of magic at times of particular stress, such as denunciations of astrologers. Yet to label anyone who practised alchemy or astrology as a 'magician' would be thoroughly misleading and historically inaccurate, even if those who engaged in these practices thereby made themselves more vulnerable to accusations of magic.

Until the second half of the twentieth century, a moralising and rationalist approach to magic prevailed, and historians tended to disparage it as a false and discarded belief-system. The use of value-laden terminology such as 'superstition' and 'credulity' as catch-all terms for puzzling beliefs does nothing to explain *why* anyone believed anything, and a focus on what people *believed* is a decidedly modern preoccupation. It was more often what people *did* that mattered to the authorities in the Middle Ages.[35] Defining the extent of definite and conscious *belief* in magic, either in the early modern or contemporary world, is well-nigh impossible. Furthermore, before we can ask *why* the people of the past believed something, we must try to understand exactly *what* it was they believed, as far as possible in their own terms. Passing moral or rational judgements on the private beliefs or practices of long-dead people is a futile exercise that makes for bad history. Magic has its own flexible internal logic, and magical thinking remains one possible response to modernity,[36] lingering in a society long after conscious belief in its power has disappeared.

Behaviour may be a better guide to someone's attitude to magic than the beliefs he or she explicitly articulates. Because the operation of magic is inherently mysterious, believing that it is just possible that magic *might* work amounts to much the same thing as believing that magic does work. The responses of government officials to magical threats may not always have been underpinned by committed belief in magic on the part of those officials, but throughout history magic has flourished in the grey area between definite belief and instinctive, inarticulate suspicion.

Magic implicated in political crime could take many forms, although the most common accusations concerned conjuration of demons associated with astrological calculations of a ruler's death and the construction of an effigy in order to harm a ruler by sympathetic magic. Sometimes people were accused of doing both of these things. Spirit conjuration and astrology were elite activities, and those accused of using them for treasonous purposes were usually either educated individuals or elite individuals who hired an educated astrologer or necromancer to perform magic on their behalf. Effigy magic did not, in and of itself, require education or skill and was associated with witchcraft. However, it could also take sophisticated forms and featured in books of necromancy, enhanced by complex astrological and demonic rites. Many practices were not ritual magic under the strict definition of conjuration of spirits, but nevertheless involved ritual elements.[37] In the majority of cases in which people were accused of effigy magic against the monarch and other officials it seems that the construction of the effigy was accompanied by the celebration of masses, observance of astrological times and magical figures drawn on the effigies. However, the taint of base witchcraft that accompanied the making of effigies added to the stigma associated with the activity.

MAGIC AND WITCHCRAFT

Distinguishing magic from witchcraft is a particularly difficult problem for the historian of supernatural beliefs in England, but one that cannot be avoided. Outside England, the key difference between accusations against witches and accusations against magicians was that witches were supposed to be 'members of great cults of sorcerers' who met at orgiastic Sabbaths, while magicians were not.[38] Witches were members of devil worshipping cults while magicians committed the sin of honouring demons without being full-blown diabolists. However, Ronald Hutton has argued that witches in England (apart from Cornwall) were almost always thought of as solitary individuals, and no idea of witches' Sabbaths exists in English tradition.[39] Nevertheless, early modern English people did not consider witchcraft and magic to be the same thing, and to lump the two terms together is to disregard the mental landscape of people in the past.

The anthropologist Garrick Bailey distinguished between 'sorcery' as 'the performance of rites and spells intended to cause supernatural forces to harm others', and 'witchcraft' as 'the use of psychic power alone to cause harm to others'.[40] This definition is problematic as applied to medieval and early modern England, where the word 'witch' was used more broadly than just to refer to people who were thought to harm by projected thought (ill-wishing or 'malefice'). Someone might be accused of being a witch for creating an effigy as well as mere ill-wishing, and virtually the same ritual methods used to cause harm (such as constructing a wax effigy) might also be used to attempt healing (indeed, medieval books of magic advise that a person harmed by means of effigy magic can also be healed by it). Furthermore, counter-magic directed *against* harmful magic often simply reversed the procedure originally used to harm, yet was not considered witchcraft.

From the sixteenth century onwards, the English words 'witch' and 'witchcraft' had purely negative connotations. Magic, by contrast, could be performed for both good and evil purposes. However, magic performed for evil might also be called witchcraft. A distinction between witchcraft and magic in purely functional terms is therefore problematic. Another approach is to accept that the words used to describe a supernatural accusation against someone in early modern England said more about who that person was than the practices of which he or she was accused. Thus an uneducated person, especially a woman, might be accused of witchcraft, while an educated man was more likely to be accused of magic. There are notable exceptions to this general observation, such as the 1645 witchcraft trial of the clergyman John Lowes,[41] but it provides a basic framework within which the historian can work. Accusations of witchcraft rarely included any mention of the ritual practices characteristic of magic, while accusations of magic did not include the idea of the explicit Satanic pact that often underpinned witchcraft accusations. To classify witchcraft as a kind of magic or magic as a kind of witchcraft is to turn one or other word into a 'greedy concept' that is at risk of devouring the distinctions (albeit fluid and inexact) that early modern people themselves drew between magic and witchcraft.

The contrast between witchcraft and magic was reflected in the way people accused of the offences were treated. England never experienced a national panic over magicians on the scale of France's 'affair of the poisons' (1676–82), and even the events of 1578–81 did not lead to a large number of trials for magic or witchcraft. Indeed, Davies has shown that it was rare for professional magicians (cunning-folk) to be prosecuted as witches.[42] One possible interpretation of this difference in judicial treatment between magicians and witches, in spite of the fact that both conjuration and witchcraft were punishable under the same statute, is that witches were thought to make a pact with the devil. The pact was not mentioned in the 'Witchcraft Acts' of 1563 and 1604, and scholars are divided on exactly when pact witchcraft first made an appearance in England. On the Continent the idea of a pact can be traced to a series of bulls issued by Pope John XXII in the 1320s,[43] but a pamphlet of 1589 represents one of the earliest mentions of the idea in England.[44] Even then, accusations of pact witchcraft only came to the fore in England in the 1640s, and instances of witchcraft without an explicitly diabolic element continued to be part of the English tradition.[45]

Nevertheless, by the middle of the seventeenth century English lawyers understood a clear distinction between witchcraft and conjuration (i.e. necromancy), based on the nature of the Satanic pact, as a legal manual of 1645 explained:

> The conjurers believe that by certain terrible words they can raise the Devil and make him to tremble ... and having raised the Devil, they

seem, by prayers and invocation of God's powerful names, to compel the Devil to do and say what the conjurer commandeth him. The witch dealeth rather by a friendly and voluntary conference or agreement between him or her and the Devil or familiar to have his or her turn served, and in lieu thereof the witch giveth or offereth his or her soul, blood, or other gift unto the Devil.[46]

Furthermore, conjurers and witches differed in their intentions, since 'the conjurer compacteth for curiosity' but 'the witch of mere malice'.[47] In 1716, just a year before the last English witch trial, William Hawkins distinguished three types of supernatural offenders:

(1) Conjurers, who by force of certain magic words endeavour to raise the devil, and compel him to execute their commands.
(2) Witches, who by way of friendly conference are said to bargain with an evil spirit to do what they desire of him.
(3) Sorcerers or charmers, who by the use of certain superstitious forms of words, or by means of images, or other odd representations of persons or things, etc., are said to produce strange effects above the ordinary course of nature.[48]

Hawkins's interpretation was hardly justified by the contents of the 1604 statute on which he was commenting, which made no mention of witches making a pact with the devil. Yet Hawkins's definition of conjuration as a practice based on specific words does reveal a significant difference between the way in which magic and witchcraft were imagined in early modern England, because it was perfectly possible for a bewitchment to happen without words. Witchcraft in English tradition was first and foremost 'ill-wishing'; only later were embellishments such as the Satanic pact, the witch's mark and the imp/familiar added to the story. The power of witches was mysterious and supernatural in nature, but – unlike the sorcerer or conjurer – the witch did not need to possess any special skill or knowledge. A witch was a *kind of person*, whereas a magician was a person who practised a particular *kind of activity*. Although there were certainly instances of witches engaging in magical activity, witchcraft in England was not traditionally 'book magic', the kind of magic that literate people might attempt.[49] The meaning of the words 'witch' and 'witchcraft' also changed over time. As the suffix '-craft' suggests, in medieval England 'witchcraft' was a word that might be applied to popular magical remedies.[50] This meaning survived into the early modern era; in 1566 Elizabeth Mortlock of Pampisford, Cambridgeshire, was 'noted to the office of a witch' because she offered women magical girdles to protect them in childbirth.[51] However, by around 1600 the word had come to be associated almost exclusively with evil and ill-wishing.

MAGIC AND TREASON

There was no sense in which magic in medieval and early modern England was regarded as treasonous *by definition*, and it is important not to sensationalise magic in pre-industrial England. In both rural and urban communities, magic was more often than not a thoroughly ordinary, mundane business. It was used to find lost goods, locate thieves, protect cattle from disease and cure bewitched people or animals. However, magic had uses for the individual as well as the community. It was in these kind of activities that magic had the potential to come into conflict with the ever-encroaching claims of central government. People who dug treasure out of the ground, guided by spirits, were taking 'treasure-trove' that belonged to the crown; people who pulled down landmarks in the belief that treasure was hidden under them hindered the progress of travellers on the king's highway; and people who used fragments of medieval liturgy in charms and spells were defying centrally enforced religious policies.

If someone could use magic to kill a neighbour over a boundary dispute, there was no reason (in theory) why magic might not be used to kill a social superior, or even the king himself – who was, after all, just a human being. In a world before effective autopsies, where there was little or no understanding of the causes of illness, sudden and premature death was a common occurrence. A few instances of a magical ritual, followed by the intended victim's death, were enough to convince many people of magic's ability to kill. Furthermore, serious illnesses were so prevalent that the chances of a magical attempt on the monarch's life coinciding with a royal health scare were high; this happened in 1578 when a discovery of suspicious wax images coincided with an illness that Queen Elizabeth was suffering as a result of an abscess in her teeth.

The expansion of literacy triggered by the English Reformation also had significant consequences for magic.[52] Magic remained something that required specialist knowledge and it retained much of its mystique, but by the end of the sixteenth century it was no longer confined to the clergy, or even those with knowledge of ancient languages. Magic offered an opportunity to those who felt powerless against the seemingly limitless reach of early modern governments. Whereas in the Middle Ages magic had been treated as an irritating infraction against religious discipline, in the sixteenth century it had the potential to become a socially destabilising force. In an era when even unthinking speeches uttered in drink could bring a charge of *lèse majesté* or treason, it is hardly surprising that early modern governments were concerned about the seditious potential of magic. Until the late seventeenth century (and indeed beyond) it seems likely that most English people entertained the possibility that magic might work; many were absolutely convinced that it worked. In the light of this prevailing climate of credulity, it would have been the height of folly for a government charged with protecting the realm to fail to act against magical attempts to subvert the social and political order. Even if ministers themselves were sceptical of magic, they could not afford to be seen as weak by a population that largely accepted its reality. Indeed, so strict were the laws in Tudor England that even seeking information that *could* be used to make a magical attempt on the monarch's life, by casting his or her horoscope, was forbidden.

In early modern England, as today, a variety of views on the reality and effectiveness of magic existed, even if figures like Reginald Scot, the Kentish magistrate who argued in 1584 that all magic was fraudulent, were at the outer fringes of opinion. Most people believed that magic was possible, even if most practising magicians they encountered were frauds – after all, until the mid-seventeenth century there was no established and credible natural philosophy that could offer an alternative to belief in magic. King James VI and I believed passionately in the reality of magic, but thought it impossible for magicians to kill a divinely ordained king. Likewise, many jurists held that witches and magicians were powerless against the authorities who apprehended and tried them. Still others, like Scot, thought that magicians were fraudulent but that they should nevertheless be punished for their presumption.

Scepticism about magic in early modern England existed primarily for religious rather than philosophical reasons. For Scot, a major reason to reject magic was its association with Catholicism; stamping out belief in magic was the logical progression of a Protestant Reformation that had stamped out belief in false religion. King James's belief that magic could not touch him personally was bound up with his theopolitical conception of the divine right of kings. The power of God, who had chosen him as king, would always be greater than that of magicians and witches. Ironically, it seems that some early modern people with the most intense religious beliefs were *less* likely to be afraid of magic, on account of their enhanced sense of the power and majesty of God. Accordingly, some condemned excessive belief in the power of magic as an instance of faithlessness. It was the puritan minister John Gaule, concerned that witchfinders were polluting the word of God, rather than sympathetic defenders of accused witches, who eventually turned public opinion against 'Witchfinder General' Matthew Hopkins in the 1640s.[53] Many Protestants believed that magic had power only over the sinful, who were already in the devil's power.

To some extent, magical treason was the creation of the governments that tried to stamp it out. It is likely that many of those arrested and tried were not remotely trying to kill the monarch by magic, but simply found themselves on the wrong side of policy at the wrong time. However, it would be a mistake to suppose that magical treason was nothing more than a paranoid fantasy of civil servants, albeit a deadly one. There can be little doubt that people really did set out to attack monarchs by magic, which raises the question of what motivated plotters to resort to such methods rather than straightforward assassination or rebellion. Ronald Hutton has observed that magic was the method of treason favoured by the 'weak' – women, priests and old men[54] – since it offered the possibility of a remote assassination with minimal danger to the magician, or the individual who hired him or her. Those accused of magical treason were not always 'weak', however, and magic sometimes accompanied more conventional methods. In these cases it would seem that magical operations were added to a diversified portfolio of treason as an additional guarantee of success.

The vast majority of medieval magicians were monks, friars and ordained clergy. One reason for this was simple; a magician had to be able to read and write (Latin as well as English), and the church was the major source of education. Another reason was that magicians needed to harness the intrinsic power of the church's ceremonies, and therefore it helped if a magician could perform those ceremonies himself. The most powerful ceremony of all was the mass, in which the words spoken by the priest at the consecration of bread and wine transformed them into the body and blood of Christ. Many pre-Reformation books of magic required the magician to say a mass (or several), thereby requiring him to be a priest, and both priests and deacons had the power to bless and exorcise. Some magical formulae even involved the use of consecrated hosts.[55] All of this was strenuously condemned by the church, but the differences between the 'official magic' of the church and the unofficial magic of conjurers were slight.[56] Many ordinary people, and some of the clergy themselves, either did not understand or had little regard for the distinctions made by learned theologians between licit and illicit practices.

The early modern popular image of the magician as a morally abandoned, overreaching character like Christopher Marlowe's Doctor Faustus did not necessarily reflect the reality. Magicians were just as likely to be motivated by simple curiosity, petty lust and pecuniary greed as by a desire for cosmic power. Magic offered the clergy an opportunity to make a little money on the side, trading on their literacy and spiritual prestige. The sheer mundaneness of the spells in many books of magic suggests a degree of complacency on the part of some magicians about the spiritual forces they might be awakening. In other words, there is no reason to think that magicians were more inclined than anyone else to treason and plotting. They were simply individuals in possession of a unique and specific skill set. As Sophie Page has shown in her recent study of magical books in the library of St Augustine's Abbey in Canterbury, natural magic of all kinds (even the creation of unnatural 'monsters') seems to have been practised without restriction by medieval monks.[57] The more acceptable forms of natural magic included astral magic, which sought to bring down the influences of stars and planets to achieve marvellous effects on earth, as well as herbalism and lithomancy, which drew on the inherent virtues of plants and minerals placed in them by God. However, the monks of St Augustine's did not include books of ritual magic or necromancy in their library catalogue, since this was a form of magic more readily perceived as illicit.

Whereas much natural magic could be traced back to the works of Pliny the Elder and other ancient sources, along with Arabic manuscripts, medieval necromancy was ultimately of Jewish origin. Translation and repeated copying had produced a distinctively Christian form of necromancy, but many formulas were still attributed to King Solomon or Moses, while angels and demons retained Hebraic names.[58] The few surviving books of necromancy rarely contain magical operations designed specifically to kill,[59] since magic of this kind was usually used with the intention of influencing a person's behaviour. Therefore, although necromancy might be used to coerce a monarch's judgement or procure favour, it was generally unsuitable for magical assassinations.

Ironically, methods for killing by magic could be found in the practices of the less controversial natural magic. Sympathetic magic, the idea that something done to an image of a person or an object associated with that person would result in actual effects on that person, could be employed with sinister intent. Books of magic sometimes contained rituals for making more effective the manufacture of a wax effigy which could then be used to harm or even kill someone, and many accusations of magical treason focussed on such procedures. However, this was by no means the only method that could be used to harm or kill a monarch, and other cases involved magically formulated poisons and demons summoned to announce or hasten the monarch's death.

STRUCTURE OF THE BOOK

The structure of the book is chronological, with Chapter 1 beginning with the earliest verifiable instances of magic with a treasonous element in the fourteenth century, and covering the remainder of the Middle Ages up to the death of the first Tudor king, Henry VII, in 1509. Chapter 2 covers the early Reformation period, beginning with Henry VIII's earliest religious and political changes in the 1530s and taking the story up to the death of Queen Mary I in 1558. Chapter 3 covers the first phase of the reign of Elizabeth I, between 1558 and 1577, while Chapter 4 begins with the great magical treason panic of Elizabethan England, the affair of the Islington effigies, and traces its aftermath up to the queen's death in 1603. The chapter also addresses the possible influence of reported treasonous magical conspiracies on the early works of Shakespeare. Chapter 5 addresses the theme of magic as a political crime in early Stuart England, between the accession of King James VI and I to the English throne in 1603 and the outbreak of civil war in England in 1642, while Chapter 6 concludes the story by considering the marked decline of political accusations of magic in the post-Civil War and post-Restoration eras. The chapter addresses English involvement in the French 'affair of the poisons' as well as the lingering legacy of magical treason into later eras.

CHAPTER 1

'Compassing and Imagining': Magic as a Political Crime in Medieval England

The idea that magic could be a 'political crime' – except in the general sense that magicians were criminals and therefore a threat to civil society – did not emerge in England until the fourteenth century. The simplest reason for this is that the practice of magic came under the jurisdiction of the law of the church (canon law) rather than the king's law, and therefore magic was scrutinised by the ecclesiastical authorities for its violations of divine law. A more complex reason is that the fourteenth century marked a turning point in attitudes towards magic across Europe. As a consequence of anxieties about the Cathar heresy in southern France and northern Spain, the Fourth Lateran Council produced a dogmatic definition of demons in 1215 and the church began to re-emphasise the devil's activity in the world. As a result, the church was less likely to write magic off as empty superstition and came to view it as something definitively inspired by the devil – and therefore something capable of actual harm.[1]

One striking English example that shows the magnitude of the shift in attitudes towards magic can be found in accounts of William the Conqueror's siege of the island of Ely in the Cambridgeshire Fens in 1070. William's siege was failing to dislodge the English warrior Hereward 'the Wake'. The Norman knight Ivo Taillebois told William that he knew an old woman 'who by her art alone could shatter the strength and stronghold [of the English] in the isle'. William hesitated, perhaps because he had a reputation for ignoring superstition,[2] but in the end he instructed his soldiers to fetch the woman in secret. The old woman was set in a high place, 'and having gone up, fulminated for a long time against the isle and its inhabitants, making many destructive spells, likenesses and fantasies of their overthrow'.[3] However, just as the woman was about to launch her third attempt at a magical attack against the defenders, they crept out of the reeds and set fire to the trees at the edge of the fen. The woman was so terrified that she fell from her place and was killed:

> And that aforesaid poisoner, having been set in a more eminent place over everyone else, so that she might be freer in her incantations, fell from the height by terror, as if struck by a hurricane. And thus, by a broken neck, she who had come beforehand to kill others lost consciousness and perished.[4]

The willingness of a king who claimed to be England's legitimate ruler to use magic against his enemies bespeaks much more ambivalent cultural attitudes towards magic in Norman England than existed by the fourteenth century. The early medieval tradition of classifying magic as a collection of dangerous pretences began with the *Etymologies* of Isidore of Seville (*c.* 560–636), subsequently passing into the influential writings of Hrabanus Maurus, Burchard of Worms, Ivo of Chartres, Hugh of St Victor and John of Salisbury, as well as into the definitive textbook of medieval canon law, Gratian's *Decretum*. These authors 'debated the legality of magic but not its efficacy; magic was a form of moral and religious perversion, but it was not, perhaps, something that needed to be explained'.[5] Commentators of the early and high Middle Ages were clear that dabbling in magic was a sin, but theological enquiry into the demonic causes of magical phenomena as experiential realities (demonology) did not truly exist as a mainstream scholarly pursuit until after the Fourth Lateran Council of 1215.

In 1281, under the influence of a harder line being adopted against magic by ecclesiastical authorities across Europe, Archbishop John Pecham of Canterbury drew up a constitution that identified magic as an infringement of the First Commandment, against idolatry: 'You will not have strange gods before me. You will not make for yourself any sculpted thing or the likeness of anything that is in the heaven above, or on the earth beneath, or of those things that are in the water beneath the earth; you will neither adore nor worship them' (Exodus 20:3–4).[6] Yet in spite of its classification as a form of idolatry, magic was not a serious crime, insofar as it was punished only by the church and not by the king's courts. Since the church courts could not, without the collaboration of the secular authorities, impose any sentence more severe than excommunication or penance, it was not possible (in theory, at least) for anyone to suffer the death penalty for magic alone.

However, matters were not quite so simple if magic was entangled with other crimes, as it was in many medieval accusations – particularly with poisoning (*veneficium*), swindling, sexual misconduct and heresy. The association of magic with heresy was never as potent in England as in other European countries where magicians were accused of actively worshipping the devil,[7] but the advent of the Lollard heresy in the fourteenth century made the authorities more sensitive to the possibility that magic might mask other deviant beliefs. The church courts treated heresy as a violation of the Second Commandment, 'You will not take the name of the Lord your God in vain' (Exodus 20:7), because it represented a misuse of religious doctrines. The irony of trying to associate Lollardy with magic, given the Lollards' own condemnation of the church's blessings and exorcisms as 'necromancy',[8] seems to have been lost on the authorities. When Robert Barker of Babraham, Cambridgeshire, appeared before Bishop William Gray of Ely charged with magical treasure-hunting in January 1466, it was 'on account of a vehement suspicion of heresy and the art of necromancy'.[9] In condemning Robert to a penance, Gray commented on his 'superstitious, idolatrous wisdom and, as a consequence, heretical wickedness'.[10]

The fact that Bishop Gray himself presided over a simple case of magic was a sign of the hierarchy's concern (such cases were usually left to archdeacons and other commissaries[11]), but luckily for him, Barker was found guilty only of magic and not heresy. In 1401, Henry IV's Parliament introduced the statute *De haeretico comburendo* which allowed the church courts to hand over a relapsed heretic to the secular authorities to be burnt alive at the stake. Furthermore, whereas before 1401 only a synod of bishops had been able to convict for heresy, after 1401 judgement lay with the local bishop alone.[12] Yet in spite of harsher penalties for heresy and determined attempts to smear magicians as heretics, it was a great deal safer to practise magic in the Middle Ages than it was in subsequent centuries. The Friar in Geoffrey Chaucer's 'Parson's Tale' puts magic under the First Commandment, but considers it part of the sin of Wrath – one of the less serious of the Seven Deadly Sins.[13] The medieval church was protective of its right to try cases concerning magic, denying the right of secular magistrates to try a spiritual crime. Magic was the proper concern of the church, partly because clerics were often the culprits, and partly because magicians almost always constructed their ritual procedures by misusing the church's rites and ceremonies. Furthermore, canon law provided relatively little guidance on what actually constituted 'good' and 'bad' magical practices, a fact which allowed many magicians to escape justice.[14]

Since ritual magic was largely the preserve of literate individuals, it was perhaps inevitable that accusations would surface at the royal court among the king's clerks. P. G. Maxwell-Stuart has argued that the case of Adam de Stratton, a moneylender and financier to the court of Edward I, might be interpreted as an early instance of an accusation of magical treason. According to the chronicler Bartholomew de Cotton, in 1289 Stratton was arrested, taken to the Tower, and his belongings seized. Amongst them was found a 'silken box' in which Stratton kept nail-clippings, pubic hair, and the feet of moles and toads. Because the box had a seal attached to it by one of the royal justices, and Stratton threw it into a latrine (presumably in an effort to conceal it from the searchers), 'everyone considered him to be a traitor to the King, and he was accused of belonging to that group of people called *sortilegi*'.[15]

It seems likely that in this case, Stratton's 'treason' had nothing to do with the magical nature of the box's contents; rather, it derived from the fact that he threw the royal seal attached to the box into the latrine. Defacing the image of the king (especially his seal) was close to treason, and there is no suggestion that Stratton intended to use the contents of his magical box against the king. In another incident, in 1313 or 1314 a man named John Tanner (alias Canne) was hanged for trying to seize the crown by the aid of the devil.[16] This was a very general slur, however, and such an accusation may have been intended to convey Tanner's general sinfulness rather than implying the use of any form of ritual magic on his part.

JOHN OF NOTTINGHAM AND THE PLOT AGAINST EDWARD II

The first unambiguous case of an individual using magic in an attempt to kill the monarch occurred in the reign of Edward II. In fact, Edward was only a subsidiary target of a plot that was aimed primarily against the king's favourite Hugh Despenser, earl of Winchester (c. 1286–1326), who was widely hated. On the evening of 30 November 1323 a delegation of 28 citizens of Coventry called on the house of John of Nottingham, a reputed necromancer. The citizens swore John and his lodger Robert le Mareschall to secrecy and complained that the Prior of Coventry, supported by the Despensers, was extracting extortionate taxes.

The citizens asked John to use magic to kill Despenser and his father, as well as the king and the prior. In return, they promised him twenty pounds (an enormous sum at the time) and a 'reward' (*gareison*) in any religious house he chose. This probably meant a corrody (a permanent income derived from the lands of a monastery). Robert was promised fifteen pounds if he assisted the necromancer with his work. Shortly afterwards some of the citizens delivered seven pounds of wax and two ells (yards) of canvas. The canvas was probably needed for the drawing of magical circles that would protect the magician from the spirits he conjured to appear.

In a deserted, half-ruined house outside the city walls,[17] John and Robert set to work to make effigies of the four main victims as well as the prior's cellarer and steward and an unfortunate courtier, Richard de Sowe, on whom the magic was to be tested. This was a form of magic known in Latin as *invultuacio*, from the word *vultus* meaning 'face' or 'image'. The first mention of this practice in England occurs in an Anglo-Saxon penitential from the reign of King Edgar (959–75), and it was punishable by death according to the *Leges Henrici*, a code composed in around 1114 during the reign of Henry I.[18] The earliest mention of the crime being committed may have occurred in 948 but was recorded between 963 and 975 in a charter of King Edgar confirming lands to Wulfstan Ucca including the manor of Ailsworth in Northamptonshire, because 'a widow and her son had previously forfeited the land at Ailsworth because they drove iron pins into Wulfstan's father, Ælfsige. And it was detected and the murderous instrument dragged from her chamber; and the woman was seized, and drowned at London Bridge, and her son escaped and became an outlaw'.[19] Most historians interpret this incident as effigy magic, although Carole Hough argues that there is no actual mention of an effigy in the original Old English, which says simply 'they drove iron pins into Wulfstan's father' (*hi drifon serne stacan on Ælsie Wulfstanes feder*) and that a *morð* was dragged from her chamber. The Old English word *morð* usually meant 'death' but could also mean an instrument that caused someone's death. Hough suggests that the passage can be interpreted as referring to a literal physical assault on Ælfsige by the widow and her son with an iron bar.[20] However, *drifon* ('drove') would be a peculiar word to use for such a literal attack.

John and Robert must have done rather more than just make effigies, since they were working from early December 1323 until May 1324, and it is likely that John was combining traditional sympathetic effigy-magic with more sophisticated astrological techniques. A surviving manuscript in the British Library, although it dates from about a century later, contains an example of astrological magic using images. This is a Latin translation of a work by the Arabic astrologer Sahl Ibn Bishr, the *Liber imaginum* ('Book of Images'),[21] which was probably produced in London or Westminster in the mid-fifteenth century. The text contains rituals to promote concord, to make enemies stumble, for help in illness and on journeys, as well as for many other eventualities like the planting of trees and even hair loss and constipation. A common feature of all the rituals in the *Liber imaginum* is that they must be performed at certain hours of the day or night, and that they invoke the magical assistance of the 'lord' (*dominus*), meaning the presiding spirit, of that day or hour. This was an idea found across much Christian, Jewish and Arabic magic. Clearly, the correct performance of the magical operation required considerable astrological knowledge.

One example of harmful magic in the *Liber imaginum* involves the 'burial' (*sepultura*) of an image of someone who has been stung by a scorpion in order to save his or her life and drive the scorpion away. However, the rite can also be turned around to achieve the person's death. The procedure requires the magician to make two images, one of the person stung by the scorpion and another of the scorpion itself. The resulting magical images can be used both for good and ill:

> Make an image when Scorpio is in the ascendant; likewise let the moon be under an unfortunate lord [i.e. spirit] and with a malevolent aspect. Let the names of the ascendant [planets] and the name of the moon be inserted. When it is something good which someone inserts, put it on the front [of the image]; if something bad, put it on the back. Bury the image in the middle of a place and bury it with the Scorpion so that he should go back from that place and not return.[22]

The text's broken Latin then seems to instruct that the name of a spirit should be written on the head of the wax effigy of the person, as well as astrological signs for Venus and the Sun on the shoulder blade and breast, before the effigy is thrown into water to bring harm (*iniuria*) to the person it represents. Finally, the magician should hold the effigy by the feet and burn it in a fire at sunrise, when the moon is still visible in the sky:

> At a fortunate hour, at sunrise, sculpt [into] the head of the image you are moulding who should be the lord of the head ... Thus the body will be good, at sunrise, and let there be a waxing moon at the fortunate moment. Let there be on the shoulder blade and the breast at sunrise, and imprint the stomach at sunrise, in which let there be the aforesaid Venus at sunrise, in which let there be the sun. Throw into water without delay at sunrise the one in whom there should be an injury, neither draw it back nor draw it out, but throw it into the water. Come and burn it by the feet at sunrise when there is a moon. It is complete.[23]

This sort of 'astral magic' ultimately derived from an eleventh-century book of Arabic magic, *Gayat al-Hakim* ('The Goal of the

Wise'), known in the Latin West as the *Picatrix*. The Christian re-conquest of Spain brought this and other products of Islamic learning into Christendom in the eleventh century. The burial of symbolic objects occurs again and again in harmful magic based on the *Picatrix*. As Richard Kieckhefer explained,

> Burial ensures secrecy, fixes the object's location, and perhaps implies an appeal to demons or other chthonic [underworld] powers ... a buried image can work insidiously on the place where it lies. When the magic is psychological, the point is presumably to affect the victim's mind by establishing a kind of magical force field within his or her environment. One might even speak of this as environmental magic, designed to afflict individuals indirectly by planting sinister forces in or near the places they frequent.[24]

If this was the sort of learning that John of Nottingham possessed, then it represented the alliance of basic harmful magic with the most advanced medieval astronomical knowledge – a potent combination. At midnight on 27 April 1324 (the precise time again suggests astrological significance), John handed his assistant 'a curious pin wrought of sharp lead' and instructed him to drive it two inches into the forehead of Richard de Sowe's effigy. Robert then visited the nobleman and found him in a frenzy, shouting 'Harrow! Harrow!'[25] Amongst the potential purposes of harmful magic was causing madness,[26] so this was an encouraging sign.

The magic was evidently working, so on 20 May John pulled the pin out of the forehead and stuck it in the effigy's heart. Three days later Richard was dead. By November, however, Robert had turned evidence against his master and told the whole story to a coroner, perhaps hoping to save his own skin.[27] By the time John, Robert and the Coventry citizens came to be tried for murder in June 1325, John had already died in prison. The Coventry men were found not guilty for lack of evidence. Whether this was simply because the effigies had disappeared, or because the jury was unconvinced that Richard de Sowe really died because of magic practised against him, is unclear. In any case, the magician's assistant, Robert le Mareschall, did not escape unscathed, and in 1326 he was hanged on the basis of his own evidence.[28]

MAGIC AND THE STATUTE OF TREASON

The case of John of Nottingham turned the spotlight on the possibility of malicious magic and its potential to touch even the highest in the land. Hugh Despenser, paranoid for his own safety, even wrote to Pope John XXII appealing for aid against the magic that was being practised against his life. Worryingly, if courts were required to prove that malicious magic was effective, it was possible that no-one would ever be found guilty. A law was needed that outlawed uttering the words of magic themselves. Subsequent governments learnt from the fact that Edward II was murdered not long after this abortive magical attempt on his life. His brother even asked a friar to conjure a demon to find out whether the king was dead.[29] No-one could be allowed to touch the king's life with impunity if the kingdom was to remain secure, and the Statute of Treason of 1351 was the result.

The Statute of Treason (albeit slightly modified) remains one of the most ancient laws still on the statute book in England and Wales. The statute formally defined high treason for the first time, which took place when:

> ... a man doth compass or imagine the death of our Lord the King, or of our Lady his Queen or of their eldest son and heir; or if a man do violate the king's companion, or the king's eldest daughter unmarried, or the wife of the king's eldest son and heir; or if a man do levy war against our Lord the King in his realm, or elsewhere ... or if a man slay the Chancellor, Treasurer or the King's Justices ... being in their places, doing their offices ... it is to be understood, that in the cases above rehearsed, that ought to be judged treason which extends to our Lord the King, and his Royal Majesty.[30]

Medieval jurists identified several 'branches' of treason within this law, the first of which was the 'thought-crime' of 'compassing or imagining' the death of the king, from the Norman French *conpasser et ymaginer*. *Ymaginer* meant something similar to the modern English sense of 'imagine': it was treason to cherish and dwell on a fantasy of the king's death.[31] *Conpasser* literally meant 'to walk around', with the sense of planning or taking steps (*pas*) to bring about the death of the king, so 'compassing' was something more active than 'imagining'.

Most medieval and early modern prosecutions for treason were based on this 'compassing and imagining' clause of the statute, since it was possible to interpret it in a multitude of different ways. Some jurists even argued that insulting or demeaning the king could destroy the love between the king and his subjects and therefore counted as treason, because the king would become sad and die sooner. Such dubious treason cases were known as 'constructive treason', because an otherwise innocent action could be construed as treason by any lawyer who was clever enough to do so.[32] Technically, the original statute required the court to prove that someone had compassed or imagined the death of the king by some 'overt act'. Richard II suspended this requirement in 1397, but the change was so unpopular that the original requirement was restored by Henry IV in 1399. However, there was no reason why the 'overt act' of treason could not be speech, meaning that the law's applicability was still extremely wide.[33] If a magician made a wax effigy of the king, then he was imagining the king's death by an overt act. The elegance of the Statute was that the jury was required to make no judgement on whether magic *worked* (a theological issue beyond the expertise of laymen) – it just had to decide whether malice and harm was intended to the king by the words uttered or actions done.

APPLICATION OF THE STATUTE OF TREASON

The Statute did not immediately result in a flurry of prosecutions of magicians, and Henry IV (reigned 1399–1413) seems to have been the first monarch to realise its potential for criminalising magicians. Henry declared that the predecessor he deposed, Richard II, had been under the influence of magic. Accordingly, a suspicious scroll covered in strange figures was produced from the chest of one of Richard's chaplains, John Magdalene, and handed to Parliament in the autumn of 1399. Magdalene was called before an ecclesiastical court, but other councillors of the late King Richard were less lucky when the new king's councillors ordered a round-up of those who had supposedly driven Richard mad 'by sortilege or false and fallible calculations'.[34] However, such accusations seem to have been believed by some; Thomas Walsingham, a monk of St Albans Abbey, thought that

Richard was unable to oppose the unsuitable marriage of Robert de Vere, duke of Ireland in 1387 because he was 'held fast by the magic spells of a friar in Robert's service, and so completely unable to discern or follow the good or the right'.[35]

All of this was politically useful to Henry IV's government. The claim that Richard II had been attacked magically was not so much a cry of treason as a necessary gesture to show that Richard had been rendered incapable of ruling by forces beyond his control, thereby justifying Henry's coup. However, early attempts to prosecute magical treason in the courts in Henry IV's reign were a failure. In 1401 a clerk, John Inglewood, along with Robert Marner, a canon of Ipswich, and a preaching friar who had been a confessor to the deposed Richard II were accused of plotting the death of the new king, Henry IV, 'by necromancy and enchantment'. The alleged method of assassination, which involved poisoning the saddle of the king's horse, counted as *veneficium*, a concept that covered both magic and poisoning. However, Inglewood, Marner and the friar were acquitted because their accuser, Thomas Samford, had a criminal record and could not be trusted.[36]

In spite of the Statute of Treason, the church was prepared to assert its right to punish magical offences even when these were potentially treasonable in nature, especially when the culprit was a cleric. In 1376 Parliament was informed that a Dominican friar who served as physician to Alice Perrers, the mistress of Edward III, was really 'an evil magician, dedicated to evil-doing, and it was by his magical devices that Alice had enticed the king into an illicit love-affair with her'.[37] It turned out that the friar

> ... had made wax effigies of the king and Alice, and that, as once that infamous magician Nectanebus king of Egypt had done, he used these, with the juices of magical herbs and his words of incantation, to enable Alice to get whatever she wanted from the king. He had also devised rings that caused forgetfulness or remembrance, just as Moses had once done, so that as long as the king wore them he would never forget this harlot.[38]

The friar was trapped when two knights, Sir John de la Mare and Sir John Kentwood, arrived at Alice's estate of Pallenswick, near Fulham, carrying jars of urine and claiming that they had come to seek a cure.

When the friar came downstairs they arrested him. John of Gaunt, duke of Lancaster, the king's third son, arranged the friar's capture and wanted to burn him, and it was only with difficulty that the archbishop of Canterbury managed to extricate the Dominican. In the end, the friars themselves were told to keep the miscreant under 'strict supervision'. The secular authorities could ask the church to round up magicians, such as in the commission issued to the bishop of Lincoln on 2 January 1406 'to apprehend all sorcerers, magicians, enchanters, necromancers, diviners, ariolers and phitoners' in his diocese.[39] Ultimately, however, the punishment of magicians lay outside the king's direct control.

The only exception to the church's jurisdiction were clear-cut cases of magical treason directed against the monarch. In the summer of 1419 Henry V was facing increasing financial pressures from his war with France and his forthcoming marriage with Catherine of Valois. It seems that the solution Henry hit upon to solve his money worries was seizing the goods of his stepmother, Joan of Navarre. Joan had married Henry's father, Henry IV, in 1402 and Henry V's relations with her had hitherto been good, but in August 1419 he ordered the goods of her chaplain, a Franciscan friar named John Randolph, to be confiscated. Randolph was arrested and, under questioning, accused the king's stepmother of 'compassing and imagining' Henry's death by magic.[40] Once more, it would seem, Randolph was trying to save himself by pre-empting allegations that were inevitable. He was a celebrated astrologer and, as later events would prove, this was a profession that attracted accusations of sorcery like no other.

Joan was arrested and her assets seized, and on 1 October she was taken under guard to Pevensey Castle in Sussex. Joan would remain under comfortable house arrest at Pevensey and at Leeds Castle in Kent until six months before Henry V's death in 1420. The case against Joan of Navarre was never brought to trial, making it highly likely that the charges against her were entirely fabricated. On the other hand, Henry seems to have been genuinely anxious about magic being used against his person. A mandate from the archbishop of Canterbury to the bishop of London requesting prayers for the king on his French campaigns mentioned 'superstitious operations of necromancers, especially such as (according to report) have lately been devised by some persons for the destruction of his person'. Perhaps Henry's belief that his stepmother was practising against him was sincere. In any event, Randolph got off lightly by being committed to life imprisonment in the Tower. Imprisonment in the Tower could mean anything from abject incarceration in a dungeon to house-arrest in a comfortable apartment, depending on the wealth and status of the prisoner, but in Randolph's case his confinement was cut short when he was murdered by the Tower's chaplain.[41] The chaplain was apparently mad, but Randolph's fate was a grim reminder that necromancy – even of the suspected kind – always had consequences.

Henry V died at Vincennes just outside Paris in August 1422 during a final campaign against the French. He was succeeded by his nine-month-old son, Henry VI. England was ruled by a regency headed by the duke of Bedford and, when Bedford was fighting in France, the king's great uncle Humphrey, duke of Gloucester. Bedford struggled to hold the English empire in France together against determined resistance from the French, inspired by Joan of Arc. The king's council was convinced Joan made use of magic to win her victories, but they also worried about magical plots at home. In 1429 Agnes Burgate of Exeter, along with a group of knights, clergy and gentry, was accused of making a wax image of a boy, representing Henry VI, and placing it over a fire on a spit of alder 'so as to weaken the King's body and cause his death'.[42] The next year seven 'witches' (*maleficae*) were apprehended from different parts of England and accused of using magic to kill the king.[43] The rule of the infant king was fragile in the extreme, and his ministers correspondingly paranoid. As it turned out, the allegations against Joan of Navarre were little more than a dress-rehearsal for the fifteenth century's most famous case of magical treason, which dramatically demonstrated the limitations of the secular courts when faced with the church's competing jurisdiction over magical crimes.

THE CASE OF ELEANOR COBHAM

Eleanor Cobham was successively a lady-in-waiting to the duke of Gloucester's first wife, then the duke's mistress, and finally his wife.

Eleanor and her husband, who was the heir apparent to the throne, were the glittering focus of a cultivated and cosmopolitan miniature court in Greenwich that mirrored the royal court at Westminster, where the young, feeble and childless king was proving a disappointing successor to his father Henry V, the celebrated victor of Agincourt. The Gloucesters were interested in astrology and were connected to the actors in the Joan of Navarre scandal: Humphrey had intervened to protect John Randolph, and his library contained a set of astronomical tables authored by Randolph.[44] Eleanor was one of the chief mourners at Joan's funeral.[45] Eleanor also owned an Arabic text of astrological medicine, and Roger Bolingbroke, who would later become involved in her downfall, dedicated a work on geomancy to her.[46] Geomancy at this time was a form of divination based on the casting of lots, which were then made to correspond to astrological principles.

Eleanor was desperate both to bear Humphrey's child – a child that could have been second-in-line to the throne – and to know whether Henry would live long. By 1440, however, Humphrey was being sidelined by other members of the king's council, especially Cardinal Beaufort, the unscrupulous bishop of Winchester, and the archbishop of York, John Kemp.[47] The fiercely ambitious Beaufort belonged to a semi-legitimate branch of the royal family descended from John of Gaunt, and both bishops saw Gloucester as a spent force and a representative of an older generation who needed to be removed. Eleanor gave them the excuse they needed when, in April 1440, she began to approach astrologers about casting the king's horoscope.[48]

Astrology was not magic, but astrologers were still in possession of dangerous information that could be used to foment rebellion or weaken the monarch. In the first century CE the Roman Emperor Augustus wisely decided to make his horoscope public as the best way to neutralise the threat of hostile astrologers, but he still made it illegal for slaves to consult astrologers about the deaths of their masters or for citizens to investigate the death of the emperor. Astrologers were regularly expelled from Rome and Roman jurists were divided on whether mere knowledge of astrology was necessary to justify expulsion, or evidence of practice or malicious intent was required.[49] Augustus began a tradition of official suspicion of astrologers – not because they were thought to invoke demons, but simply because they were believed to have access to information about the monarch's life and death.

Some astrologers just told their clients what they wanted (or needed) to hear, rather than attempting a genuine interpretation of the stars. Unfortunately for Eleanor, the two astrologers she consulted were too honest for their own good. They were both clerics of learning and influence: Thomas Southwell, a high-profile physician and a canon of St Stephen's Chapel in the Palace of Westminster, and Roger Bolingbroke, the head of an Oxford college. Southwell and Bolingbroke cast Henry's horoscope and, having examined it carefully, they concluded that the king would face a serious illness in the near future. Such a gloomy prediction was bound to leak out, and it soon reached the king's ministers. The council commissioned a rival astrologer to cast an alternative horoscope with a contrary interpretation of future events, but they then went further and brought in Southwell and Bolingbroke for questioning on 28 and 29 June 1441. We do not know exactly what the astrologers said, but twelve days later they were arrested and charged with necromancy and heresy.

Because Southwell and Bolingbroke's offence concerned the king, it fell within the purview of the law of treason. The clause in the 1351 Statute of Treason against 'compassing or imagining' the death of the king made astrological prognostications touching the king very risky indeed. In casting anyone's horoscope, an astrologer was 'compassing' that person's destiny, including his or her death; and if the astrologer added a specific interpretation of the astrological chart concerning that person's death, then the astrologer was certainly 'imagining' it. A lawyer could easily argue that casting the king's horoscope was treason by definition. However, the initial charge against Southwell and Bolingbroke was necromancy, even though there was technically no statute under which this crime could be prosecuted. However, the accusation painted Southwell and Bolingbroke as worse than they were and let the reputation of astrology in general off the hook, at least partially. It was certainly not the case that all astrologers were thought to be magicians, but there was a widespread assumption that anyone who possessed the skills to cast a horoscope could also probably practise black magic if he so chose.

One of Eleanor's servants brought her the news of Southwell and Bolingbroke's arrests while she was at dinner with her friends at an upmarket tavern, the King's Head in Cheapside. Eleanor fled immediately to Westminster Abbey for sanctuary. As soon as Eleanor touched the great bronze ring on the west door of Westminster Abbey she was under the abbot's protection. So far, however, Bolingbroke had only admitted that Eleanor asked him questions about her own future fortune; this was not a crime in itself, but since her fortunes might well involve her husband's succession to the throne and therefore Henry's death, she had been asking dangerous questions.

The council ordered Southwell to be imprisoned in the Tower on 10 July. Bolingbroke remained at liberty, but a royal servant, Bartholomew Hallay, was instructed to follow him on 12 July.[50] Under examination in the Tower between 10 and 23 July, Southwell named Eleanor as the instigator of the casting of the king's horoscope. This may have been when Bolingbroke was accused of necromancy that made use of the mass, as one chronicler suggested:

> It was said that the said master Roger should labour to consume the king's person by way of necromancy, and that the said master Thomas should say masses in forbidden and inconvenient places, that is to say, in the lodge of Hornsey Park beside London, upon certain instruments with which the said master Roger should use his said craft of necromancy against the faith and good belief.[51]

The perversion of the mass, although an ecclesiastical rather than a civil offence, was the most serious kind of black magic, and the introduction of this accusation into the proceedings was probably intended to leave no doubt that Bolingbroke and Southwell were necromancers. To make matters worse, Hornsey Park, which was about six miles north of the medieval city, belonged to the bishop of London. The lodge, which would originally have been where the bishop stayed while hunting, may already have been a ruin when Southwell and Bolingbroke visited. John Norden observed the ruins of this building in 1593 and concluded,

[It] seemeth by the foundation that it was rather a castle, than a lodge, for the hill is at this day trenched with two deep ditches, now old and overgrown with bushes: the rubble thereof, as brick, tile, and Cornish slate, are in heaps yet to be seen, which ruins are of great antiquity, as may appear by the oaks, at this day standing (above 100 years' growth) upon the very foundation of the building.[52]

The workings of magicians were associated with deserted houses, like the one in which John of Nottingham and Robert le Mareschall performed their operations in 1324. There was nothing illegal about saying mass in remote places. Hermits did so every day, but it was against canon law to say mass on something that was not a consecrated altar without a papal dispensation. It is possible that Southwell simply selected the lodge as a place where he thought he would not get caught. However, in the sixteenth and seventeenth centuries parks became associated with the fairies; they were places outside the civilised life of cities and the cultivated environment of farmland, and the ideal place to make contact with other worlds.[53] Hornsey lodge may have been 'forbidden and inconvenient' because it was a reputed haunt of fairies and evil spirits.

On 15 July Henry rode into London, but was met with a severe hailstorm, which Londoners concluded had been caused by witches and clerics dabbling in magic. It may have been at this point that the authorities arrested another actor in the drama, Margery Jourdemayne, the 'witch of Eye'.[54] On Sunday 23 July, Bolingbroke was forced to stand on a high stage in St Paul's Churchyard while the bishop of Rochester preached against sorcery at St Paul's Cross, the adjacent open-air pulpit. The audience included most of the king's council: Cardinal Beaufort, Archbishop Chichele of Canterbury, the bishops of London and Salisbury and the earls of Northumberland and Stafford.[55] They were treated to the spectacle of

> Master Roger with all his instruments of necromancy – that is to say a chair painted, wherein he was wont to sit when he wrought his craft, and on the four corners of the chair stood four swords, and upon every sword hanging an image of copper – and with many other instruments according to his said craft, stood in a high stage above all men's heads in Paul's churchyard before the cross while the sermon endured, holding a sword in his right hand and a sceptre in his left hand, arrayed in a marvellous array wherein he was wont to sit when he wrought his

necromancy. And after the sermon was done, he abjured all manner [of] articles belonging in any wise to the said craft of necromancy, or misowning to the Christian faith.[56]

According to one witness there were also 'images of silver, of wax, and other metals', which presumably included the effigy of the king that was supposed to cause his death. Necromancers were believed to conduct a rite in which the effigy of the person to be killed would be baptised in their name – another perversion of the church's official rites – in order to enhance the sympathetic correspondence between the effigy and the person.[57]

One mid-fifteenth-century manuscript book of magic surviving in Cambridge University Library contains magical procedures that may have been similar to those alleged against Southwell and Bolingbroke. The *Liber de angelis, annulis, karacteribus & ymaginibus planetarum* ('Book of Angels, Rings, Characters and Images of the Planets') was supposedly authored by someone called 'Messayaac', the sort of invented Jewish name that made a book of magic sound impressive and exotic.[58] It was copied by 'Bokenham', who may have been William Bockenham, a monk from Norwich with a medical degree from the University of Bologna.[59] It is certainly plausible that a book of this kind could have ended up in the hands of a physician, as the boundary between astrological medicine and forbidden magic was a porous one.

The *Liber de angelis* contained instructions for making an image out of red wax 'in the hour of Mars' (*in hora Martis*), which was to be submerged in running water, 'and by this same image you can ruin or destroy whatever you wish'.[60] However, the most sinister piece of magic in the *Liber de angelis* was something called 'The Trojan Revenge' (*Vindicta Troie*). This was perhaps an ironic allusion to the fact that Troy was destroyed by means of an image, the wooden horse in which Greek soldiers were hiding, but there is another interpretation. In Book 8 of Virgil's *Aeneid* (lines 839–40), the Sibyl informs Aeneas that a new leader will arise in Italy, 'of the race of Achilles, strong in arms, having avenged the ancestors of Troy and the defiled temples of Minerva' (*genus armipotentis Achilli, / ultus auos Troiae templa et temerata Mineruae*). The theme of the future rise of Rome as Troy's revenge against the Greeks runs throughout the *Aeneid*, the most widely read secular Latin text in medieval Europe. Richard Kieckhefer has noted that some spells in grimoires came with a sort of 'historical testimonial', claiming that a similar spell had been used by a historical character,[61] and the title of the 'Trojan Revenge' could be interpreted in this way. The Trojans' ultimate victory over the Greeks by becoming the ancestors of the Romans embodies a fear that the weak and defeated will somehow find an insidious means to overcome the strong and victorious.

The 'Trojan Revenge' took two forms. The first was intended to inflict a fever on someone rather than kill him or her,[62] but the second was very dark magic indeed. Entitled 'The experiment of Saturn to bring hatred or infirmity to someone in some member or in the whole body', it required the magician to obtain 'wax foul or decayed with age, especially funereal wax' (*ceram inmundam siue uetustate consumptam, et maxime ceram funeris*). This was the wax used for waterproofing the cerecloth in which bodies were buried, so the magician might have to engage in some grave-robbing. The magician shaped the wax into the form of the victim, saying:

> Oh most shining and powerful spirits of Saturn, descend now from the higher places! Oh sad ones, be present, wrathful, disquieting N the son of C; and descend in hate and usefulness, for as long as this image shall endure in the power of its creator, on N the son (or daughter) of C in whose name I now draw out this image.[63]

Then, when the magician had made the image as ugly and disfigured as possible, 'that is to say with a twisted face, with hands put in the place of feet and feet contrariwise in the place of hands',[64] he was to write the name of the victim on the image's forehead, with the name of Saturn on the figure's chest and the sigil of Saturn between the shoulder-blades. Then 'it should be suffumigated with horses' hooves, old shoes, rotten tin, human bones and hair. After this, wrap the image in a shroud and bury it in a horrible, fetid and unclean place, face down in the earth'.[65] Before burial, the image could be pierced with a pin to ensure disease in a particular part of the body, impotence, and even death: 'And if you want to hand him over to death, fix the pin upon the spine from the head to the heart'.[66]

Even then, however, the magic was potentially reversible, if the image was disinterred from the ground, the name and the pin removed, and the image washed in spring water.

The rather unusual phrase used by the chronicler to describe Bolingbroke's crime, 'misowning to the Christian faith', is an indication of the fine line between magic and heresy in fifteenth-century England. To 'disown' the Christian faith was to renounce belief in Christ and the Trinity, the crime of apostasy; clearly, Southwell and Bolingbroke were not guilty of this if they still believed in the effectiveness of the church's ceremonies. To 'misown', a word that has not survived into modern English, meant to profess the Christian faith in a perverted fashion, 'against faith and good belief'. In other words, Southwell and Bolingbroke were guilty of superstition, the wrong kind of religious belief. A superstitious person believed the accepted orthodox faith but added 'vain observances' on top, such as the belief that specific prayers had guaranteed effects. A heretic, by contrast, questioned the content of accepted orthodoxy itself.

There was nothing intrinsically heretical in believing that magic worked. Medieval theologians were divided on the extent to which God permitted the devil and his assistants to exercise power in the world, and some disputed the idea that human beings could recruit demons to assist them. However, this was usually expressed in the idea that magicians were deluded into thinking that they controlled the demons, when in reality the demons were controlling them. As long as magicians existed, it was perfectly plausible that demons would continue to seduce them to greater sins by giving the appearance of co-operation. On the other hand, the belief that God or his angels could be compelled to assist magicians was in an entirely different category. The sacraments of the church, taught the great Scholastic theologian Thomas Aquinas, gained their effectiveness from the fact that they were performed according to the correct form by a priest, and this doctrine strengthened the faith that magicians had in consecrated hosts. However, Aquinas also taught that it depended on God whether a person who received the host also received any grace; and this was where the magicians went wrong, assuming that the mass could be used as an instrument to control God.[67]

Because Eleanor was under the church's protection, she could only be tried by a church court, especially since she had committed a crime that was (insofar as it involved necromancy) under the church's jurisdiction. Accordingly, Eleanor was examined by a panel of bishops in St Stephen's Chapel, Westminster on 24 and 25 July. She eventually admitted to five of the 28 charges against her, and was committed to imprisonment in Leeds Castle in Kent to await trial. Southwell and Bolingbroke, meanwhile, were given a secular trial on 26 July where they were accused of having used magical figures, vestments and instruments in three London parishes to invoke evil spirits and calculate the death of the king. Southwell's part in the affair had been to sing masses for the protection of Bolingbroke, who had performed the actual conjurations. The two priests had made a wax figure of the king and calculated that he would die of 'melancholia' in May or June 1441. Witnesses claimed that Eleanor had aided and abetted all this, while the rumour of the king's impending death was circulated in London.[68]

Southwell and Bolingbroke were indicted for high treason and Eleanor was named as an accessory. Knowing that it could only impose a penance, Eleanor insisted that she should receive a trial in an ecclesiastical court since she had already submitted herself to the judgement of the bishops. When she appeared before the court on 21 October Eleanor denied treasonable necromancy but admitted that she had asked Bolingbroke for advice on how to conceive and obtained potions that would help her bear Duke Humphrey's child from Margery Jourdemayne. This was also an intelligent (albeit cynical) decision on Eleanor's part; had she denied everything, the church court could have discharged her to the civil authorities; had she admitted everything, the court could have deemed her offences so serious that she should be passed to the secular court. However, by admitting to a lesser offence, Eleanor obliged the church to impose a penance on her that served as a symbolic punishment for her misdemeanour.

On 9 November the procession of senior clergy filed into St Stephen's Chapel to pass sentence on Eleanor: Archbishop Chichele, Cardinal Beaufort, Archbishop Kemp, and the bishops of London, Salisbury and Norwich. Chichele annulled Eleanor's marriage with the duke. This was significant, because it implied that Eleanor had seduced Gloucester by magical arts and therefore he had not given his true and free consent to marriage. Furthermore, Eleanor was ordered to make a public spectacle of herself by walking barefoot to three London churches, on three successive market days, carrying a lighted taper. She was subsequently condemned to a luxury version of life imprisonment in a series of royal castles, with a pension of 100 marks (a mark was three quarters of a pound). Southwell, Bolingbroke and Margery Jourdemayne were not so lucky; Southwell died in the Tower of London, following a prophecy he had made 'that he should die in his bed, and not by justice',[69] leaving Bolingbroke to suffer the full penalty for treason.

On 18 November the unfortunate astrologer appeared before the Chief Justice of the King's Bench, Sir John Hody, along with two other men who had been implicated in the scandal: John Holme, one of Eleanor's chaplains, and a squire named William Wodham. Both Holme and Wodham were pardoned, but Bolingbroke was sentenced to death. Later that day he was drawn on a hurdle from the Tower to Tyburn, where he made a final profession that 'he presumed too far in his cunning ... whereof he cried God's mercy'. He was then hanged, drawn and quartered and his quarters sent to Oxford, Cambridge, York and Hereford while his head was displayed on London Bridge.[70] For the first time in English history, a magician had suffered the full penalty for treason.

Margery Jourdemayne was burnt alive at the stake in Smithfield market on 27 October. Burning was the punishment for a woman found guilty of petty or high treason, but Margery was apparently burnt because she 'relapsed', usually a term applied to heretics. A heretic brought before a church court for the first time would be required to recant and let off with a penance. If he or she then subsequently relapsed into heresy, the penalty was burning. Margery had already appeared before a church court for 'sorcery' in 1430,[71] so she was certainly a relapsed sorcerer, and it is possible that Margery was burnt following the example of Joan of Arc, who was burnt at the stake by the English at Rouen in 1431, accused of being a witch. If this was the case then Margery's execution was of dubious legality, because no capital crime of witchcraft existed in

1441, and the statute *De haeretico comburendo* gave no indication that witches were heretics.

There is no evidence that Margery was condemned to death for any identifiable heresy,[72] and indeed chroniclers of the time were clear that she suffered for 'false belief and witchcraft'. The absence of any record of her sentence in surviving Middlesex indictments would suggest that she was sentenced entirely by a church court for an ecclesiastical offence, and indeed in the seventeenth century Sir Edward Coke claimed that he had seen a document stating that Margery was burnt under *De haeretico comburendo*.[73] If true, the case of Margery Jourdemayne is one in which the practice of magic was regarded as explicitly heretical, a breach of the First as well as the Second Commandment. Maxwell-Stuart argues that the images made by Margery were intended for harmful magic against the king rather than fertility magic,[74] but it is unlikely that contemporaries thought of Margery as a witch in the later, early modern sense of that term. She was, rather, a cunning woman who specialised in love magic and aphrodisiacs, and Jessica Freeman saw her as a convenient scapegoat owing to her lower social status.[75] Whatever the truth, Margery was certainly the victim of Eleanor's plan to save herself.

The government's anxiety about magical treason did not stop at the executions of Bolingbroke and Margery Jourdemayne. Henry VI ordered a broader inquiry into 'all manner [of] treasons, sorcery, and all manner of things that might in any wise touch or concern harmfully the King's person'.[76] The government's concern even extended to hecklers. In 1443 Henry was riding through the streets of London when a woman named Juliana Quick called out at him, 'Harry of Windsor, ride soberly, thy horse may stumble and break thy neck'. Challenged by a courtier, John Beauchamp, Juliana further insulted the king, 'Thou art a fool, a known fool throughout the kingdom of England'. Juliana also referred disparagingly to the king's imprisonment of Eleanor Cobham, suggesting that the duchess of Gloucester may have enjoyed some popularity with ordinary people. Juliana was brought to trial with several others 'for secretly plotting the death of the king'.[77] Whether Juliana's initial words were treated as a form of curse or ill-wishing is unclear, but she refused to plead in court and so was condemned to *la peine forte et dure* ('the strong and hard penalty'), in which the accused was placed under a board and slowly crushed to death by weights placed on top of it.[78]

It seems highly likely, given what we know of Eleanor's ambitious character and Margery Jourdemayne's history of trouble with the church courts, that Margery was helping Eleanor with love potions and potions designed to promote conception. Assessing the guilt of the two astrologers, Southwell and Bolingbroke, is a harder task. That they cast a horoscope for the king is certain, and the display of magical instruments on the stage with Bolingbroke appears to show that they were using magic. Consecrated swords, wands and lamina (metal plates engraved with astrological signs) were indeed paraphernalia used by ritual magicians. However, the display at St Paul's Cross described by the chroniclers seems, if anything, a little too theatrical. Even if some of the equipment displayed to the curious public really did belong to the astrologers, it is by no means impossible that the authorities 'enhanced' that Sunday afternoon's entertainment by making Bolingbroke wear a fantastical robe. As for the wax images, they are mentioned only by one chronicler. Southwell and Bolingbroke may well have dabbled in magic, like many learned clerics and especially those learned in astrology, but the evidence that they actually used black magic to try to kill Henry VI is by no means convincing.[79]

MAGIC IN THE WARS OF THE ROSES

The second half of the fifteenth century saw the outbreak of the series of dynastic struggles that have become known as the Wars of the Roses. All of the players in this conflict were descendants of King Edward III (reigned 1327–77), whose grandson Richard II was overthrown in 1399 by Henry Bolingbroke (becoming Henry IV). Henry IV's claim to the throne was a tenuous one; he was the son of John of Gaunt, duke of Lancaster, the third son of Edward III. The famous victories won by Henry IV's son, Henry V, meant that there was little opposition to his reign, but the weakness of Henry VI in the 1450s and the loss of English territorial gains in France produced widespread disorder. In the summer of 1450 a rebellion broke out in Kent led by Jack Cade, who formed an army which briefly took control of London and forced Henry VI to flee to Warwickshire. Henry initially pardoned Cade and his followers, but later issued a proclamation calling for Cade's arrest. Amongst other things, this document claimed that Cade, by using magical books 'reared up the devil in the semblance of a black dog in his chamber where he was lodged at Dartford'.[80] Whether this was merely the use of accusations of magic to discredit a rebel or a reflection of genuine government fear that Cade possessed magical powers is unclear.

The political chaos of the 1450s tempted Richard Plantagenet, duke of York (1411–60), to assert his genealogical claim to be considered Henry's heir apparent. Richard was descended on his father's side from the fourth son of Edward III, Edmund of Langley, and on his mother's side from Lionel of Antwerp, the second son of Edward III. Richard believed that his combined paternal and maternal descent from Edward III gave him a better claim than Henry, although at first he was content to be recognised as heir apparent and accorded the political influence befitting such a status. Henry's mental breakdown in 1453 temporarily solved the potential conflict, as it allowed Richard of York to take control of the kingdom as Protector of the Realm. However, when Henry recovered his sanity in 1455 the kingdom erupted into full-blown civil war. Richard of York was killed at the battle of Wakefield in 1460 but his son, Edward of York, continued the fight, this time openly claiming the throne and displaying the white rose badge of the House of York. Henry VI's supporters became known as Lancastrians because of the king's descent from John of Gaunt, duke of Lancaster. Edward IV's victory in the battle of Towton in 1461 established him on the throne, for the time being at least.

On 22 January 1470 Thomas Wake was examined before the bishop of Carlisle, before whom he accused Jacquette of Luxemburg, widow of the duke of Bedford and mother of the queen, Elizabeth Woodville, of casting lead images of the king and her daughter. Wake had brought a parish clerk from Northamptonshire, John Daunger, to testify to the fact, but Daunger's evidence contradicted Wake's and the king's council set aside the case as 'unproven'. However, as Maxwell-Stuart notes, 'an accusation of image-magic could be made [against the queen's mother] and taken seriously by such people as the Archbishop of Canterbury, the Archbishop of York, the

Chancellor, the bishops of Ely, Rochester, Durham, and Carlisle, and several secular lords'.[81] Jacquette was acquitted.[82]

In October 1470 Edward IV was forced to flee to Burgundy when he was overthrown by the earl of Warwick, partly because Warwick resented Edward's marriage to Elizabeth Woodville. Warwick briefly restored Henry VI as a puppet king before Edward defeated the Lancastrians once again at the battle of Tewkesbury. Edward then ruled in relative security until his death in 1483. Edward IV's second reign was not entirely without its troubles, however, and in 1477 the spectre of magic as political crime returned. Edward's brother, George, duke of Clarence, had supported Warwick's restoration of Henry VI and, although Edward and Clarence were reconciled, the brothers' relationship must have been strained, to say the least. On 19 May 1477 an accusation of treason was made against Thomas Burdett, one of Clarence's retainers from his Warwickshire estates. Burdett was accused of engaging two Oxford men, John Stacy and Thomas Blake, one a layman and the other a priest, 'to calculate the nativities of the king, and of Edward, prince of Wales, his eldest son, and also to know when the king would die', in November 1474. It was further alleged that on 6 February 1475 Stacy and Blake 'worked and calculated by art magic, necromancy and astronomy, the death and final destruction of the king and prince'.[83] Burdett and Stacy were found guilty of high treason and hanged, drawn and quartered on 20 May 1477.

Initially, no link was made between Burdett's plot and Clarence himself, but Clarence unwisely arranged for a declaration of innocence made by Burdett just before his execution to be read to the council. Clarence's actions resulted in a summons to the Palace of Westminster, where Edward IV accused him of 'most serious [misconduct] ... in contempt of the law of the land and a great threat to judges and jurors of the kingdom'. Curiously, Clarence was accused of saying that Edward IV was trying to kill people by magic: he allowed his servants to say 'that the king our sovereign lord wrought by nigromancy and used craft to poison his subjects, such as he pleased', and claimed 'that the king intended to consume him in like wise as a candle consumeth in burning', a clear reference to practices of effigy-magic.[84]

Clarence was imprisoned and a special session of Parliament found him guilty of high treason at the beginning of 1478, before he suffered the bizarre execution of being drowned in a butt of sweet fortified wine on 18 February.[85] Clarence was never personally accused of treasonable necromancy and his death was only indirectly connected to the actions of Thomas Burdett, but the case demonstrated the powerful potential of accusations of necromancy to bring down the highest in the land in the fifteenth century. However, the case of Thomas Burdett is interesting in another way, because for the first time, astrology was equated with necromancy in the charges levelled against him. The wording of the accusation, equating 'art magic', 'necromancy' and 'astronomy', suggested that calculating the king's horoscope was here regarded as an intrinsic part of the act of trying to kill him by magic, rather than a necessary preparatory act to more sinister rites (as in the accusations against Southwell and Bolingbroke).

According to Thomas More's historically dubious biography of Richard III, in June 1483 Richard was convinced that Elizabeth and Edward IV's mistress, Jane Shore, had collaborated to kill him by magic, claiming 'That sorceress and that other witch of her counsel ... have by their sorcery and witchcraft wasted my body'.[86] According to one interpretation, Richard pretended to be under magical attack after eating some strawberries, to which he knew he was allergic, a gift from the bishop of Ely, John Morton.[87] After eating the strawberries, Richard is supposed to have bared his withered arm and accused William, baron Hastings of trying to kill him by witchcraft.[88] This accusation was followed by Richard declaring himself king in his own right (rather than regent for Edward IV's young son Edward V), partly on the grounds that the marriage of Edward V's parents (Edward IV and Elizabeth Woodville) had been brought about by love magic.[89] Canon law did not give clear guidance on the validity of marriages contracted whilst under the influence of magic,[90] and Richard also made the case that Edward's marriage to Elizabeth was null and void because he was already married to Eleanor Butler when he met Elizabeth.

Contemporary sources recording the arrest of Hastings and Morton do not mention any connection with accusations of magic or witchcraft. However, John Leland has argued that, if it happened, the charge of witchcraft against Elizabeth Woodville was more than the 'standard medieval smear' it seemed to be, since it led directly to Richard seizing the throne in his own right.[91] If, as Jonathan Hughes claimed, fear of witchcraft was the actual cause of Richard seizing the throne,[92] then the accusations against Elizabeth count as some of the most important charges of magical treason in English history. On 10 June Richard wrote to the city of York, asking for its help against Elizabeth and her relatives 'which have intended and daily doth intend to murder and utterly destroy us and our cousin the Duke of Buckingham and the old royal blood of this realm, and as it is now openly known by their subtle and damnable ways forecasted the same'.[93]

Richard was claiming that Elizabeth had employed astrology to know if an assassination of Richard would succeed ('forecasted'), but the use of the word 'damnable' implied that more than astrology was involved here. Richard seems to have been implying astrology allied with necromancy, as in the Eleanor Cobham case. When Henry Stafford, duke of Buckingham rebelled against Richard in the autumn of 1483, one of the rebels was 'Thomas Nandyk, late of Cambridge, nigromancer', who may have been in the service of one of the other rebels, Bishop Morton of Ely.[94] Nandyk or Nandyke was a physician and was present at Brecon at the time of Buckingham's rebellion, and later at Colchester when the Brandon family launched another revolt. Nandyke was subsequently outlawed by act of Parliament. Leland has speculated that Nandyke could have been the astrologer who 'forecasted' on behalf of Elizabeth Woodville against Richard.

Another anti-Ricardian physician and astrologer was Lewis of Caerleon, who was popular amongst the Lancastrian nobility, including the earl of Richmond, the son of Edmund Tudor and Lady Margaret Beaufort, who would go on to become Henry VII. In 1483 Lewis was implicated in a plot by Richmond and the duke of Buckingham to overthrow Richard III and was incarcerated in the Tower. It seems likely that he would have been accused of treasonable necromancy, given his profession, but as it happened his patron won the battle of Bosworth and Lewis was made a knight of the king's alms at Windsor in 1486.[95] However, Leland has noted that Lewis had a particular interest in past magicians accused of treason; he owned a manuscript discussing the horoscope of Henry VI prepared by Southwell and Bolingbroke and a set of astrological tables prepared for Humphrey, duke of Gloucester by John Randolph.[96]

THE REIGN OF HENRY VII

Henry VII was not immune to magical attempts against his life, and in 1494 a remarkable conspiracy was launched in Rome to poison the king with a magical ointment. The conspirators were John Kendal, grand prior of the Order of St John of Jerusalem in England,[97] his nephew John Thweng (also a knight of the order), William Horsey, the archdeacon of London, and his nephew John Horsey. Also party to the plot were two servants (named Walter and Lilly) and a secretary, William Witton. The eighth and final conspirator was a Frenchman, Bernard de Vignolles. The group planned to kill by magic the king, his children, his mother Lady Margaret Beaufort, 'and those who thought themselves close to his person and counsel'. Archdeacon Horsey had already tried this once before; he went to stay in the house of an 'astrologer', Rodrigo, who promised to carry out the deed. Rodrigo, however, took his money and did nothing. The conspirators then sent Bernard to another Spanish 'astrologer', known only as Juan. It is likely that both Rodrigo and Juan were *conversos*, converted Jews fleeing the persecution of the Spanish Inquisition; Spanish Jews had a Europe-wide reputation for magical skill.

As a demonstration of his powers, Juan the magician promised to bring about the death, remotely and by magical means, of a young man acting as a personal servant to Çem, the brother of the Ottoman Sultan Bayezid II, then being held as an honoured prisoner in the Vatican Palace by Pope Alexander VI. The conspirators agreed to pay Juan the sum of money they had promised, then despatched Bernard with instructions to give it to the astrologer, along with instructions for a magical assassination of Henry VII. As an extra guarantee, Prior Kendal left one of his servants, a Sardinian named Stefano Maranicho, at the astrologer's house.

Once they had made their preparations the conspirators returned to England, where they waited for two years before they met together again, probably at the headquarters of the Order of St John in Clerkenwell. Rodrigo, the first astrologer they had asked to carry out the act, was spreading the rumour in Rome that there was a plot to kill the king of England. Archdeacon Horsey was getting very nervous indeed, and put pressure on Prior Kendal to send Bernard back to Rome to silence the unsatisfactory magician – this time by the rather less magical means of cutting his throat. Bernard was also to go to Juan, the other astrologer, and ensure that he carried out what he had been paid to do; money was no object. Bernard accordingly went back to Italy and asked Juan whether he could kill the king without personally visiting England, 'from fear that he was not known there'. The astrologer replied that he had to visit Henry's palace, disguised in the habit of a friar, if the plan was to work. In the event Juan never did go to England, although Bernard thought this was simply because the conspirators were not paying him enough.

Promising to follow him to England, Juan gave Bernard a small box containing an ointment that, if smeared along the step of a door or gate that the king might walk over, would cause his closest friends to turn on him and kill him. Going back to his room, Bernard opened the box out of curiosity, and was so disgusted by the smell of the contents that he threw it away. However, he was afraid that Juan had already written to Kendal explaining that Bernard was the courier for a magical ointment, so Bernard bought a replacement box from an apothecary at Orleans. He faked the colour of the magical ointment by mixing mercury with earth, soot and water. Bernard made his way to the prior's lodgings at Clerkenwell and presented Kendal with the box, giving the precise message that Juan had told him to pass on, 'that there was great danger in touching it for those that had the desire to do evil with it, and that if it remained for twenty-two hours in his house, this would be to his great danger'. Terrified, the prior refused to accept the box and told Bernard to throw it away.[98] Bernard made a long confession of this whole affair to the authorities in 1496. Henry VII does not seem to have taken the matter seriously and Kendal was pardoned on 18 June 1496.[99]

CONCLUSION

It is not particularly surprising that, given the dramatic changes in political fortune that could affect anyone in fifteenth-century England, high-ranking figures at court consulted astrologers for some consolation about the future. However, by the end of the fifteenth century it had become possible to 'demonise' astrology, equating it with the 'black art' of necromancy. Part of the reason for this may have been simple ignorance. To the untrained eye, the circular form taken by an astrological chart would have resembled the magic circles drawn out by magicians, which were supposed to afford protection from the spirits they called up. It was well-known that magicians relied upon the correct calculation of the phases of the moon and the position of the stars to make their rituals effective. However, high-profile events like the Eleanor Cobham affair also served to bring astrology into disrepute; the idea that astrologers might also be magicians was eminently plausible in the popular imagination.

The insecurities of fifteenth-century governments and the esoteric interests of members of the court together created the perfect conditions for accusations of magical treason. However, fifteenth-century accusations of political crime involving magic differed in two important respects from later cases. Sixteenth- and seventeenth-century magicians accused of conspiring the death of the monarch were condemned under the law of treason and never under the heresy laws. Furthermore, where fifteenth-century anxieties focussed on the king's stability on the throne and the survival of the regime, the sixteenth century saw the development of much more far-reaching existential concerns. Henry VIII continued to worry about potential challenges from rival Yorkist claimants, but it was the religious upheavals across the sea in Germany that really discomfited his ministers. When Henry took the momentous step of allowing these new currents of thought to take hold in his own kingdom, the very foundations of society, authority and belief were unsettled.

CHAPTER 2

Treason, Sorcery and Prophecy in The Early English Reformation, 1534–58

Traitors and potential traitors were always amongst a sensible monarch's first priorities, but the Tudors expanded the boundaries of what counted as the business of central government, and with it the boundaries of what might be considered a political crime. As Chapter 1 has shown, acts of magical treason were not a distinctively early modern phenomenon, but the anxiety they produced in the sixteenth century was unprecedented, perhaps because the ruling elite had begun to fear dark forces of disorder at work in a world that was changing at a bewildering pace. Lacey Baldwin Smith connected growing interest in both treason and illicit magic with religious changes, suggesting that

> The refusal to accept the operation of chance and free will and the even more depressing logic that all misfortune stemmed from the slug of depravity inherent in every Christian soul, which ... drove Tudor England to seek an explanation and remedy for personal failure in the existence and punishment of witches and warlocks, may also have encouraged the conviction that the enemy with his sinister conspiracies was for ever stalking innocent, unsuspecting and loyal-hearted people.[1]

A further contributing factor to the association between treason and magic was the fact that early modern England was 'a world addicted to making connections on the basis of correspondences' between things that contemporary viewers might regard as entirely different.[2] An attack on a symbol might be equated to a literal attack on the object it represented. It was treason to harm a ward of the monarch, and likewise a serious offence to injure or kill a messenger in royal livery. Anything that represented the monarch was, in a sense, the monarch him or herself.[3] Thus, the counterfeiting of currency was a crime closely assimilated to high treason because it involved disrespect to the image of the monarch, and it was treated not so much as a form of fraud as an affront to the monarch's person and authority. However, counterfeiting was also closely linked to alchemy and magic, insofar as it required the ability to simulate the appearance of gold and silver.

The same sort of thinking that lay behind the extension of treason to cover affronts to the monarch's honour or personal image also lay behind sympathetic magic, most notably the attempt to harm someone by using an effigy. It should not be surprising that accusations of treason so often involved magic; after all, the sacredness of the monarch against which traitors offended was itself 'magical' insofar as it mysteriously extended beyond the king's person, and in an age when 'constructive treason' was a favourite device of despotic monarchs, no accusation was more damaging, scandalous or easier to fabricate against someone than treasonous magic. Magical acts that could be construed as treason had been prosecuted in the courts since the fourteenth century, but strictly speaking it was *only* when magic was involved in treason that it was a criminal matter before 1542, when Parliament passed the first act explicitly directed against magical practices. The criminalisation of magic meant, in one sense, that magic became a political crime by definition, since Parliament considered it a potential threat to good order in the commonwealth. However, although political motivations did lie behind the 1542 act, magic as a political crime might also be punished as *lèse majesté*, sedition, misprision of treason or as high treason itself under the extended definitions of that crime developed in the reign of Henry VIII. Politicisation of magic in the Reformation period clearly did not extend to every magical act, and although allegations of magic were increasingly deployed against conservative critics of religious reform, they also remained rooted in an earlier medieval tradition of suspecting the monarch's enemies of dark supernatural dealings.

THE TUDORS AND THE ENGLISH REFORMATION

When Henry VII's second son Prince Henry succeeded him in 1509, England hoped for the dawning of a golden age. The young Henry VIII had little interest in politics and delegated the everyday running of his kingdom to Cardinal Thomas Wolsey, the butcher's son from Ipswich who became England's greatest Renaissance magnate. However, Henry was interested in theology and even authored a book against the new Lutheran heresy which had sprung up in Germany, *The Assertion of the Seven Sacraments* (1521). This gained him a reputation as one of Europe's most devout Catholic princes and the title 'Defender of the Faith' from the pope. Through his marriage to Catherine of Aragon he aligned England with Spain, recently united into a single kingdom and Europe's fastest rising power with a newly discovered empire in the Americas.

Yet there was a cloud on the horizon. Henry VIII's interest in politics and in the future of his own dynasty was kindled in the late 1520s by the unavoidable biological fact that Catherine was reaching an age when she would be unable to bear him a son. So far, she had borne him a single daughter, Mary, and suffered numerous miscarriages and stillbirths. At around the same time, Henry became infatuated with a lady of the court, Anne Boleyn. Henry was reminded of the fact that Catherine had been briefly married to his eldest brother, Prince Arthur, before his death in 1502, and began to worry that a verse of Leviticus that threatened a curse of childlessness on a man who married his brother's widow might apply to him. Henry instructed Wolsey to obtain an annulment of his marriage from the pope. This was not an unreasonable request in principle; Rome had obliged monarchs in similar situations before, and a case against the validity of Henry and Catherine's marriage could certainly be made. However, by a fatal historical accident, the pope was at the time under the complete control of Catherine's nephew, the Emperor Charles V, who would never allow the disgrace of having his aunt cast off by the king of England.

Attempts to obtain the divorce (or more properly annulment) stalled and by 1533 Henry, in consultation with his ministers, had decided on a radical constitutional solution to his marital problems. Unable to annul his marriage to Catherine, Henry would instead annul England's marriage to Catholic Christendom. In 1532 the Statute in Restraint of Appeals prevented any English subject from appealing the decision of an ecclesiastical court to the highest authority, the pope. Then the Act of Supremacy of 1534 declared Henry the Supreme Head of the Church of England on the rather flimsy historical grounds that England had never truly been subject to the pope's jurisdiction anyway. An Oath of Supremacy declaring Henry to be the Supreme Head of the church could now be tendered to anyone, especially the clergy. Finally, a new Treason Act in 1534 defined refusal to recognise the king's new status as treason, and no-one was exempt; Henry's former Lord Chancellor, Sir Thomas More, and the bishop of Rochester, John Fisher, both lost their heads on Tower Hill in the summer of 1535.

Henry's policy of religious change was far from over. Conscious that they constituted a focus of opposition to his new religious policy, and desperate for funds to support his war with France, Henry instructed his new first minister, Thomas Cromwell, to dissolve and seize the lands of England's monasteries. Cromwell began with the smaller abbeys and priories in 1536. The larger abbeys followed a few years later and the dissolution process was complete by 1540, cutting a swathe through almost a thousand years of religious history and wiping out the charitable work of the monasteries, the closest thing to a medieval welfare state. No government could attempt so radical an assault on local communities without being challenged, and a protest movement sprang up in the north known as the 'Pilgrimage of Grace', opposing the dissolution and looking alarmingly like the armed rebellion it claimed not to be. The dynastic wars of the fifteenth century had been bloody, certainly, but sixteenth-century England was entering a profound and hitherto unparalleled crisis of the soul.

Henry's Reformation was a piecemeal affair, an effort at reform by a Catholic king forced by circumstance into schism with Rome and manipulated by ministers both Catholic and Protestant – if the words

'Protestant' and 'Catholic' can be used meaningfully at this early stage. The terms 'reformers' and 'conservatives' better describe the participants in the religious debate. After 1535 everyone in government accepted the royal supremacy, at least in practice, but some were keen to retain all Catholic rites, doctrines and practices while others, like Cromwell and the new archbishop of Canterbury, Thomas Cranmer, were keen to see reform along the lines of what had taken place in the German Lutheran states and Huldrych Zwingli's Zurich. Henry himself picked and chose the doctrines he liked; purgatory, the doctrine that the souls of sinful but repentant Christians underwent a period of purification before entering heaven, was abolished. Bizarrely, however, the sacrifice of the mass, which was believed to relieve the souls in purgatory, remained. Still more perversely, Henry ordered that the English Bible translated by William Tyndale should be made available in all churches, yet burnt as heretics those who chose to interpret it for themselves.

Henry's church lurched away from the path of reform in the king's twilight years, but things changed dramatically after his death when the dukes of Somerset and Northumberland ruled successively on behalf of the young King Edward VI. Somerset and Northumberland launched a campaign of religious reform before which Henry's efforts paled into insignificance. A new, plain English liturgy replaced the mass and churchwardens in every parish in England were instructed to remove all unnecessary vessels, images of the saints, rood lofts and stone altars from churches, whose walls were whitewashed and adorned only with biblical inscriptions in blackletter script. The Edwardine Reformation was amongst the most radical in Europe, and was partly inspired by the ideas of the austere Swiss reformer Zwingli. When Edward VI died of tuberculosis on 6 July 1553 at the age of seventeen, Northumberland made a desperate attempt to preserve his Reformation by promoting Lady Jane Grey, the granddaughter of Henry VIII's youngest sister Mary, as the new queen. Popular opinion, however, was on the side of the Lady Mary, Henry's daughter by Catherine of Aragon.

Mary, who had never truly accepted her father's reforms, rapidly swept away opposition and began the process of returning England to the Catholic faith. In this she was assisted by Cardinal Reginald Pole, papal legate and archbishop of Canterbury (who also happened to be a member of the once rival Yorkist dynasty). Mary repudiated the title of Supreme Head of the English church, arranged for the restoration of church goods and prohibited the English liturgy. In January 1555 Parliament revived the fifteenth-century laws against heresy, along with the penalty of burning that had been repealed under Henry VIII and Edward VI. During the course of Mary's reign, around 300 people were tried and found guilty of heresy in ecclesiastical courts and handed over to the civil authorities to be burned alive. For centuries, this one aspect of Mary's reign completely overshadowed her reputation, in spite of the fact that she was not the only Tudor monarch to burn people for heresy. However, John Foxe's *Actes and Monumentes* (first published in 1563), which portrayed the heretics burnt in Mary's reign as the latest in a long line of martyrs created by a corrupt Catholic church, became a defining document of English Protestant Christianity.

In Mary's reign England was joined to Catholic Christendom once more and experienced Renaissance art and culture, and by her marriage to Phillip II of Spain in 1554 Mary brought England into an alliance with the Habsburgs, the family that ruled the New World and more than half of Western Europe. England became an early proving ground for the Catholic Counter-Reformation, the church's counter-attack against Protestantism, and many of the foremost figures of the Marian church went on to lead the Counter-Reformation in Europe. Yet a true evaluation of the potential of Mary's Catholic regime is prevented by the fact of its abrupt end. The childless queen died in an influenza epidemic on 17 November 1558, followed by Cardinal Pole a few hours later.

Divided by religion, Henry VIII, Edward VI and Mary shared an exalted view of the prerogatives of monarchy that made them and their governments especially sensitive to treason. The greater the monarch's power, the greater the threat of magical treason seemed, as other more overt means of undermining the state, such as armed rebellion, became increasingly unrealistic. The Henrician and Edwardine reformations, by eroding the authority of the church, removed powers from the church courts and made it necessary for Parliament to legislate in areas that had previously been the sole concern of the church's canon law such as sexual behaviour, religious belief and the use of magic. The medieval church was certainly no bastion of personal liberty, but the early modern state's intrusion brought harsh penalties for offences that would once have been dealt with by the imposition of a penance. Judicial punishment, unlike penance, was final and represented a retributive rather than a redemptive ideal of justice.

PROPHECY AND TREASON

The earliest opposition to Henry VIII's new religious policy took the form of prophecy rather than magic, although the two soon became intertwined. In 1533 a nun from Kent, Elizabeth Barton (the 'Holy Maid of Kent'), who already had a reputation for receiving visions and was well known to William Wareham, the archbishop of Canterbury and John Fisher, the bishop of Rochester, began speaking against the king's marriage to Anne Boleyn and predicted his death. Barton was arrested and examined by the Court of Star Chamber in November 1533, but the judges would not find her guilty of treason just for uttering words *prophesying* the king's death because these were not necessarily uttered with malice.[4] In February 1534, during or after Barton's second treason trial, Cromwell wrote at length to Fisher, criticising him for choosing to believe her prophecies. Cromwell accused Fisher of not subjecting Barton's prophecies to proper scrutiny and accepting her truthfulness on hearsay, asking pointedly, 'Whether if she had showed you as many revelations or the confirmation of the king's grace's marriage ... as she did to the contrary, you would have given as much credence to her as you have done[?]'. In Cromwell's view, Fisher had cynically chosen to exploit Barton's prophecies for political advantage.

Fisher's greatest crime in Cromwell's eyes, however, was to have withheld the content of Elizabeth Barton's revelations, especially where they concerned the king's death, from Henry himself: 'You were bound by your fidelity to show to the king's grace that thing which seemed to concern his grace and his reign so nearly'.[5] Fisher's communications with Barton, according to Cromwell's interpretation, began to look uncomfortably like 'compassing or imagining' the king's death. Barton was found guilty at her second trial, apparently on the grounds that her words were likely to cause a division between the king and his people, and she was executed as a traitor on 21 April 1534. After her death, Barton was widely portrayed as a witch by Tudor propagandists.[6] Although her punishment had eventually been secured, the case of the 'Holy Maid' revealed to Henry and Cromwell that there existed a loophole in the law of treason that could allow someone to prophesy the king's death with impunity.

Parliament responded in November 1534 by revising the Statute of Treason. It was now treason to 'maliciously wish, will or desire by words or writing, or by craft imagine, invent, practise, or attempt any bodily harm to be done or committed to the king's most royal person'. It was also treason to express anything in words or writing to the effect that the king was 'a heretic, tyrant, schismatic, infidel or usurper of the crown'. The act also abolished sanctuary for those accused of high treason, making it impossible for anyone to place themselves under the protection of the church, as Eleanor Cobham had done in 1441. The fact that attacks on Henry's claim to the throne were condemned in the same breath as attacks on his religious policy was significant; Henry's break with Rome faced some of the severest criticism in the North, where support for the Tudors was also weakest. The Pilgrimage of Grace, which was preceded by unrest in Lincolnshire, began in Yorkshire in October 1536. Its leaders proclaimed that it was not a rebellion against the king, but rather against the evil counsel of his ministers and opposed only one policy, the dissolution of the monasteries. However, it cannot have been lost on Henry that the North, and Yorkshire in particular, was the home of Yorkist magnates who had never truly accepted the Tudor dynasty.

By the new statute of 1534, treason was expanded from protection of the king's person to include protection of his policies,[7] since it was difficult to disagree with the break with Rome without implying that the king was a heretic and schismatic. As in 1351, the new definition was not immediately followed by a rush of prosecutions and it may have been as much a symbolic gesture as an attempt to ensnare a whole new category of traitors. The addition of the word 'maliciously' to the definition of treason by 'wishing' makes it doubtful that

Elizabeth Barton could have been prosecuted under the new statute anyway. However, the statute may have aided the conviction of William Byrd, the vicar of Brodford in Wiltshire, who in November 1536 instructed his chaplain and others to use magic to discover how long the king would live. Byrd issued a veiled threat against the king's life if he were ever to visit the North: '[I]f the King go thither himself he will never come home again ... and in truth it were pity he should every [sic.] come home again'. However, the execution of the law was inconsistent and the London priest William Barton and his associate Richard Smith seem never to have come to trial for declaring that 'the King was a cuckold and should worthily die'. Like Byrd, Barton and Smith were also involved in magic and Smith had made a special magical chain, composed of precious metals, which was supposed to be a gift to the king and would cause his death by a fall.[8]

The evidence suggests that the same disaffected individuals who were attracted by the idea of prophecies were interested in magic as well. Prophecy and magic were different in theory, since prophecy involved knowing the future rather than trying to control it, but it is not difficult to imagine how the one desire might turn into the other. In 1536 an informant named Richard Branktre made numerous accusations against William Love, the Cistercian abbot of Coggeshall in Essex. The principal accusation against Love was his reading of anti-royal prophecies, but Branktre also claimed to know from testimony given by John Sampford, a previous abbot, and a servant called Nicholas Crane that Love had given a drink to a young woman to cause a miscarriage. She nearly died as a result, and the abbot and others made preparations to bury her in the wood yard if she did. The procurement of abortions was closely associated with cunning-folk and was intended to imply that the abbot was dealing in magic.

Love was also accused of homosexuality or pederasty: he 'did unlawfully use one Rob[er]t Goswill, then young and now a monk there; this was about ten years past'. Finally, Love was accused of locating lost objects.[9] What Branktre probably had in mind was the 'Bible and key', a popular and enduring form of divination that involved placing a key on a verse of the Bible. The book was then closed with the key protruding, bound together, and suspended by a cord. The diviner took hold of the key's bow and spoke the name of a thief or the location of a lost item; if he spoke correctly, it was believed that the Bible and key would turn. The curate of Rye, William Inold, was accused of preaching against Henry's religious changes and refusing to read the Bible in English; he also observed forbidden holy days, such as the feast of St Thomas Becket, and promoted veneration of images and relics which had officially been outlawed. All of these offences were reported to Cromwell by Inold's parishioners, who also labelled him a 'witch' because he tried to cure a child called Hamper of the 'chyne cough' (probably whooping cough) by encouraging him to drink three times from the chalice at mass.[10]

Neither William Love nor William Inold was accused of doing anything that a cunning man or woman would not have done; theirs was not the ritual magic of necromancers. However, the accusations against them are indicative of a pattern that developed during the 1530s whereby 'superstitious' practices, including magic, were routinely attributed to opponents of religious change. Maxwell-Stuart has described this process as the 'politicisation of magic',[11] and the 1530s marked the beginning of a vociferous and actively escalating campaign by proponents of reform to discredit Catholic ceremonies as magic. As Helen Parish has observed, however, the reformers were caught between their desire to accuse conservative clergy of being magicians in league with the devil on the one hand, and their desire to portray Catholic ceremonial as nothing more than empty 'juggling' on the other.[12]

It seems unlikely that Cromwell believed that the likes of Love and Inold were about to attempt treasonable acts of magic, but the government increasingly viewed the new category of traitors created by Henry's laws (dissident religious conservatives) as potentially capable of any form of religious deviance, including magic. The connection between magic and clerical disobedience was confirmed by cases like that of Sir William Richardson, a priest who celebrated the feast of St Thomas Becket on 1 July 1537, in defiance of royal edict. Richardson had previously been accused of sorcery, but escaped justice because Lady Lisle had interceded for him, and she now promised to do the same again.[13]

The government's interest in magicians extended to those who sought to foresee and control the acts of the king and his ministers as well as those who were trying to kill him by magic. On 30 July 1537 James Mayhow of Rochester, Robert Hogekyn of Flushing and Arnold Hopkin of Sittingbourne met with an English priest living in the Low Countries named Doctor Clene, who was otherwise known as 'Sir John Skarme', 'because he can cumber the devil as is said'. This was a reference to the popular but unofficial English saint 'Sir John Schorne', who was supposed to have put the devil in a boot.[14] The word 'conjurer', as applied to Doctor Clene, was ambiguous: a priest with a reputation as an exorcist might equally have a reputation as a magician. Clene told his visitors that he had used a crystal to see whether the leaders of the Pilgrimage of Grace were still alive, and had discovered that one was still at large and would kill the king not more than eleven days before Christmas.[15] Use of a crystal implied that Clene had summoned a spirit and therefore performed necromancy.

Clene also said that he had once worked for Cardinal Wolsey, for whom he made a magical ring 'with a stone that he wrought many things with', but suffered imprisonment in the Fleet as a consequence. Devices that could win favour with the king or protect the wearer from condemnation in court (or even from execution) were a staple of early modern magic. One grimoire of the period advised, 'If thou dost desire the love of any worshipful man, write his name and his mother's name and bend it under thy right armhole and bear it with thee, and thou shalt have his love'.[16] The belief that Henry's favourites, Wolsey and Cromwell, were only able to achieve what they did by magic rings seems to have been widespread. It was an indictment of Henry's notorious caprice and fickleness that people believed his favour could only be retained for long periods of time by using magic. Wolsey and Cromwell were his longest surviving ministers, but there is no evidence that they really did try to use magic to maintain their positions.[17]

The suggestion that people were trying to control the king remotely by magic was a disturbing one; technically, it did not violate any existing law, but it implied potential harm to the monarch and therefore fell within the ambit of a treason investigation. A magical ring was part of the potentially treasonous dealings of Sir William Neville, the brother of John Neville, Lord Latimer. The Nevilles were a junior branch of the family of Richard Neville, earl of Warwick (1428–71), who famously affected the course of the Wars of the Roses and was known as the 'Kingmaker'. Sir William seems to have been inspired by his family's glorious history to consult two magicians, Richard Jones and William Wade, to predict his future and provide him with various magical paraphernalia, including a cloak of invisibility. The magicians predicted that Neville would become earl of Warwick and were tempted into ever more rash prophecies, eventually declaring that Henry's reign would end in 1533 and that Neville would organise the subsequent succession to the throne.[18]

Neville asked Jones to make him a magical ring like one that Cardinal Wolsey was supposed to have possessed, 'that whatsoever he asked of the king's grace, that he had'. Neville thought that Cromwell had also consulted 'one that was seen in your faculty' (i.e. magic). When he was later questioned about this allegation, Jones admitted that 'I showed him that I had read many books, and specially the works of Solomon, and how this ring should be made, and of what metal; and what virtues they had after the canon of Solomon'.[19] However, Jones denied having actually made the ring. The earldom of Warwick had last been held by Edward of Warwick (son of the duke of Clarence), a Yorkist pretender who died in the Tower in 1499, so any attempt to revive it 'by sorcery or possibly by force' had more than a whiff of treason about it. Fortunately for Neville, Cromwell recognised that he was not a deliberate traitor and he remained in the king's favour.

One group especially suspected of magic and defying the government in the 1530s were friars. There were a number of separate orders of friars in England in the 1530s, who included the Blackfriars (Dominicans), the Greyfriars (Franciscans), Observant Friars and Whitefriars (Carmelites).[20] Friars were mendicants, meaning that (in theory) their only income was from alms rather than from lands belonging to their priories. Unlike monks, the friars were supposed to move from place to place, preaching and living lives of Christian simplicity. In practice, however, soon after their first appearance in England in the thirteenth century, the friars had been at the forefront of advanced education in the universities.

The Dominicans and Franciscans both had houses at Oxford and Cambridge and many friars were highly educated, holding doctorates of divinity. All of the leading minds of medieval scholastic philosophy were either Dominican or Franciscan friars, including Thomas Aquinas, Bonaventure, Duns Scotus and William of Ockham.

John Randolph, the astrologer who suffered for his association with Henry V's stepmother, Joan of Navarre, had been a Franciscan friar, and the friars' extensive knowledge gave them a not altogether undeserved reputation for necromancy. Part of the reason for this was the friars' interest in the entirety of nature. Medieval Franciscans pioneered alchemy (accidentally inventing the distillation of alcohol in the process), and one of the most popular stories of sorcery in medieval England concerned a magical talking bronze head supposedly made by the thirteenth-century Franciscan Roger Bacon.[21] Franciscans adopted a materialistic approach to the spiritual world that led them to promote devotional practices close to or indistinguishable from magic.[22] To make matters worse for the friars in England, their continued existence in the realm challenged the break with Rome. Unlike Benedictine monks, friars belonged to centrally organised, world-wide orders,[23] and their loyalties were suspect in the extreme as far as the government was concerned.

Franciscan confidence in the reality and effectiveness of magic made the friars celebrated exorcists of evil spirits, but it also meant that some friars became interested in magic themselves. Cromwell commissioned an agent named Gervase Tyndall to investigate a group of friars who were suspected of necromantic activities, which Cromwell suspected were aimed at undermining the regime.[24] When in June 1535 a government informant named Jasper Fyloll 'stopped at the Black Friars here of London, friar Dr Maydland said he would like to see the head of every maintainer of the new learning upon a stake ... and to see the king die a "violent and shameful" death; also, "to see that mischievous whore the queen to be burnt"'. According to Fyloll's account, Maydland declared that 'he knew by his science of necromancy that the new learning should be suppressed, and the old restored by the king's enemies from beyond the sea'.[25] Maydland's prophecy was probably a reference to the widespread belief that the

Holy Roman Emperor Charles V would intervene in England and overthrow Henry.

Some of Henry's humblest subjects felt strongly enough against his religious changes to attempt to direct supernatural power against him. On 7 September 1537 John Lokkar, a farmer at Rysome Grange in Holderness, the part of Yorkshire on the north side of the river Humber, had a surprise visitor:

> One Mabel Brigge came to the house of John Lokkar at Reysome Grange, a se'nnight before Cross Day [14 September] last, with two children, and immediately afterwards one Nelson, the farmer of Risome Garth, sent his maiden, one Margaret, to the aforesaid Lokkar, desiring that the above named Mabel might remain and he would see her costs paid. John and Agnes Lokkar then perceiving that the said Mabel fasted the next Friday, Saturday and Sunday till mass was done, asked her why she did so. She replied it was a charitable fast, and said she had never so fasted before but once for a man, and he broke his neck ere it were all fasted, and so she trusted that they should do that had made all this business, and that was the King and this false Duke [of Norfolk].[26]

As a laywoman, a directed fast was the most powerful spiritual weapon that Mabel had at her disposal. It is unlikely that she would have seen her actions as magical, but her expectation that the fast would have automatic and specific consequences makes it an instance of religious practice that is hard to distinguish meaningfully from magic. Lockar, horrified by Mabel's plan, paid a visit to Isabel Bucke, the woman whom Mabel said had hired her. According to Lokkar, Isabel confessed that she wanted the deaths of the king and the duke of Norfolk, who had been sent to put down the Pilgrimage of Grace, but Isabel's husband William begged Lockar to keep the matter secret and tried to bribe him with three shillings and two yards of cloth.

Mabel then moved to the house of William Fletcher in nearby Welwick, where she began what she called the 'Black Fast', eating and drinking nothing but bread and water on one day a week for five weeks. This, she believed, would oblige everyone in Holderness to pray for her and Isabel. Mabel and Isabel were both arrested and questioned on 28 January 1538 by a commission convened to investigate the matter composed of Thomas and James Ellerkar, John Goldwell and Patrick Tomson. The government took this threat seriously because Holderness was just across the Humber Estuary from Lincolnshire, where rebellion against Henry's religious changes first broke out in October 1536. The spirit of rebellion had spread north into Holderness, and from there infected Yorkshire, becoming the Pilgrimage of Grace.

Under questioning on 4 February, Isabel claimed that she originally asked Mabel to fast for her around 24 June 1537 so that she could locate some money which had been stolen. She was not, in other words, denying the magical intention of the fast – ritual methods for finding stolen goods were a staple of common magic – but she denied that she had ever asked Mabel 'to fast St Trynzan's fast for a wreck-taking of the King's Highness and the Duke of Norfolk'. Isabel originally intended to fast herself, but obtained permission from Thomas Marshall, a chantry priest at Holmpton whom she described as her 'ghostly father', to ask Mabel to fast in her stead because she was feeling faint. Clearly, from the priest's point of view this was a legitimate reason to perform the devotion of a fast dedicated to 'St Trynzon', the Irish saint Trinian. The suspects were taken to York on 11 March, where Mabel was indicted for high treason and executed, presumably by burning, but Isabel was reprieved. The chantry priest and William Bucke, who tried to bribe Lokkar, were convicted of misprision of treason (knowing that treason was being committed and doing nothing about it).[27]

The two priests involved in the case of Mabel Brigge exemplify the opposing forces at work in Henry's Reformation. Ralph Bell, the vicar of Holme, clinched the case when he revealed what the suspects had told him under the seal of the confessional. This would have been unthinkable just four years earlier, but Henry's religious changes clearly made some clergy abandon the old conventions of the priesthood. The chantry priest Thomas Marshall, on the other hand, stood for the old church with his willingness to endorse Mabel and Isabel's belief in the power of the fast, a sure sign of conservative religious attitudes. Chantry priests, unlike parish priests, existed only to say private masses for the dead. They were supported and paid for by endowments left by donors in their wills, and were a crucial part of the 'spiritual economy' of pre-Reformation England. Many were sponsored by guilds to say masses for the deceased souls of members. The very existence of chantry priests implied belief in purgatory, since without purgatory there was no need to say masses to speed a soul's journey to heaven. Nevertheless, the chantries survived the dissolution of the monasteries and were not abolished until 1547, in the reign of Edward VI.[28] Chantry priests had no spiritual authority over parishioners and the fact that Isabel took advice from him suggests that he was her personal confessor. Chantry priests were 'generally poorly educated, poorly paid, underemployed and often not particularly pious or well-behaved',[29] and one possible form this bad behaviour might take was involvement in magic.

MAGIC AND TREASON AT COURT

At some time between 1538 and 1560 the ex-Carmelite friar and enthusiastic reformer John Bale (1495–1563), who became bishop of Ossory in Ireland in 1552, wrote a history play, *Kynge Johan*, in which he attempted to overturn the traditional perception of King John as a wicked ruler. Bale recast John as a defender of Gospel purity against a Catholic church riddled with superstition, and his play mingled human characters with allegorical figures representing vices and virtues. Bale resurrected the rumour that John was poisoned on his visit to the Cistercian abbey of Swineshead in Lincolnshire in 1216, and blamed the crime on the monks. The events as Bale portrays them have strong overtones of magical treason. The vices are discussing ways to oppose and get rid of John, when 'Dissymulacyon' makes an appearance. 'Sedicyon' asks where 'Dissymulacyon' has been and receives the answer 'In the gardene, man, the herbes and wedes amonge; / And there have I gote the poyson of toade. / I hope in a wyle to wurke some feate abroade'.[30] The monk Simon of Swynsett then gives the king the poison to drink in his cup.[31]

Against the background of the stereotyped ritualism and superstition of Bale's monks, Dissymulacyon's loitering 'the herbes and wedes amonge' is strongly suggestive of witchcraft, as is the use of a toad as the source of poison. Whether or not Bale composed *Kynge Johan* during Henry VIII's reign or not, the resemblances between Bale's John and Henry are clear. Bale attempted to present John as a precedent for Henry's strong opposition to ecclesiastical authority and for the claims of the crown over against the church. In the play, unscrupulous monks are in league with barons determined to bring over Lewis, dauphin of France and dethrone John. The play's adoption of the Swineshead conspiracy theory betrayed Henrician reformers' concerns that an alliance between the conservative nobility and clergy had the potential to reverse the Reformation but also to generate magical plots, fuelled by popish superstition, directed against the king.

In April 1536 allegations of magic erupted in the heart of the king's household and, indeed, his bed. By far the most famous, but also the most problematic treason trial in Henry's reign to feature an allegation of 'witchcraft' was that of his second wife, Anne Boleyn, who was accused of treason, incest, adultery and 'witchcraft'. The Holy Roman Emperor's ambassador to Henry's court, Eustace Chapuys, reported in a letter to the emperor on 10 February 1536 that Henry believed he had been 'seduced and forced into his second marriage by means of sortileges and charms'.[32] This was an allegation against queens and royal mistresses familiar from the Middle Ages and Chapuys, as an opponent of Henry's marriage to Anne in the first place, would have been open to such rumours.[33] Cromwell alluded vaguely to 'the Queen's abomination, both in incontinent living and other offences towards the King's highness' in a letter of 14 May to Stephen Gardiner, bishop of Winchester.[34] Affecting the king's romantic judgement by magic was a serious matter, but it was not the same as trying to kill him, and did not necessarily make Anne a witch. In fact, although Anne was accused of bewitching the king, this was not one of the formal charges on which she was tried; it seems most likely that it was intended as a catch-all allegation of involvement in illicit magic, primarily alleged attempts at poisoning and an interest in love magic.

There is no firm evidence to suggest that Anne was considered a witch during her lifetime, although some historians have speculated that Henry believed she was a witch because he allowed her to be accused of causing his impotence; this was a standard accusation against malefic witches in Continental Europe.[35] Henry was prepared to admit to impotence because he did not want to admit to fathering the 'shapeless mass' of flesh to which Anne gave birth in January 1536; the monstrous birth, in Henry's view, had to be the consequence of adultery or incest.[36] Early modern people believed that monstrous births were punishments for sexual sins, and since Henry did not want to admit to sexual sins, it followed that Anne had to be guilty.[37] However, whilst monstrous births, sexual misconduct and impotence were all associated with witchcraft, they do not amount to a certainty that Henry or his ministers believed that Anne was a witch. This idea seems to have appeared several decades after her death and was derived from a Latin account of the English Reformation written by a Catholic in exile, Nicholas Sander, in 1585.

Sander was keen to discredit Anne as the heretical mother of Elizabeth I, but even he never directly called Anne a witch; rather his account gave her a deformity that suggested this identification to others. According to Sander, 'on her right hand a sixth finger was beginning to grow; under her chin grew a swelling, I know not what'.[38] The Latin word used by Sander to describe the state of Anne's sixth finger, *agnascebatur*, suggests that it was rudimentary or only partially formed. According to the widely held doctrine of physiognomy, a person's evil character was displayed in deformities, and witches especially were supposed to be betrayed by their bodily blemishes. The unnatural excrescences on Anne's body bring to mind the idea of 'the witch's mark', which some demonologists believed took the form of a 'teat' or flap of flesh on a witch's body. Whether Sander meant to imply any of this is unclear; it is likely that he made up or exaggerated Anne's deformities, since there is no reason why he alone should have had access to this information about her so long after her death. Whatever Sander's intentions, the idea that Anne Boleyn was a witch with six fingers on one hand has proved an enduring myth.[39]

The accusations against Anne Boleyn are of comparatively slight significance in the history of treasonous magic. If Anne was involved in any sort of magic at all, it was love potions made by cunning women, not the learned magic with which Eleanor Cobham and the duke of Clarence became associated in the fifteenth century. Anne was not the first royal wife or mistress to dabble in love potions, and she would not be the last. Given the fatal consequences of her eventual fall from favour, it is hardly surprising that Anne was prepared to do anything to retain Henry's affections. There is no evidence that her involvement in magic was treasonous in nature, and it was the accusations of adultery and incest against her that ultimately sealed her fate; the insinuations of 'witchcraft' were so much padding.

Anne was barely cold in her grave when Henry married his third wife, Jane Seymour, in May 1536. On 12 October 1537 Jane gave birth to a son, Prince Edward (the future Edward VI) and died shortly thereafter. The infant prince was now Henry's greatest single asset and his life was infinitely precious to the king. Consequently, it was a matter of great concern when an attempt was apparently made to kill Edward by magic. On 3 January 1538 some passers-by caught sight of what appeared to be the half-buried body of an infant in a London churchyard. The parish clerk dug the body up and found that inside the winding sheet was not the body of a real baby but a wax model with two pins stuck in it. One of the witnesses, Fulk Vaughan, took the wax effigy to a local scrivener named Poole living in Crooked Lane, who was known to have some knowledge of magic (a scrivener was a professional copyist of legal documents).

Poole was rather unimpressed; the effigy had certainly been intended to 'waste' someone, but whoever had decided to have it buried 'was not his craft's master'; in other words, an incompetent magician. Poole insisted that the proper procedure was to bury the wax image in horse dung, whose natural heat would slowly melt the effigy and with it destroy the person's health. Rumours quickly spread that the effigy represented the prince, although there was no evidence to suppose that it did. Nevertheless, the incident brought about an official investigation led by Cromwell's secretary, Thomas Wriothesley,[40] and was apparently not the only one of its kind. A porter at Corpus Christi College, Oxford, gossiped in 1538 that a wax image supposed to represent Prince Edward had been found with a knife in it.[41]

Allegations that emerged in the summer of 1540 demonstrated that there remained individuals at the heart of Henry's court interested in using magic to calculate his death. In January 1540 Henry reluctantly married his fourth wife, Anne of Cleves, a match meticulously engineered by Thomas Cromwell, soon to be earl of Essex. Cromwell famously persuaded Henry to marry Anne on the strength of an excessively flattering portrait by Holbein and Henry's need for a German alliance. On their wedding night, however, Henry found himself unable to consummate his marriage with Anne: 'I have felt her belly and breasts,' he declared to Cromwell, 'and thereby as I can judge she should be no maid, which struck me so to the heart when I felt them that I had neither will nor courage to proceed any further in other matters'.[42] Although these words suggest that Henry simply found Anne sexually unattractive, he sought an annulment from the bishops on the grounds of 'relative impotence', meaning that he was unable to maintain an erection to consummate his marriage, but only in the specific case of Anne.[43] Relative impotence was usually attributed to harmful magic, and, although neither Henry nor Cromwell accused anyone in particular of causing the king's condition, it raised fears that someone might be directing spells against Henry.

The failure of Henry's marriage to Anne of Cleves emboldened Cromwell's opponents, the religious conservatives, to move against him, and he was arrested for treason on 10 June 1540. Anyone closely associated with Cromwell was tainted as well. Five days after his arrest the king's council began to investigate colourful accusations made against one of Cromwell's closest assistants, Walter Hungerford, baron Hungerford of Heytesbury, by a certain 'Mother Huntley'.[44] Lord Hungerford was a wealthy landowner in Wiltshire and Somerset who had been one of Cromwell's trusted agents at court since 1533. He dealt with disobedient priests, settled matters arising from the redistribution of monastic land to the gentry and acted to arrest individuals suspected of seditious speech, including prophecies against the regime.[45] However, Hungerford's reputation was somewhat unsavoury. In 1536 his wife Elizabeth Hussey had complained to Cromwell that her husband incarcerated her for four years in a tower at Farleigh Castle, Hungerford's country seat in Somerset, and that during that time he had tried to poison her via his chaplain. Elizabeth begged Cromwell for a divorce, which at that time could only be obtained by act of Parliament. Cromwell commissioned William Petre and Thomas Benet to advance a bill in Parliament for Hungerford's divorce in February 1540, although the type of divorce proposed would not have allowed Hungerford or his wife to re-marry.

Hungerford was accused of having instructed his chaplains at Farleigh Castle, Hugh Wood and Doctor Maudlin, to predict the length of the king's life and the likely success of the rebels in the Pilgrimage of Grace on 22 March 1537. Hungerford also instructed the priests to work with a certain 'Mother Roche', probably a cunning woman with a reputation for such dealings. If one of Hungerford's chaplains had already been prepared to poison Lady Hungerford, it is not surprising that he was implicated in magic as well. The mention of the Pilgrimage of Grace in the charges against Hungerford was significant; Hungerford's father-in-law had been executed for his part in the Lincolnshire Rising, a rebellion that preceded the more famous northern rebellion. This tainted Hungerford by association, and made the accusations against him more plausible.

Hungerford's treason consisted in his use of magic to 'compass or imagine' the king's death, along with the fact that he had allowed a chaplain, William Byrd, to remain at Farleigh Castle in spite of his known opposition to the royal supremacy. Byrd was the same man who had tried to conjure the king's death in 1536.[46] Hungerford was further accused of being involved with known heretics. The third charge against him was that he had 'exercised, frequented, and used the abominable and detestable vice and sin of buggery with William Master [and] Thomas Smith', two of his servants.[47] 'Buggery', had intimate associations with heresy;[48] the word itself was derived, via Norman French, from the word 'Bulgar', a synonym for the dualist Cathar heretics of southern France who were accused of practising homosexuality. Buggery was made a capital crime in 1533, although the statute defined it vaguely as involving unnatural sexual acts without specifying anal sex, the term's more recent meaning. Until 1533 buggery had been punished, like most other infractions against the era's sexual morality, in the church courts. Hungerford became the first ever victim of the new Statute of Buggery.

Hungerford died on the scaffold along with his patron, the earl of Essex, on 28 July 1540. The next day the French ambassador, Charles de Marillac, noted in a letter describing Cromwell's execution that 'with him was apparently beheaded Lord Hungerford, a man aged forty years, convicted of sodomy, of having forced his own daughter and of having used magical arts and the invocation of devils'.[49] It is possible that Hungerford's indictment for heresy inspired Cromwell's enemies to add that charge to the fallen minister's indictment as well. It was a commonplace of medieval and Renaissance thought, derived from Plato and Aristotle, that if a person had one vice then they were likely to be corrupt in every way. The unity of the vices mirrored the unity of the virtues, and the case of Hungerford proved that a man who abandoned restraint in the area of sexuality could be expected to fall into treason, magic and heresy as well. Indeed, the use of the term 'treason of buggery' by contemporaries drew attention to the fact that treason, like buggery, was a rebellion against nature. So, by extension, was magic.[50] As Baldwin Smith has argued, 'sympathetic and cosmic logic' lay behind Hungerford's execution: 'treason was a universal perversity; buggery was an unnatural act; therefore, buggery was treason'.[51] However, it is also possible that Henry was angered by Cromwell's support for Hungerford's divorce when he gave no help to the king in getting rid of Anne of Cleves. On this reading of events, both Cromwell and Hungerford were victims of Henry's spite.[52]

Existing laws proved adequate when it came to prosecuting Lord Hungerford, but for reasons that still remain obscure the Parliament of 1542 introduced a new law that made virtually *any* magic a felony and therefore a capital offence. 'The bill against conjurations and witchcrafts and sorcery and enchantments', which may have been drafted as early as 1533,[53] provided that

> ... if any person or persons, after the first day of May next coming, use, devise, practise or exercise, or cause to be used, devised, practised or exercised, any invocations or conjurations of spirits, witchcrafts, enchantments, or sorceries, to the intent to get or find money or treasure, or to waste, consume or destroy any person in his body, members or goods, or to provoke any person to unlawful love, or for any other unlawful intent or purpose, or by occasion or colour of such things or any of them, or for despite of Christ, or for lucre of money, dig up or pull down any cross or crosses, or by such invocations or conjurations of spirits, witchcrafts, enchantments, sorcery, or any of them, take upon them to declare where goods stolen or lost shall become, That then all and every such offence and offences, from the said first day of May next coming, shall be deemed accepted and adjudged felony.[54]

Since no record survives of the debates that led up to this act, the only clues as to the reasons for the first English statute to make an explicit mention of magic are contained within the text of the bill itself. Firstly, it seems likely that 'invocations or conjurations of spirits', 'witchcrafts', 'enchantments', and 'sorceries' were intended as synonyms for a single type of activity, since the use of multiple redundant terms for the same thing was a characteristic feature of the language of Tudor statutes. A consequence of this is that the appearance of the word 'witchcrafts' for the first time in a statute is of no special significance; the context of the rest of the act makes it highly unlikely that 'witchcrafts' here means malefic witchcraft, the act of an ill-favoured person wishing harm on others. Historians have tended to treat the act of 1542 as a forerunner to the better known 'Witchcraft Acts' of 1563 and 1604, but this glosses over the fact that no-one accused of the crime of witchcraft (as later understood) was ever tried under the 1542 statute.

The emphasis of the 1542 act was firmly on magical treasure-hunting. This is the only kind of magic to receive two mentions in the act; magic 'to get or find money or treasure' is the first kind listed, and the mention of those who 'for despite of Christ, or for lucre of money, dig up or pull down any cross or crosses' is a reference to the same practice. Harmful magic, love magic and the magical detection of stolen goods were relegated to a secondary position. This might seem strange, given Henry's preoccupation with harmful magic aimed at himself, but it is to be remembered that the use of harmful magic against the king was already covered by the treason laws. Technically, even harmful magic deployed by wives against husbands or by servants against masters was already outlawed before 1542 as petty treason.

Maxwell-Stuart has noted that the 1542 act was aimed more at the kind of activities undertaken by men than by women, and has suggested that the Hungerford case may have influenced Parliament.[55] However, it seems that no single reason can plausibly account for Parliament's concern about magical treasure-hunting in 1542, and the act was probably the product of multiple factors. The wording of the act suggests that the government was concerned about the impiety implied by people pulling down wayside crosses 'for despite of Christ'. Although the cross would later be deliberately removed as an idolatrous image in the reign of Edward VI, Henry's government was more conservative. It is possible that in an age of poor roads and perilous travel the government was also concerned that crosses should remain as landmarks for people to find their way around the landscape. However, magical treasure-hunting was also stealing from the king, and in at least one case, Henry Cowpar, parson of Ockley was accused of finding treasure by magic *and* uttering prophecies against the king.[56] Contempt for the king's property went hand-in-hand with contempt for his person.

It seems likely that magical treasure-hunting preceded killing someone by magic in the list because it concerned the king and the realm. The wording of the act allowed magical killing to be interpreted as the consequence of the 'ill-wishing' of malefic witchcraft as well as the traditional 'effigy magic' used in the Middle Ages. The final prohibitions against love magic and magical property-detection were virtually unenforceable, as these kinds of popular magic could be practised everywhere and, in the case of finding stolen property, by anyone capable of preparing the 'Bible and key' or 'sieve and shears'. In the absence of any evidence of the parliamentary debates, it is difficult to ascertain the extent to which the act was motivated by fear that magic actually worked, or alternatively guided by a desire to punish fraudsters and charlatans. It is almost certain that both imperatives were at work in the drafting of the act, since the social problem of fraudulent cunning-folk justified the legislation, quite apart from the danger of magic actually working. However, the act's penalties were extraordinarily harsh, and a blanket death penalty for magic has never been imposed in England before or since. The act's harshness may well have deterred its execution and there is no definite case of a successful conviction under the 1542 statute.[57]

THE REIGNS OF EDWARD VI AND MARY

Henry VIII died on 28 January 1547, having appointed a sixteen-member Council of Regency to rule on behalf of the young Edward VI. Sixteenth-century governments had a tendency to portray their predecessors as unreasonably harsh, and Edward's first Parliament repealed the 1534 Treason Act, along with several other pieces of draconian Henrician legislation, as 'very strait, sore, extreme and terrible' in December 1547.[58] Along with the Treason Act went the act against conjuration and witchcraft of 1542, 'almost by default'.[59] Sadly, there is no sixteenth-century Hansard that recorded the details of parliamentary debates; indeed, for most laws all we have is the bill's final text. However, it seems likely that the 1542 act was repealed without individual consideration, as part of a package of liberalising measures intended to give Edward's subjects a flavour of their new king.

Sure enough, no prosecutions for magical treason took place in Edward's reign, although concern about magic remained and magicians were pursued by the church, as they had been before 1542.[60] At some point after 1547, a magician named Allen fell under suspicion, and Edward Underhill was sent by the Lord Mayor of London, with two other men, to arrest him:

> ... we met [him] withal in Paul's, and took him with us into his chamber, where we found figures set to calculate the nativity of the King, and a judgement given of his death, whereof this foolish wretch thought himself so sure that he and his counsellors, the papists, bruited it all over. The King lay at Hampton Court [at] the same time, and my Lord Protector at the Syon; unto whom I carried this Allen, with his books of conjurations, circles, and many things belonging to that devilish art, which he affirmed before my Lord was a lawful science, for the statute against such was repealed.

The Lord Protector responded by sending Allen to the Tower, where he was examined and found to be 'a very unlearned ass, and a sorcerer, for the which he was worthy [of] hanging'. However, no prosecution could be brought against him, and after about a year of incarceration Allen was freed when a friend posted his bail.[61]

In 1551 Edward's bishops began to reform the church's canon law, defining magic as 'a pact or alliance contracted with the demon, and his ministers, by spells, prayers, characters, or other similar instruments of impiety having been gathered together, which refers either to the investigation of future causes or the seeking out of certain things which we ask'.[62] This was simultaneously a very wide and a very narrow definition of magic. By including 'prayers' as magical, the new canon potentially encompassed deviant religious behaviour as well as more traditional magic. However, the purposes of magic were defined only as divination of the future and the seeking out of lost or stolen items. Divination was already dealt with in other canons, so this seems redundant, but more importantly, the canon included no mention of the attempt to use magic to kill or commit treason. The canon laid down 'the gravest penalties' (*poenas ... gravissimas*) for magic,[63] without saying what these were; but since the matter could only be dealt with in the church courts, excommunication and public penance were the harshest punishments available.

As the teenage king's health failed the government seems to have become more nervous about magical treason. On 5 April 1552 a man named Clerke 'sometime servant and secretary to the Duke of Norfolk' was accused before the king's council of being 'a reporter abroad of certain lewd prophecies and other slanderous matters touching the King's Majesty', but a further search uncovered 'certain characters and books of nigromancy and conjuration found in his lodging'.[64] Clerke's connection with the duke of Norfolk strongly suggests that he was linked to the religious conservatives. Later, on 21 May 1553, four men were incarcerated in the Tower, suspected of having said 'certain words touching the King's Majesty's person', and at the last minute a magician, Gregory Wisdom, was arrested and added to their number in the Fleet Prison.[65] The king was dead before any of the plotters could come to trial, but it is conceivable that the government could have been preparing to make accusations of magical treason against this group.

Once Mary I had disposed of her rival, Lady Jane Grey, she went even further than Edward VI in an effort to convince her subjects that she represented a return to the 'good old days' before government paranoia and arbitrary prosecutions for constructive treason. Her first Parliament repealed all treason statutes since 1351 and the queen made an explicit statement that no-one would ever be punished merely for the words they spoke under her reign.[66] In retrospect, this avowal that words against the queen would be tolerated seems grimly ironic, since Mary's government quickly set to work to ensure that death was the penalty for any words said against the church. A consequence of both the repeal of the 1542 act and the return to Catholicism was that magic reverted to the jurisdiction of the church courts, which now had real teeth with the revival of the medieval heresy laws. However, Mary's reign saw little more than the occasional episcopal fulmination against witchcraft and sorcery and a few people brought before the church courts.[67] Both the government's and the church's main priority was the extirpation of heresy, and this seems to have distracted attention from magical activity. Furthermore, some Marian Catholics consciously distanced themselves from earlier Catholic critiques of 'superstition' as magic, for instance in the works of Renaissance humanists such as Erasmus.[68]

As time went on, the hollowness of Mary's original promise of freedom of speech became apparent. Mary married Phillip of Spain, the son and heir of the Emperor Charles V, on 25 July 1554 in Winchester Cathedral. Mary was anxious that opposition to the 'Spanish marriage', combined with the ridicule that followed her 'false pregnancy' between October 1554 and August 1555, was in danger of undermining her new regime. The Parliament of 1554–55 passed 'An act against seditious words and rumours' which specified a fine of a thousand pounds, three months' imprisonment and the removal of the culprit's ears for the first offence, and death for the second. Authors of seditious writings were to lose their right hands. The same Parliament passed 'An act for the punishment of traitorous words against the queen's majesty', which made it high treason to pray 'by express words or sayings, that God should shorten [the queen's] days or take her out of the way'.[69]

This latter act represented the first reaction of a Catholic government to a new religious phenomenon, similar to treasonous magic yet crucially different from anything that had gone before. Whilst the majority of Mary's subjects seem to have been contented with (or at least indifferent to) her restoration of Catholicism, the radical Reformation in Edward's reign had created a hard core of 'Gospellers' (the word 'Protestant' was not yet in general use). These were both clergy and ordinary people who rejected the reinstatement of the mass, vestments in the liturgy, statues in churches and the suppression of the English Bible. Their views differed widely; some were loyal to Henry's old religious policy, some to Northumberland's, some may have been survivors of the Lollard sect, and some were Anabaptists with extreme religious views such as the rejection of infant baptism and the divinity of Christ. A common feature of the Gospellers was their hostility to 'superstition', meaning that they were hardly likely to use magic based on Catholic rituals to express their disquiet at government policy. On the contrary, they viewed the mass as little more than a worthless conjuring trick. Instead of working magic against Mary, the Gospellers prayed for her demise which, if not magic, could certainly have been construed as a form of verbal treason under the statute of 1351. In order to avoid any ambiguity, Mary's Parliament passed a separate law to deal with such cases.

Mary's phantom pregnancy gave rise to the sole true magical scandal of her reign in the spring of 1555. Mary's half-sister and heir apparent according to Henry VIII's will, Princess Elizabeth, was an embarrassment to the queen for her ambivalent attitude towards Catholicism. As a princess of the blood royal she was entitled to maintain her own household, but she was also effectively a prisoner at Woodstock Palace. Elizabeth was naturally concerned about the possibility that Mary might be pregnant, since it would deprive her of her place in the succession, and for reassurance she turned to a young man named John Dee. Dee was a brilliant mathematician who had studied at Cambridge and Louvain. The impressive mechanical automata he had made for an entertainment at Trinity College, Cambridge had gained him a reputation as a conjurer, and like many mathematicians of his day he made use of his skills to cast precise judicial horoscopes. Judicial astrology sought to give answers to specific questions about a person's destiny, as opposed to ordinary horoscopes which made general predictions about a person's future based on the position of the stars at the hour of their conception or birth.

In April 1555 Elizabeth summoned Dee to Woodstock, where, in the presence of her auditor, Sir Thomas Benger, and two other members of the princess's household he started casting horoscopes for Elizabeth, Mary and Phillip. On 17 April Elizabeth was summoned to Hampton Court to witness the birth of Mary's anticipated child, and Dee went with the rest of her household. Later he carried on the calculations at Benger's own home at Great Milton in Oxfordshire. Dee returned to London in May, where he resumed his calculations in rented rooms which were raided 'on suspicion of magic' on 28 May by pursuivants sent by the Privy Council. The pursuivants sealed Dee's rooms, either for fear of their potentially magical contents or in order to prevent Dee's friends from interfering with the evidence.[70] Dee had become the victim in a larger political game: emboldened by what they believed was the forthcoming birth of an heir for Phillip and Mary, the Council was seeking grounds to accuse Elizabeth of treason. Information given by Thomas Prideaux and George Ferrars, the MP for Markyate and Flamstead in Hertfordshire, gave a glimmer of hope that Elizabeth might be involved in a magical plot. In Dee's own words, the accusation was 'that I endeavoured by enchantments to destroy Queen Mary'.

Dee was interrogated, probably at Hampton Court or St James's Palace, by two Privy Councillors, Sir Francis Englefield and Mary's principal secretary, Sir John Bourne. Dee managed to incriminate his assistant John Feild, as well as Sir Thomas Benger and Christopher Carye, a distant relative of Elizabeth through the Boleyns. A few days later one of George Ferrars's children was dead and another went blind, apparent confirmation that Dee the conjurer was taking magical revenge for his imprisonment. Dee was at first presented with 'four articles', and presumably pressured into signing them, but the articles later multiplied to eighteen, suggesting that the accusations were piling up against Dee. Taken by boat along the Thames to the City of London, Dee appeared before Lord Broke, Justice of the Common Pleas. Dee and the others confessed to 'lewd and vain practices of calculating and conjuring' on 5 June. The words 'lewd and vain' imply that Dee's accusers regarded his practices as offensive to public decency, fraudulent and deceitful – but not treasonous.

Something changed over the next two days, as on 7 June the prisoners were accused of 'conjuring and witchcraft', a more serious charge than 'calculating and conjuring' as it implied an intention to harm, and therefore treason. Perhaps Ferrars, fearful for the safety of his remaining children, was putting pressure on the Council; perhaps the Councillors themselves smelled blood. The French ambassador, whose job was to relay English gossip back to Paris, reported that Dee and the others had tried to kill Phillip and Mary with the help of wax images, and rumours spread that the group had conjured a demon.

Dee's interrogators made repeated attempts to force him to admit to the involvement of evil spirits, but he refused. On 9 June the Council authorised the use of torture on the suspects, although it is unclear whether this ever took place. At the last minute, it would seem that Dee was rescued by an unusual saviour: the bishop of London, Edmund Bonner.

Bonner gained a reputation during and after Mary's reign as an enthusiastic and brutal persecutor of heretics. However, he also thought he was Dee's distant relative, and this may have saved the young astrologer. According to Dee, writing in 1599, he 'was sent to the examining and custody of Bishop Bonner for religious matters', and was imprisoned with the future martyr Bartlet Green. By the beginning of July, however, Dee was one of the bishop's chaplains at Fulham Palace. It seems peculiar that a prisoner could become a trusted servant quite so readily, and it is possible that Dee portrayed himself as Bonner's prisoner when in fact he was all too willing to serve him. Bonner's reputation in Elizabethan England was so black that such a deceit is understandable, but it has muddied the historical record.

On 29 August, Dee and the other prisoners appeared before the Court of Star Chamber where they were discharged of all suspicion of treason, and released on bonds for good behaviour until Christmas. The reason for this sudden change of heart from the Council may have been Bonner's intervention; on the other hand, it may be that Phillip, realising that Mary was not going to give birth, had realised the need to effect a reconciliation with Elizabeth as heir apparent.[71] Nevertheless, Dee's deliverance was nothing short of miraculous; he came within a hair's breadth of being the latest astrologer to fall victim to an accusation of magical treason. Ironically, Dee would one day play a key part in defending his patroness, soon to become Queen Elizabeth, from an apparent magical attack mounted by Catholics.

CONCLUSION

The reigns of Henry VIII, Edward VI and Mary I saw a sustained attempt by a series of regimes to conflate prophecy with magic and to associate both with treason. In the 1530s, for the first time, the practice of magic against the life of the king became associated with a specific set of theo-political beliefs: those likely to be accused of magical treason were religious conservatives who opposed the dissolution of the monasteries and the royal supremacy. Furthermore, the reign of Henry VIII saw the punishment of magic shift from the church to the state, with the first parliamentary legislation against magic passed in 1542. Nevertheless, numerous forms of magic remained under the jurisdiction of the church courts and the 1542 act was short-lived, being repealed in 1547. Magical scandals rumbled on into the reigns of Edward VI and Mary I, and John Dee came close to being accused of trying to kill Mary by magic, but Edward and Mary saw nothing like the elaborate magical conspiracies that would be directed against their successor, Elizabeth I.

CHAPTER 3

Elizabeth versus The 'Popish Conjurers', 1558–77

Elizabeth I was perhaps the most magically attacked monarch – at least while on the throne of England – in English history. The early, perilous years of her reign saw many treasonous plots that included illicit astrological calculations of the queen's death, conjuration of demons to ask questions about the succession, and traditional effigy magic. Elizabeth's political opponents were almost always individuals with Catholic sympathies who favoured the dynastic claims of her Catholic cousin Mary, Queen of Scots (1542–86), although treasonous plots sometimes revived memories of the Wars of the Roses by involving surviving Yorkist claimants as well. 'Popish conjurers', whether in reality or in the imaginations of Elizabeth's counsellors, continually menaced the queen's health and wellbeing, although the most prominent serial magical traitor of her reign, John Prestall, had a knack for escaping justice.

THE ELIZABETHAN REFORMATION

The only surviving child of Henry VIII and Anne Boleyn succeeded to the throne at the age of 25 in the winter of 1558, according to the terms of her father's will. Both Catholics and Protestants hoped that Elizabeth would back their cause, but by the end of 1559 her first Parliament had produced a religious compromise that, in its essentials, endures to this day in England's established church.

At first, there was only one group in England that opposed Elizabeth's religious policy, conviction-Catholics who refused to attend their local parish churches and hear the new English liturgy, hence their title of recusants. At first, recusants were punished only with fines; Elizabeth's government seems to have believed that they would come round eventually, just as many of the recusants believed that the restoration of Catholicism was just on the horizon.

As it became clear that Elizabeth was going to reign for a long time, and that the religious settlement was there to stay, laws and attitudes hardened. The penalties for recusancy escalated; Catholics began to be imprisoned without trial for long periods and to have their property (and even their children) taken away from them. A Catholic rebellion broke out in the north of England in 1569, and in 1570 Pope Pius V promulgated the bull *Regnans in excelsis* ('Reigning on high'), which excommunicated Elizabeth, declaring her a heretic and a bastard with no right to rule, and releasing her Catholic subjects from any obligation to obey her. A minority of Catholics saw the bull as a justification to support plots in favour of rival claimants to the English throne, most notably Mary, Queen of Scots, who was the granddaughter of Henry VIII's sister, Margaret Tudor.

Elizabeth's regime was diplomatically isolated in the face of a mighty Catholic Spanish and Habsburg Empire, led by Elizabeth's one-time brother-in-law and former king of England, Phillip II of Spain. Phillip was simultaneously trying to turn the tide of a brutal religious war in France in favour of Catholicism and fighting Protestant rebels in the Low Countries who wanted their independence from Spain. Both France and the rebel Netherlands, England's potential allies, were being squeezed by a would-be world emperor with seemingly limitless resources. Elizabeth's dominions, too, were under attack, as the pope personally sponsored an invasion of Ireland to support a native rebellion there. When Englishmen trained as Catholic priests in the new Continental seminaries began trickling into England in the late 1570s, they were met with savage brutality. The law defined it as high treason to obtain Catholic priestly orders abroad and return to England, meaning that English-born Catholic priests were committing treason just by setting foot on English soil.

To make matters worse, refusal to attend church services began to spread to opponents of Elizabeth's new church at the opposite end of the religious spectrum. Elizabeth insisted that no-one could preach without a licence, leaving most parishes reliant on the officially approved *Book of Homilies*, from which the vicar was expected to read every Sunday. In a world where the pulpit was the source of news, gossip and political commentary, Elizabeth considered preaching far too dangerous an instrument to put into the hands of a dubiously loyal and half-educated clergy. However, the ban on preaching went against the original spirit of Edward's reformation and some clergy defied it, just as they refused to wear surplices as relics of popish superstition. A minority of 'puritan' laypeople started refusing to go to church because they disapproved of the ceremonies and the attitudes of the 'non-preaching' parsons.

THE ACCESSION OF ELIZABETH

Without the benefit of hindsight, in the 1560s and 1570s, Elizabeth's reign seemed insecure at best, and doomed at worst, on account of her reluctance to make a dynastic alliance through marriage. For two decades, England teetered on the brink of a religious civil war like the ones that were raging north of the border in Scotland and across the Channel in France. England was an insignificant country at the fringe of Europe that could only survive, many thought, through aligning itself with one of the greater powers. Yet there were also more insidious threats at work against Elizabeth's government than the war-mongering of Phillip of Spain. In 1582, the Jesuit priest Robert Parsons, writing from the security of the French city of Rouen after returning from his first attempted mission to England, complained that English Catholics were being blamed for terrorising Queen Elizabeth and her subjects with acts of malicious magic. He denounced '... that ridiculous and wanton manner of chatting of our adversaries (as our most ancient enemies were wont to do) in slandering Catholics to be of familiar acquaintance with devils. And I might sooner lack time than matter, if I should reckon up all the surmises, and fables which they have forged, touching this point.'

Parsons's reference to 'our ancient enemies' was an allusion to the early Christian author Minucius Felix, who claimed that the enemies of the Christians thought they were cannibals who performed human sacrifice and magical rites. It remains unclear whether any pagan Roman ever did believe what Minucius Felix said they did, but that scarcely mattered; Minucius blackened his enemies by recounting the absurd delusions they had about *their* enemies. Parsons was perfectly at home in this sort of game, trading rumour for rumour and turning the very existence of a rumour into the material for his argument. Parsons ridiculed Protestants for blaming an apparently magical attack on St Paul's Cathedral on Catholics, as well as noting the sudden and inexplicable deaths of court officials involved in the trial of a Catholic bookbinder, which were also blamed on magic.[1] He mocked the credulity of those who believed that magic really lay behind these events, but there was a sting in the tail of Parsons's message: these things did indeed have a supernatural cause, but it was God himself. Misfortunes of this kind were a judgement on Elizabethan England for abandoning the Catholic faith.

Catholic authors like Parsons, gloating over every bad harvest, urban fire or collapsed building as an example of 'providential' divine judgement, did little to allay Protestant fears that Catholics were enemies of the state, not just because they were disloyal but also because their immersion in an ancient world of superstition gave them potentially dangerous knowledge of magic. As soon as it became apparent that Elizabeth had no intention of maintaining her sister Mary's allegiance to the Catholic faith, her government felt itself to be under attack from the lingering ghosts of the old regime: priests who still believed in their power to abuse the Catholic sacraments for magical ends, old women who made malicious use of Latin prayers and defiant Catholics in the provinces whose devotion to 'holy' images was joined to a more sinister interest in image magic.

England in 1559 was a country in spiritual crisis. Looking back on the first year of Elizabeth's reign, a repentant magician, Francis Coxe, described a nation more willing to rely on magic and prophecies than on God:

> [Magic] grew into such credit with men, that not only they judged the course of natural things thereby to be governed, but also that part which God hath and doth reserve to himself ... Nay they ceased not here, but so blinded and bewitched the wits of men, that scant durst they credit God himself, if it seemed that their blinded prophecies any time would make contradiction.[2]

Although Elizabeth had brought back the Protestant religion and the English Bible,

> ... yet did the people so waver, the whole realm was so troubled and so moved with the blind enigmatical and devilish prophecies of that heaven gazer Nostradamus ... that even those which in their hearts could have wished the glory of God and his word most flourishing to be established were brought into such an extreme coldness of faith, that they doubted God had forgotten his promise.[3]

Coxe was in no doubt that 'the infection of these pestilential poisoned lying prophecies' lay behind the country's crisis of faith.

THE FORTESCUE CONSPIRACY

Combatting treasonous magic was amongst the most urgent priorities of Elizabeth's new government. Just days after Mary's death on 17 November 1558, pursuivants sent by the Privy Council swooped on the Spanish ambassador's house and arrested Anthony Fortescue, John Prestall and Thomas Kele for 'conjuring'.[4] Years later, in 1569, Thomas Norton would claim that Prestall and Kele held 'a lewd conjurers' conference with the devil'.[5] Fortescue had been comptroller of the household to Mary's archbishop of Canterbury, Cardinal Reginald Pole, and was also a member of the Pole family through his marriage to the cardinal's great-niece; he was arrested on 22 November. Since they were unable to prosecute them in the secular courts, on 25 November the Privy Council sent the two conjurers, Prestall and Kele, to the bishop of London for punishment 'according to the order of the ecclesiastical laws, as he shall think meet'.[6] It was potentially a provocative gesture; the bishop of London was still Edmund Bonner, the leading persecutor of Gospellers in Mary's reign, and the Councillors may have been taunting Bonner by asking him to punish known Catholics. On the other hand, if the Privy Council wanted the conjurers to be punished they had no choice but to send them to Bonner. In the absence of a statute against conjuration at this period, magicians could be tried only by their local bishop in a church court.

The arrest of John Prestall in December 1558 was the first appearance of this remarkable yet largely forgotten magician, perhaps the single most persistent magical traitor in English history. A 1584 list 'of all such as are certified in the Exchequer to be fugitive over the seas' described him as 'John Prestall of L[ambeth], gent[leman]'.[7] The description 'gentleman' suggests that Prestall was from a family with at least some inherited land and property. Given his subsequent history, Prestall clearly had an advanced training in mathematics and astrology like his lifelong nemesis, John Dee, but there is no evidence that he attended either Oxford or Cambridge. He may, therefore, have trained like Dee at a foreign university such as Louvain, a noted centre of mathematical learning. Unlike Dee, there is no evidence that Prestall was ever ordained.

Prestall's ongoing association with Anthony Fortescue suggests that he could have been somehow connected to Cardinal Pole's household during Mary's reign, although evidence for this is lacking. The cardinal was a contradictory figure: he was the architect of the Catholic Counter-Reformation in England and a figure of towering importance to the global Catholic church, yet he was also suspected of doctrinal unorthodoxy and even leanings towards Lutheranism. Pole came extremely close to being elected pope in 1549–50, and on the death of Pope Julius III in 1555 a member of Pole's circle in Rome, Alvise Priuli, was found with a book of astrological prophecies that foretold Pole would be elected as an 'angelic Pope'. On the other hand, Pole himself is supposed to have rebuffed an astrologer who predicted great things for him by suggesting that the baptism or 'new birth' of a Christian negated the influence of the stars at his actual birth.[8] Whatever the nature of his relationship with the Pole family, it seems safe to say that Prestall belonged to a new category of disenfranchised Englishmen who had strongly identified with the Marian regime and now felt like strangers in their own land under Elizabeth's Protestant rule.

After his release from prison in around 1560, Prestall married Isabel (or Elizabeth) Catesby, the widow of one of his creditors, Sir John

Owen. Prestall assumed guardianship of his fourteen-year-old stepson Henry Owen, the heir of Sir John's estates. Henry later claimed that, on Prestall's return from his first period of exile, the magician had run up enormous debts. When confronted by his creditors, Prestall declared, 'I am indebted unto you and am not able for to pay you, and yet being honest, if you should lose your money, [know] this that you will let me have more money, and if you use the matter wisely, you shall see what I will do. I will bring you a young man, lately come to his lands ... to be bound unto you for the whole'. The 'young man' was, of course, Prestall's stepson Henry Owen. Prestall proceeded to persuade Henry to mortgage his lands, and defrauded him of over 2000 marks.[9] In light of later evidence regarding Prestall's character, Henry Owen's accusations do not seem at all improbable.[10]

THE 1559 BILL AGAINST SORCERY, WITCHCRAFT AND BUGGERY

Elizabeth's new bishops were just as enthusiastic about prosecuting magicians as their Catholic predecessors, if not more so. John Jewel, the new bishop of Salisbury and the foremost apologist of the Elizabethan Reformation, wrote to the Italian Protestant academic Pietro Martire Vermigli, then living in exile at Oxford, to describe his first episcopal visitation in 1559. In Jewel's view, by sanctioning 'superstition' officially in the form of Catholic worship, Mary had opened the floodgates to magic of all kinds. His outlook was based on his reading of the Old Testament; every time the kings of Israel turned away from the worship of God, their people fell back on oracles, soothsayers and sacrifices to pagan gods. It was also influenced by his Calvinist theology, which held that human beings were naturally evil, depraved and inclined to idolatry. Without active preaching of the Gospel, it was inevitable that the uninstructed would revert to heathen beliefs. Jewel complained of Catholic devotions and witchcraft in the same breath: 'We found in all places votive relics of saints ... and I know not what small fragments of the sacred cross. The number of witches and sorceresses had everywhere become enormous'.[11]

Similarly, Richard Cox, bishop of Ely, complained to the Privy Council that Catholics were being treated so leniently when they were the 'dreamers', 'false prophets' and workers of false wonders of Deuteronomy 12, and argued that the death penalty for Catholics was sanctioned in the Old Testament:

> I would wish the twelfth Chapter of Deuteronomy to be read over, wherein it is thus written: If there arise among you a prophet or a dreamer and showeth thee a sign or a wonder, and that sign or wonder shall come to pass which he showeth thee, and sayeth, let us go after strange gods: that prophet or dreamer shall be slain, because he hath spoken to turn thee away from God, that he might drive thee from that the which the Lord hath commanded thee, and so thou shalt take away the mischief from the midst after ... God be merciful unto us that we have suffered his enemies so long trail abroad, that the false prophets, and the head papists we have nourished, some in prisons, some with Bishops, as who should say we cannot tell what to do with them, when God himself our heavenly father hath taught us by his blessed word how to use and deal with them.[12]

In 1559 Elizabeth's bishops were instructed to find out 'any that do use charms, sorceries, enchantments, invocations, circles, witchcrafts, soothsaying, or any like crafts or imaginations invented by the devil, and specially in the time of women's travail'. Just as magical treasure-hunting was the preoccupation of the 1540s, so magical girdles given to women to guarantee their safety in pregnancy seems to have been a preoccupation of the 1560s.[13] An increasingly misogynistic rhetoric was portraying popular magic as the preserve of women, a crucial step on the road to the first witchcraft prosecutions in 1566.

Protestants perceived Catholicism as soft on magic and witchcraft – an unfair assessment, given the vast number of women burned as witches under Catholic authority in fifteenth-century Germany. However, the Protestant rediscovery of the Bible meant a renewed emphasis on such verses as Leviticus 20:6: 'If any turn after such as work with spirits, and after soothsayers to go a whoring after them, then will I set my face against that man, and will cut him off from among his people', and Exodus 22:18: 'Thou shalt not suffer a witch to live'.[14] Protestant translation choices may have played a role in raising the profile of witchcraft. Although the Latin Vulgate used the term *malefici* in Exodus 22:18 (the same word used by Catholic inquisitors to describe witches in the fifteenth century), at I Samuel 15:23 it used the term *peccatum ariolandi* ('the sin of soothsaying'), which the Geneva Bible (and the Authorised Version after it) chose to render as 'the sin of witchcraft'.[15] The somewhat ambiguous statement *quoniam quasi peccatum ariolandi est repugnare* ('For to fight back is like the sin of soothsaying') thus became a damning and unambiguous indictment of traitors, 'For rebellion is as the sin of witchcraft'. The translators thus imposed new layers of meaning, producing a verse that reflected early modern preoccupations.

Perhaps as a result of the courts' inability to punish Kele and Prestall, members of Elizabeth's first Parliament introduced a bill calling for 'punishment of sorcery, witchcraft and buggery by felony', with death by hanging as the penalty for any of them. The bill passed the House of Commons but Parliament was prorogued a week after the bill arrived in the House of Lords. The acts needed to re-establish the royal supremacy and the Protestant faith had taken priority in Parliament's order of business.[16] The abortive bill of 1559 may have been motivated by a zealous Protestant desire to rid the nation of idolaters, as well as the 'Erastianism' of the Elizabethan regime (the doctrine that the power of the church should be limited by or transferred to the state). The bishops in Elizabeth's first Parliament rejected the Act of Uniformity, which passed only because so many sees were vacant at the time and therefore there was a shortage of bishops in the House of Lords. The queen's loyal supporters may not have trusted the bishops to punish serious crimes like witchcraft, sorcery and buggery in the church courts, and there is certainly no evidence that Bonner ever proceeded against Kele and Prestall.

THE WALDEGRAVE AND POLE CONSPIRACIES

In April 1561 disturbing evidence emerged of a magical conspiracy that involved contact with foreign powers. On 14 April a former monk called John Coxe, otherwise known as Devon, was arrested by customs officers at the port of Gravesend, in the Thames estuary, while trying to find a ship that would take him to the Spanish Netherlands.[17] Although the dissolution of the monasteries had been completed in 1540, Mary re-founded a single Benedictine monastery during her reign, Westminster Abbey.[18] Since Coxe was described as 'young' in one document it seems likely that he was a monk of Westminster rather than a surviving monk of one of the pre-Reformation monasteries (no Englishman joined a Continental monastery until 1589[19]). Westminster Abbey was still the home of the monks when Elizabeth was crowned there on 15 January 1559, but it was dissolved for the second time on 12 July 1559 and the monks were forced to seek preferment within the new Church of England, enter a secular profession, or go into exile abroad.

When Coxe was searched he was found to be carrying letters to Catholic exiles living in the Low Countries. Hauled before a local magistrate in Kent, Coxe was questioned and admitted to saying mass contrary to the Act of Uniformity and believing that the new religion of England was not the true religion; he also revealed that many prominent Essex families, including some of Elizabeth's Privy Councillors, supported a network of 'massing priests' in the countryside. Coxe also confessed to saying mass as part of love magic. On the face of it, Coxe's most serious crime was the suspicion that he might be a courier for disloyal subjects. It was a crime to say mass, but there was no law against using the mass for magical purposes. The revelation about the network of massing priests was interesting, but not in itself evidence of treason.

However, Elizabeth's new chief minister, William Cecil, was determined to investigate further. The Privy Council commissioned John de Vere, earl of Oxford, to go into Essex, where he was one of the leading magnates and the Lord Lieutenant of the county, 'to enquire for mass mongers, and conjurers'.[20] Oxford's men searched the homes of Sir Edward Waldegrave at Borley and Sir Thomas Wharton at Beaulieu (or New Hall), a former palace of Henry VII where Mary Tudor had been imprisoned during the reign of Edward VI. During Mary's reign, Waldegrave had been involved in pursuing Gospellers attempting to leave the country and Wharton had taken part in local interrogations of heretics, suggesting that both were enthusiastic Catholics.[21]

Waldegrave and Wharton confessed to hearing mass and were punished at the Brentwood assizes. However, papers seized at Borley and Beaulieu led to the arrests of four priests: William Jolly,

John Sherman, John Ramridge and Leonard Bilson. Some of these had been important clergymen in their heyday: Ramridge, like Coxe, was a former monk of Westminster,[22] while Bilson was a former prebendary of Salisbury Cathedral and chaplain to Stephen Gardiner, bishop of Winchester under Henry, Edward and Mary and a leading conservative. To their number was added an Oxford-trained doctor of medicine, Doctor Frear. Along with the priests and the physician, two noblemen were arrested: Sir Edward Hastings and Arthur Pole.

These men had a special significance to Elizabeth's government because they were both potential claimants to the throne. Hastings was the brother of Henry Hastings, earl of Huntingdon, whose mother Catherine Pole was the granddaughter of Margaret Pole, countess of Salisbury (1473–1541). Margaret, who was executed by Henry VIII for her refusal to acknowledge his supremacy, was the sole surviving child of George, duke of Clarence – the brother of Edward IV who died in a butt of malmsey wine. Margaret Pole was also the mother of Cardinal Pole. Sir Edward Hastings had been an enthusiastic supporter of Mary's regime and served as her Master of the Horse and Steward of the Duchy of Cornwall, before being created Baron Hastings of Loughborough in 1558. He was also a persecutor of heretics. Arthur Pole was the son of Sir Geoffrey Pole, Margaret Pole's youngest son, and the great nephew of Cardinal Pole.[23]

The Poles' association with the dead cardinal was enough to render them suspect on religious grounds alone, but in their case the Elizabethan government's concern about religious dissent masked an older, more primal royal fear that the White Rose of York might return to assert its superior claim to the throne. Since the sons of Edward IV and Richard III perished and left no heirs, the descendants of the duke of Clarence represented the senior line of the House of Plantagenet. Henry VIII's decision to execute the countess of Salisbury in 1541 had been motivated by more than just a concern for his ecclesiastical supremacy; there was a real fear that Margaret could become a rallying point for discontent. Twenty years later, Elizabeth's childlessness and the absence of an heir apparent rendered her especially vulnerable to dynastic threats that had the potential to resurrect the Wars of the Roses.

As early as December 1559, before the discovery of Coxe's letters, the Spanish ambassador to England, Alvaro de la Quadra, bishop of Aquila, reported that Elizabeth was 'displeased that some of them [her courtiers] are greatly caressing a nephew of Cardinal Pole ... and she suspects all of those who surround him and particularly Lord Hastings'. De la Quadra testified to the instability of Elizabeth's early reign when he airily commented, 'Let her take what care she may, she cannot prevent the river overflowing its banks one of these days and, on my faith, I think that her own co-religionists may bring this about before the Catholics'.[24] De la Quadra may have been referring to the arrests of Fortescue, Kele and Prestall, who had now attached themselves to Arthur Pole as head of the House of Plantagenet. The contents of the letters apprehended in Coxe's possession suggested that the river was indeed overflowing its banks. Hastings was encouraging Pole to marry the sister of Thomas Percy, earl of Northumberland. Percy was the leading Catholic magnate of the north, and one of the few men in England with the political clout to be able to mount a credible rebellion against Elizabeth – which, in fact, is exactly what he would do unsuccessfully in 1569.

There was no sign that Percy had agreed to his sister's marriage, and he remained in the queen's favour, but rumours circulated at court that the cloth for the wedding dress had already been bought. Pole actually married Anne Holland, the daughter of the earl of Northumberland's aunt, but it is possible that rumour exaggerated his wife's status and made her the earl's sister. Still more worryingly, the letters indicated that 'conjurers were sought ... to know how long the queen should reign, and what should become of religion'.[25] The magical twist in the case was picked up by the Spanish ambassador, who noted on 21 April that several Catholic gentlemen had been arrested, and that

> ... on account of the confession of one of the chaplains, who was going to Flanders, they have been accused of having held mass in their houses. Yesterday they were dragged to London with a great guard and then conveyed with great mockery through the middle of London to another prison. Two of those who came were taken also. Today they have taken Arthur Pole, a great-nephew of Cardinal Pole, because they say he heard mass, and they have commanded Lord Hastings, who was Lord

Chamberlain to Queen Mary, to come; I think he will soon be in the Tower as well. They call many others and say that there is a large number of them named in this matter, and the queen thinks that there is conjuration and conspiracy against her.[26]

A few days later, on 28 April, De la Quadra wrote to Margaret of Austria, governor of the Spanish Netherlands, to inform her that 'They have also arrested six or eight very honoured clergymen, two of whom are Oxford doctors, and made it public that they are necromancers and that they have conjured demons to have the queen die; for which they have been derided and, by report, are more hated by the people'.[27] De la Quadra naturally wanted to believe (or wanted his political masters to believe) that the English people despised the new Protestant regime.

Later, De la Quadra wrote to Phillip himself, informing him that the arrested priests had been discovered in possession of horoscopes for Elizabeth and her favourite, Robert Dudley, whom Elizabeth later created earl of Leicester in 1564.[28] Dudley was a regular target of plots by those jealous of the unique position he enjoyed in the queen's favour. In a letter to Sir Nicholas Throckmorton, the English ambassador to the French court, one civil servant wondered whether the plot was part of a co-ordinated strategy organised by the pope: 'The coming of the pope's nuncio into the Low Countries, the arriving of a like good fellow into Ireland, and the concurring of a nest of conjurers and mass mongers here giveth me occasion to think that our men here, had more in their minds than their old mumpsimus'.[29] 'Mumpsimus' was a pejorative reference to the Latin mass.

On 23 June 1561 nine people appeared before the Court of Queen's Bench and admitted their involvement in magic, and were made to swear on the Gospel that they would have no more traffic with evil spirits. The nine were pilloried at Westminster on the same day, and again at Cheapside on 25 June for their involvement in 'conjuring and other matter', in spite of the fact that conjuration was not against the law at the time.[30] They were Francis Coxe (the author of the exposé of magic), an innkeeper named Hugh Draper, the priests John Coxe and Leonard Bilson, an ironmonger named Robert Man, a miller from Fakenham in Suffolk named Rudolf Poyntell, a cleric from Harnington in Worcestershire named John Cockoyter, a Clerkenwell salter named Fabian Withers and the Westminster goldsmith John Wright.[31] The pillory was an unpleasant form of public humiliation but hardly a serious punishment. Arthur Pole could not be linked directly to the magical plot, and at his trial he was found guilty only of hearing mass contrary to the Act of Uniformity. He was soon released from prison, and went to stay with Lord Hastings at Stoke Poges in Buckinghamshire. In Devine's view Pole's release was deliberate, and intended to draw others into a trap bated by Cecil.[32]

In July 1562 Pole asked his brother-in-law, Anthony Fortescue, to arrange for him to enter the service of Spain in the Netherlands. Fortescue accordingly approached De la Quadra, who refused to help Pole unless he first left England. De la Quadra needed proof that Pole was in earnest, and he knew that he could be ejected from the country if he was found to be abetting treason on English soil. On 1 September Arthur and his brother Edmund met with Fortescue, John Prestall, Humphrey Barwick, Edward Cosyn, Richard Byngham and Anthony Spencer at Lambeth, where they 'conspired to depose the queen, change the state of the realm, compass the queen's death, make Mary, Queen of Scots, queen of England and raise insurrection in the realm'. The association with Mary, Queen of Scots made the Poles even more dangerous than their link with the Percys, since Mary was not only the Catholic ruler of England's volatile northern neighbour but also the preferred claimant to the English throne, as far as most Catholics were concerned. The conspirators agreed to go to Flanders where they planned to proclaim Arthur Pole duke of Clarence and send letters to Catherine de Medici, then ruler of France, along with the king of Navarre and the duke of Guise, asking for help and support. With the duke of Guise they plotted to marry Arthur's brother Edmund to Mary, Queen of Scots and obtain an army of 5000 or 6000 men, which would land in Wales and then invade England.

On 10 September Edward Cosyn and John Prestall met at Southwark, where 'they practised invocations of evil spirits and asked of an evil spirit the best way to carry out their treasons'. Prestall calculated that Elizabeth would die in March 1563. What the conspirators did not know was that one of their number, Humphrey Barwick, was a spy inserted into the group by Cecil.[33] A month later, the two magicians went ahead to Flanders to make preparations, and the day after their departure, on 11 October, Fortescue arranged for a small boat to meet the remaining conspirators at St Olave's Stairs in Lambeth and take them down the Thames to Gravesend, where the *Hoy of Flanders* was to take them to the Low Countries. The men loaded arms, money and supplies in the boat while they stayed at a local inn, the Dolphin, but after three hours they were surprised by the authorities.[34] Cecil was forced to arrest the conspirators at this point because a few days earlier Elizabeth had fallen ill with smallpox – a frightening illness from which she was just as likely to die as recover. Whether or not Cecil believed that the smallpox might have been brought about by Prestall's conjurations, he knew that if he allowed Pole to escape and the queen died, the chances of a successful Catholic invasion increased exponentially.

At his trial on 26 February 1563, Arthur Pole was found guilty of high treason and sentenced to death, but the sentence was commuted to life imprisonment, either on account of his royal blood (as William Camden claimed),[35] or in response to a petition from Sir John Fortescue, Elizabeth's Keeper of the Great Wardrobe.[36] Pole languished in the Tower and died at an unknown date before 1570, like dozens of forgotten royal prisoners before him. Overall, it seems unlikely that Prestall and Cosyn used necromancy (the invocation of evil spirits) to calculate the date of the queen's death, the likelihood of a return to Catholicism and the chances of their plan succeeding. All of these things could have been done by casting questionary horoscopes, something that Prestall was perfectly capable of doing. As so often, what the magicians really did was painted in the blackest possible light by their opponents, and astrology was demonised once again, as it had been in the fifteenth century.

Nevertheless, the investigation into the Pole conspiracy produced disturbing evidence that seditious priests and sorcerers were engaging in magical practices with impunity. Under examination in the Court of Star Chamber on 20 June 1561 by Edmund Grindal, Bonner's successor as bishop of London, Leonard Bilson had refused even to make an 'abasement' (bow to the court), but the monk John Coxe confessed to saying mass at Bilson's home, 'for hallowing of certain conjurations to those of the said Bilson who practised by those means to obtain the love of my Lady Cotton, the late wife of Sir Richard Cotton, Knight',[37] or as another source put it, 'Bilson ... to have his will of the Lady Cotton caused young Coxe a priest to say a mass to call on the devil to make her his lady'.[38]

Again, it seems unlikely that Coxe was really engaged in summoning up the devil, which was hardly necessary for a piece of love magic. However, for Grindal, who was a strict Protestant, any use of magic constituted idolatry and spiritual whoredom. Although the bishop had no love for the mass, he was nonetheless horrified that these priests could think of making use of the sacraments of the church for such unworthy ends. He wrote to Cecil, bemoaning the fact that there was no way to punish offenders like Coxe and Bilson. He even sought a legal opinion from Sir Robert Catlyn, Lord Chief Justice of the King's Bench, who managed to find a precedent from the reign of Edward III for trying someone for sorcery in the absence of legislation.[39] Meanwhile, Bilson continued to manipulate Coxe and even wrote to him in the Marshalsea prison, 'requiring him to declare by his troth, that he had wrongfully denounced him'. The former prebendary was seen walking brazenly about town wearing 'a fair gown with a large tippet and ... cap on his head' and tried to ingratiate himself with a nobleman for protection, Lord St John.[40] Nevertheless, Bilson did not escape the pillory in the end.

An early modern manuscript book of magic in Cambridge University Library dating from the mid-sixteenth century (between 1533 and 1558) contains spells that may be similar to those Coxe and Bilson employed. It is clear that anyone who used the book was expected to be a priest, not only because most of the instructions are in Latin but also because several of the operations require the use of an altar, and some involve the saying of a number of masses. The love magic ranges from simple charms to rituals involving animal sacrifice. At the simple end, the magician could 'write on an apple, or on bread, or on cheese: "Honey: Baxuti: Tetragrammaton", and your name and the name of the woman'.[41] Another spell required the magician to 'take an apple on a Friday when there is a crescent moon and make a ring in the apple and write around it, "Guel: Lucifer: Sathanas"'. Friday was associated with love because its Latin name, *dies Veneris*, meant 'the day of Venus', while apples may have been considered appropriate for love magic because Paris presented Aphrodite with an apple in Greek mythology.

Other spells, however, took on a rather more sinister complexion: 'Take three hairs from [the woman's] head and virgin wax, and make an image and enclose them in the image, and write on the front of the image "Sathan", and on the right arm "Bellial", and on the left arm "Brith", and on the right foot "Belzebub"'.[42] Had such a figure been found by the authorities, it is easy to see how it might have been interpreted as an attempt to kill by magic. Another spell was even more bizarre and must have required a strong stomach:

> Take a mole and place it in blessed jar, [make] many holes and afterwards close the mouth of that jar and put it in a place where there are many ants for ten days; afterwards take the bones of that mole and put them in running water, and retain the bones which turn against the water and touch the woman either on the face or on the hand and she will love you at once.[43]

This was not the only spell to require an animal sacrifice: another instructed the magician to 'take a staff made of hazel, one year old, and cut while growing, with the blood of a white dove, [saying] "Arax: Apeaxy: Lepeary: Femani", and touch the woman and she will be ruled by you'. Another possibility was to write out the 'Rotas Square', an ancient acrostic widely used in magic, in the blood of a white dove, dip it in holy water and place it on an altar, presumably so that mass would then be said over it, perhaps unwittingly.[44] John Coxe's love magic may have seemed relatively harmless, yet there was another magician arrested at around the same time for a much more serious offence who was also imprisoned in April and May 1561. This was Francis Coxe, not to be confused with the former monk. Francis's crime was to have plotted with two other men the death by magic of Sir William St Loe, Elizabeth's captain of the guard, butler of England, and the husband of 'Bess of Hardwick'.

This was not quite magical treason, although it was an attack on a member of the queen's household, and the attempt was exposed by an astrologer named John Man, possibly a business rival of Francis

Coxe.[45] Devine has shown that Cecil 'manoeuvred around' the lack of a statute against magic by using a precedent from 1371 and having the suspects arraigned before the Court of Star Chamber. Indeed, it was by emphasising the suspects' wider treasonable intent that Cecil managed to secure their conviction.[46] Francis Coxe appeared in the pillory with John Coxe, Bilson and the other six, but capitalised on his punishment by publishing a short broadside in which he confessed his crimes yet whetted the public's appetite for a more extensive description of the sorcerer's art. Accordingly, in 1562 Coxe brought out a book entitled *A Short Treatise declaringe the detestable wickednesse, of magicall sciences, as Necromancie. Coniurations of spirites, Curiouse Astrologie and suche lyke*, which conveniently portrayed him as a penitent sinner and earned him money at the same time. Here Coxe explained that one method used by magicians to gain power was to take a magical vow to abstain from certain foods:

> ... besides the horrible and grievous blasphemies they commit in their conjurations, they must fall to some composition with the devil, that is to promise him for his service, he will abstain from wines, or some certain meats, or drinks. As I myself knew a priest, not far from a town called Bridgewater, which as it is well known in the country, was a great magician in all his lifetime, after he once began these practices, he never would eat bread, but instead thereof did eat always cheese, which thing as he confessed divers times, he did because it was so concluded between him and the spirit, which served him, for at what time he did eat bread: he should no longer live. Yea, he would not blush to say that after a few years he should die, and that the devil for his pains that he took with him, should have in recompense his soul.[47]

The Bridgewater magician's vow to eat only cheese, whilst bizarre, would have confirmed the view of many of Coxe's readers that Catholicism, which also demanded fasts from certain kinds of food at certain times of the year, was little better than magic. However, magicians also had another, even more macabre method of obtaining power at their disposal:

> ... when the spirit is once come before the circle, he forthwith demandeth [from] the exorcist a sacrifice, which most commonly is a piece of wax consecrated, or hallowed after their own order (for they have certain books, called books of consecration) or else it is a chicken, a lapwing, or some living creature, which when he hath received, then

doth he fulfil the mind of the exorcist, for once he hath it, he will neither do, neither speak anything.[48]

The practice of animal sacrifice to evil spirits was obviously idolatry and a departure from the Christian faith. However, Coxe declined to go into much more detail about his own magical practice and instead offered anecdotes of medieval magicians who met untimely ends as a result of spells gone wrong.

One anonymous magician whose personal writings were preserved by the seventeenth-century alchemist, magician and antiquary Elias Ashmole (1617–92) was prepared to record the results of his experiments with harmful magic. The magician made a wax figure of his own daughter and found that, when the stars were correctly aligned, he could prick the wax image and 'could sensibly hurt her at my pleasure … or could procure her to sweat at my pleasure' – the latter presumably by holding the wax over a heat source.[49] Although the spell that the magician was testing was meant as a method of thief detection, it is obvious that magic of this kind was derived from the same methods John of Nottingham was practising against Edward II in the fourteenth century: a combination of basic effigy magic and more advanced astrology. The sixteenth-century magician thought that he was able to harm his daughter by 'natural magic', and that no invocation of spirits was necessary. Ironically, the most popular forms of harmful magic did not necessarily involve the invocation of evil spirits at all.

THE BURNING OF ST PAUL'S

Not long after the resolution of the first magical plot against Elizabeth, disaster struck the City of London. On the evening of 4 June 1561 lightning set fire to old St Paul's, the huge gothic cathedral in the heart of Tudor London. The lightning seems to have made contact with the cathedral's spire, a wooden structure covered with lead. It ignited the wood, which melted the lead and sent a torrent of molten metal down onto the roof of the nave; so intense was the heat that it even melted the cathedral's famous bells. As horrified crowds looked on, the spire collapsed and crashed through the long timber roof of the nave. Fire leapt along the dry medieval beams, melting the lead above them and leaving the cathedral roofless by the next morning. It was the most serious fire to affect the church until old St Paul's was completely destroyed in the Great Fire of London in 1666.

St Paul's was much more than just the cathedral of the diocese of London; it was a building at the heart of the Reformation and the social life of the city. In St Paul's churchyard was Paul's Cross, the open air pulpit where, in the fifteenth century, Roger Bolingbroke had been displayed with his instruments of magic. A century later, Paul's Cross was the mouthpiece of both Reformation and Counter-Reformation; here official religious policy was promulgated and defended, and St Paul's churchyard was hemmed in by booksellers hawking printed versions of sermons, as well as plenty of less edifying matter. The cathedral's nave, 'Paul's Walk', was also treated as a gigantic covered arcade in which people did business, exchanged gossip, planned and committed crime and even picked up prostitutes.[50] The cathedral was London itself in miniature, where the sacred and profane jostled for space.

In the years leading up to the fire the cathedral had been stripped of the Catholic furnishings restored in Mary's reign and returned to a plain, barn-like appearance. Gone were the dozens of tiny chapels where priests had each said their own individual mass, as were any members of the cathedral chapter who opposed Elizabeth's religious changes. Amongst these were John Morwen, a former prebendary of the cathedral and chaplain to Bishop Bonner, ejected for his refusal to accept the Act of Supremacy. Instead of horror at the damage done to his cathedral, Morwen reacted to the fire by metaphorically licking his lips with satisfaction. God had finally given a clear sign of his displeasure at the Protestant Reformation. In a pamphlet that Morwen distributed in Westminster, he noted that the fire took place on the eve of the now abolished Catholic feast of Corpus Christi.

It was quite common in the sixteenth century for lightning strikes to be interpreted as acts of God in the original, literal sense. Alternatively, they were interpreted as direct attacks of the devil, like the 'black dog' that burst into Bungay parish church in a thunderstorm in August 1577, leaving the marks of its claws on the singed church door.[51] All of this was part of an important strand in early modern thinking, 'providentialism', which interpreted misfortunes, disasters and strange events as signs of God's will. 'Providences' were staples of Reformation propaganda on both sides, since virtually any interpretation could be laid on otherwise inexplicable events.

Morwen's gloating attack on Protestantism was ill-timed, as evidence soon emerged that the lightning strike on St Paul's might have been the work, not of God, but of demons invoked by magic. Robert Parsons later recalled that 'certain charms or enchantments, and devices of witchcraft wound up together in pieces of parchment with figures, characters and such like fond toys' were found 'hid in the ground' near the cathedral shortly after the fire. These were, or were interpreted as, magical invocations of evil spirits to raise a storm and attack the cathedral. Suspicion fell on Morwen himself, who was not only the individual who had taken most satisfaction in the fire but also a Catholic priest who might well be in possession of magical knowledge. According to Parsons, 'The matter was supposed to have been contrived for some mischief or destruction to the Queen's Majesty', although whether this meant that the attack on St Paul's was a test-run for one on the royal court, or simply a swipe against the flagship church of the Reformation in London, is unclear.

In the event, attention shifted away from Morwen when a Protestant parson was discovered to be behind the 'fond toys'. However, the fact that the convicted sorcerers in the St Loe case were pilloried close to St Paul's may have served to emphasise the magical character of the attack on London's cathedral.[52] Twenty years later, Parsons was still fuming that people automatically jumped to the conclusion that Catholics were responsible:

> But who was he among all our adversaries which did not charge Catholics with that fact? Yet lo, not long after, it was found out and proved that a certain minister was the author and principal of this sorcery, and had diverse accomplices and accessories which were very zealous gospellers: whereupon all was hushed suddenly: yea (as busy as they were before) now they say not one word of the matter, saying that some (to turn the fault from one to another, that the blame might fall some way on Catholics) said that this minister had perhaps dissembled his religion and was a very papist in his heart.[53]

Parsons's righteous anger did little to stop the inexorable progress of the stereotype of Catholics as pyromaniacs, which was given credence by the Gunpowder Plot of 1605 and even provided the first and initially popular explanation for the Great Fire of London in 1666.

THE 1563 ACT AGAINST CONJURATION AND WITCHCRAFT

In January 1563 Parliament debated a catch-all 'Bill for servants robbing their masters, buggery, invocation of spirits, enchantments, [and] witchcraft'. Norman Jones, Glyn Parry, Peter Maxwell-Stuart and Michael Devine have seen the introduction of this bill as a direct consequence of the magical attempts on Elizabeth's life by Prestall and the other conjurers.[54] Devine has argued that 'maleficent magic was inherent in the superstitious nature of Catholicism' as Elizabeth's councillors, and particularly Cecil, saw it.[55] Malcolm Gaskill, by contrast, saw it as part of a general government reaction to the perceived proliferation of 'superstition' during the period of Catholic darkness that preceded Elizabeth's reign.[56] What is certainly clear is that the bill was addressing a legislative deficit that had existed since the repeal of the 1542 act in 1547. The bill passed to the House of Lords on 11 February, but there it was split into three separate bills, one of which was 'An act against conjurations, enchantments and witchcrafts' that is commonly known as the Witchcraft Act.

The 'Witchcraft Act' is misnamed, since it consisted of three separate sections dealing with killing by magic, harming by magic and other uses of magic including treasure-seeking or love magic. It was really a second act against conjuration, and outlawed 'any invocations or conjurations of evil and wicked spirits, to or for any intent or purpose'. The act used the terms 'witchcraft, enchantment, charm, or sorcery' in each case to refer to the activity of the offender, following the pleonastic tendency of early modern lawyers and legislators to list all synonyms they could think of for the same crime. The act used the term 'witchcraft' but failed to define it. The law made killing by magic a capital crime, while stipulating a year's imprisonment without bail for anyone who engaged in other kinds of magic, along with quarterly appearances in the pillory. The punishment for a second offence was confiscation of all goods and life imprisonment.[57]

Devine has argued that the bill was an immediate consequence of the treason of Arthur Pole and John Prestall, combined with the queen's smallpox,[58] but this interpretation is not supported by the text of the act itself. The government did not need an act against conjuration to deal with behaviour that clearly fell under the law of treason – the Statute of Treason made prosecution of magical treason perfectly possible. Furthermore, it would be strange if Prestall's actions had inspired the bill, since the bill did not mention what Prestall had actually done (calculating the length of the queen's reign); this only became a crime in 1580. It is more probable that the Privy Councillors were embarrassed that Star Chamber had been obliged to convict the suspects in the St Loe case without a statute. This, combined with Bishop Grindal's disquiet at the absence of a statute against necromancy, is likely to have provided the immediate background to the bill.

Rather than 'ensuring an indelible association between Catholicism and magic',[59] as Devine has claimed, the 1563 act revived Henry VIII's earlier legislation in a modified and more lenient form. In contrast to the 1542 act, the new law confined the death penalty to cases when evil spirits were conjured to kill someone; the earlier act had imposed the death penalty for all magical offenders. The 1563 act moved the emphasis away from magical treasure-seeking and onto killing by magic. However, the wording of the act was somewhat ambiguous; one possible interpretation is that 'invocations or conjurations of evil and wicked spirits' is a separate offence, distinct from using 'witchcraft, enchantment, charm, or sorcery' to kill, harm, find treasure or provoke unlawful love. This interpretation is consistent with the distinction made by many early modern people between magic and witchcraft. Witches did not usually 'invoke or conjure' evil spirits. The 1542 act spoke of 'invocations or conjurations of spirits, witchcrafts, enchantments, or sorceries' as if these were intended as synonyms for the same activity. The 1563 act, by contrast, seemed to designate conjuring as a separate offence: 'witchcraft' appeared in a list of subsequently forbidden behaviours.

Just as in the 1530s and 1540s, in the 1560s magic was closely associated with prophecy, and the same Parliament of 1563 saw the passage of 'An act against fond and fantastical prophecies'. This was triggered by the news that the shape of a crucifix had miraculously appeared in the trunk of a tree struck by lightning at St Donats in Wales. Catholics interpreted the appearance as a sign that the old faith was about to be restored, and the man who spread the story in London by commissioning images of the tree, Sir Thomas Stradling, was imprisoned in the Marshalsea at the same time as Francis Coxe and the other accused magicians.[60] Michael Devine has argued that, taken together, the machinations of those arrested following the capture of John Coxe and the distribution of pictures of the miraculous Welsh tree contributed to Elizabeth's decision to deny the papal nuncio entry to England and to refuse England's participation in the Council of Trent.[61]

We may never know exactly how the original legislators in the Parliament of 1563 intended the new act to be interpreted, but we do know how the courts applied it. Between 1563 and 1604, when it was replaced, the victims of the new law were not usually professional magicians like Prestall or aristocratic conspirators like Arthur Pole, but rather those accused of 'perceived maleficent anti-social behaviour at county level'.[62] In 1566 an old woman from Chelmsford in Essex was accused of killing and harming her neighbours with the help of her cat 'Satan', who was really a demonic 'familiar' in animal form. 'Satan' prevented Agnes Waterhouse from saying her prayers in English, and even when she was in church forced her to pray the old Catholic prayers in Latin.[63] It was significant that this prosecution took place in Essex, where Waldegrave and Wharton had been arrested, and that Waterhouse was accused of a superstitious attachment to Catholicism as well as witchcraft. Although she was an individual of low social status, Waterhouse may have partly served as an example to religious conservatives in Essex that Catholic practices were now unacceptable superstition.

Waterhouse was a new kind of criminal, never before seen in England. The 1563 act made no reference to the idea of familiars, a folk-belief particularly associated with East Anglia, but the judge in the Waterhouse case found the evidence convincing. By convicting her he created a precedent and defined the parameters within which the 'Witchcraft Act' would be understood by lawyers and judges, and thereby inaugurated England's era of witch-hunting. From now on, the 1563 act would be deployed primarily against female witches, not male conjurers, even though the text of the act did not explain what witchcraft was or how it worked. Theologians filled in the details. It is difficult to argue that the trial of the Chelmsford witches was of direct *political* significance; indeed, the precedent it created ensured that witchcraft was de-politicised, since it directed magistrates to look for witches among the marginalised and socially underprivileged rather than among courtiers and clergy. English witchcraft was to be a local crime, and it is primarily because of the nature of the early prosecutions in Essex that the 1563 legislation has become known as the 'Witchcraft Act'.

Agnes Waterhouse and the majority of those tried for witchcraft after her had more in common with Mabel Brigge, the woman from Holderness who fasted for Henry VIII's death, or the Gospellers who prayed for the death of Mary I, than they did with ritual magicians. There was a fine line between praying to God for aid against someone and cursing him, and a fine line between cursing and witchcraft.[64] Where the line should be drawn was open to interpretation. Even the official English prayer book contained a 'Commination, or denouncing of God's anger against sinners' that called down formal curses on those who disobeyed God's commandments, but anyone who invoked the devil in an oath was liable to be accused of a literal invocation of the evil one. This had little to do with magic, and more to do with the Reformation's re-adjustment of the boundaries between acceptable and unacceptable forms of religious speech. As the behaviour of Mabel Brigge's chantry priest demonstrated, pre-Reformation clergy were happy to indulge the personal religious preoccupations of the laity, whether a liking for prophecies or a belief in the power of fasting: post-Reformation clergy, generally speaking, were less willing.

THE ABDUCTION AND TRIAL OF JOHN STORY

In August 1570 Elizabeth's fledgling intelligence service, led by Sir Francis Walsingham, carried out one of its first major operations on foreign territory, organised by John Delves and Lancelot Bostock.[65] John Lee, a merchant at Antwerp who worked as an English agent, recruited three men to acquire a ship for him, and made contact with William Parker, a Catholic in exile in the Netherlands who was seeking a way to return home without facing a treason charge. Parker was the 'inside man' for the operation, which had as its goal the kidnap of John Story, then working as a searcher of foreign ships for the duke of Alba. Story was another former dignitary of Queen Mary's reign. He was a doctor of civil and canon law who had been Regius Professor of civil law at Oxford in the 1540s and served as an MP. Most importantly, however, Story had been Bishop Bonner's principal commissary in the 1550s for the detection and trial of heretics in the diocese of London. John Foxe's *Actes and monumentes* painted the blackest possible picture of Story as a consummate sadist, and while this was probably exaggerated, Story's past meant that he had good reason to seek refuge in the service of Spain.

Parker pretended to tip Story off about the imminent arrival of a ship with a suspicious cargo (the one commandeered by Lee), which was due to arrive at the less-frequented port of Bergen-op-Zoom. Once Story had boarded the ship to search it, Lee and his friends weighed anchor and sailed straight back to Great Yarmouth.[66] However, although Story was a hated figure as far as the Elizabethan government was concerned, there were legal problems with trying him for any of his most obvious and public crimes; it did not help that Story himself was a first-class lawyer. In the first place, everything that Story had done in Mary's reign had been legal at the time. Secondly, he had taken a formal oath of fealty to the duke of Alba which, in his view, released him from any allegiance to Elizabeth. He was a foreign subject and therefore outside the scope of the law of treason.

Naturally the court did not take this view, and decided that Story could be tried as a traitor because 'no man can shake off his country wherein he is born, nor abjure his native soil, or his prince at his pleasure'.[67] In the absolutist political culture of the sixteenth century, the idea that someone could choose to define his own nationality was nothing short of preposterous. However, the legality of Story's behaviour under Mary was irrefutable, so the prosecution decided to make the principal charge against Story one of magical treason, involving none other than John Prestall:

He was to be charged that he did traitorously conspire against the Queen's Majesty with one Prestall, an Englishman, who was a fugitive and principal devisor of the first treason intended by the young Pole eleven years past, and thereof was indicted and outlawed; and afterward of late time he practised another great treason with certain persons, whereof one disclosed the same to the Duke of Norfolk, who also very dutifully revealed the same to the Queen's Majesty.[68]

Prestall had in fact returned to England at the end of 1563, having begged Cecil in a letter of 30 November to be allowed letters of protection from the queen. These allowed Prestall to travel safely to England without being arrested. Cecil had him arrested anyway, and Prestall was incarcerated in the Tower. There he would have stayed, had it not been for Cecil's belief that alchemy might solve England's financial woes. Henry Herbert, earl of Pembroke, a close associate of Leicester, was particularly obsessed with alchemy, and although Elizabeth was somewhat more sceptical she agreed to grant a pardon to Prestall on 6 January 1567 for treason, conspiracy and 'all conjurations of evil spirits' because he offered 'to convert silver into gold'.[69]

However, Prestall was soon up to his old tricks, and became involved in a new conspiracy to put Mary, Queen of Scots on the throne. Mary fled to England in May 1568 after a failed attempt to re-establish her control of Scotland, thereby threatening the stability of the Tudor state. Leicester and Pembroke began to see Mary as a potential successor to Elizabeth, and in late 1569 Catholic resentment in the north flared into armed rebellion, threatening to plunge the country into a full-scale religious civil war. The earls of Westmoreland and Northumberland took control of Durham and restored the mass in the cathedral, a direct challenge to the Elizabethan religious settlement. The rebellion was soon defeated, but the rebels fled into Scotland, demonstrating the danger posed by the porous and unstable border between the two countries.

Prestall's part in this remains unclear, but he was certainly involved in another astrological calculation of Elizabeth's death and in the distribution of anti-government prophecies. When the authorities tried to apprehend him he likewise fled to Scotland to join the remnants of the rebel army of the Northern Earls, who were supported by Lord Maxwell. Prestall even managed to convince the Regent of Scotland, the earl of Moray, an opponent of Mary's rule, that he could successfully transmute silver into gold. Cecil contemplated a border raid into Scotland just to extract Prestall,[70] but the magician pre-empted any such attempt by taking ship to the Netherlands in June 1570, where he joined Story in exile. Shortly afterwards the pair turned up in Brussels,

> ... and there Prestall declared to certain persons, ready also to have avowed the same, that he had opened his whole purposes to Dr Story, whereto Dr Story was sworn to keep the same secret. But of the things intended by Prestall and Story at that time, neither of them would be then known, but yet Prestall affirmed he had an art to poison anybody afar off, being not present with them, and that none could do it but he.[71]

In addition to the offer to poison remotely by magic, Prestall wrote letters to Story from Scotland before his arrival in Brussels, in which he suggested an invasion of England from Scotland, a plan which was to be proposed to the duke of Alba. Prestall also told Story that 'the thing which he told ... in secret [i.e. the magical poisoning] would cost a thousand marks, and that if the Regent and the foolish boy the young King [James VI] were despatched and dead, the Scottish Queen were a marriage for the best man living'.[72] Prestall's claim to have unique power to perform a magical procedure that just happened to be extremely expensive suggests that his business sense may have been every bit as astute as his military planning.

On 24 May 1571 Story 'was arraigned, and being to be charged with treason for that he had consulted with one Prestall a man most addicted to magical illusions against his prince's life'.[73] Story refused to plead, on the basis that an English court had no jurisdiction over a subject of the king of Spain. He was found guilty and, in spite of the fact that the usual penalty for a refusal to plead was to be crushed to death in the *peine forte et dure*, Story was hanged, drawn and quartered as a traitor on 1 June. The actual evidence against Story was thin; in addition to magical treason, he was accused of cursing Elizabeth when saying grace at mealtimes, and there was no concrete evidence that he was engaged in planning an actual invasion. In Prestall's absence, anything could be said about the magician. Story's past history rendered him *persona non grata* with Elizabeth's government and, in this case, it seems that the charge of treason by magic was the most suitable for securing Story's downfall because it was easy to insinuate and hard to disprove.

By this time Prestall seems to have abandoned any political principles he might once have had. On 23 March 1572 John Lee wrote to Cecil, reporting that Prestall had set off for the Low Countries on the previous day. Prestall asked Lee 'to conceive no ungentleness in him for that he did not signify whither he went, saying he must seek his preferment by what means best he might'. Prestall took with him a large quantity of 'wildfire', a form of chemical warfare designed by alchemists and based on the ancient Byzantine naval weapon, Greek Fire. Prestall let Lee know that for a thousand crowns, an unnamed member of the Spanish court in the Netherlands would provide Cecil with intelligence. Prestall claimed that he had been asked to carry out an attack on the port of Rochester, using the wildfire, and said 'that he will do more with 500 men in the Thames mouth than the Duke [of Parma] shall with 40,000 in any other place'. The alchemical attack was to be orchestrated from within England by some of Prestall's former servants.[74]

Late in 1572 Prestall was allowed to return to England, presumably because he had informed Cecil of the wildfire attack supposedly planned against Rochester. He was imprisoned, but almost unbelievably, he was released on the payment of hefty financial bonds in July 1574.[75] The survival of John Prestall is a remarkable testimony to the power of fascination that alchemy exercised over the Tudor political elite. Yet the magical threat from Catholics, real or perceived, was far from over. On 27 and 28 June 1571 the Council instructed Sir Nicholas Poynings to send under custody to London Richard Lugge of North Nibley, a Mr Read of Littledean and John Adeane of Winchester 'with a book painted wherein the Queen's Majesty's image is with an arrow in her mouth', suggesting possible effigy magic.[76] Elizabeth's reign saw the most comprehensive development of the royal image in English history, when portraits of the queen were loaded with hidden meaning.[77] This was a practice founded on the same Hermetic-Neoplatonic doctrines of cosmic correspondences that sustained harmful effigy magic. Attacks on Elizabeth using images of the queen were the dark side of the cult of Gloriana and the royal image, and they may have been inevitable given the high profile of the queen's image.

In 1572 the Scottish Catholic bishop John Leslie turned the tables on the Elizabethan regime's anti-Catholic rhetoric of magical accusations, denouncing 'the dangerous detriments, and dishonourable infamies, that daily and hourly do spring and appear in the particular practices of this conjuration, both towards her people, her nobles, her nearest of blood, her own person and state, her posterity forever, her fame among men, and her soul before God'. These 'conjurations' were the evil advice of her ministers, 'the deadly malice of the covens and crafts' that Elizabeth was guilty of appeasing.[78] 'Can it be less, than a plain fascination and sorcery,' Leslie demanded, if the queen could not see that the Protestant rebels she was supporting in the Netherlands were opposed to the principle of government by a woman?[79] Leslie's argument that Calvinist Protestantism represented a threat to the monarchy came uncomfortably close to the truth, and he pressed the argument for all it was worth: 'What less or other can it now be, than a plain bewitching, that your Queen being of so rare a wisdom, for a woman, should yet be so circumvented and blinded, as not to see herself made the instrument of her own undoing?'[80]

THE CASE OF ROWLAND JENKS

In July 1577 the Catholic bookbinder Rowland Jenks supposedly killed an entire courtroom in Oxford by magic. Such an act fell under the original fourteenth-century definition of high treason, which made it treasonable to 'slay the Chancellor, Treasurer or the King's Justices [i.e. judges] ... being in their places, doing their offices'. This case, however, was not all it seemed. There are at least two contradictory accounts of what actually happened at the Oxford Assizes in the summer of 1577. According to Robert Parsons, Jenks was convicted at the assizes and sentenced to the pillory for seditious words against the Protestant religious settlement. This usually involved the prisoner having his head, hands and feet confined in wooden blocks while the crowd mistreated him as they chose, but in Jenks's case there was an additional and very unpleasant punishment. When the stocks of the pillory were closed over his head, his ears were nailed to the wood on either side and Jenks was given a knife, forcing him to cut off his own ears to free himself. The mutilation of ears was traditionally the punishment for forgers, but it was also occasionally used (along with mutilation of the tongue) for people convicted of seditious words against the government. In the event, Jenks met with sympathy rather than ridicule from the people of Oxford, who considered the sentence excessively severe.

It was then that, in Parsons's view, a 'wonderful judgement of God' visited the judges: 'For within few days after, the two judges, and well nigh all the jury, many of the justices and freeholders, with very many other of them which had been present there, died all of a strange kind of disease, some in the said city, and some in other places'. However, Parsons lamented that 'all the blame for this was laid upon Catholics: all this was imputed to magic and sorcery, as practised by Catholics'.[81] No evidence survives of contemporary Protestant commentators drawing this conclusion; the chronicler John Stowe simply recorded that there was a severe outbreak of gaol fever at the time, and made no mention of magic.[82] The filthy and disease-ridden conditions of Tudor prisons were an occupational hazard for judges, jurors and court officials as well as the prisoners themselves, since the assize system meant that a large number of trials would take place one after the other when prisoners had been incubating diseases like typhus and tuberculosis for months.

However, rumour gave life to the Jenks case and in 1589 a woman called Mrs Dewse, who was hiring a magician to take vengeance on her husband's enemies, cited what Jenks had supposedly done: according to her, Jenks made a candle 'from strange and frightful materials' and lit it at the moment of his condemnation. The magical candle raised a damp mist which killed his enemies.[83] By 1636, when a medical writer cited the case, it had become established folklore that Jenks used sorcery to raise a mysterious mist 'within the Castle yard and court house' where his trial was taking place; the judges fell down dead in their seats according to this account, making Jenks's act high treason.[84]

It seems likely that Parsons, who was recounting events only five years in the past, gave a more accurate account of the Jenks case, even if he was unable to pass up the opportunity to use it as Catholic propaganda. Parsons's description of the deaths of the judges as providential, like Morwen's pamphlet on the burning of St Paul's, was counterproductive to his argument that Catholics were not guilty of magic. The Elizabethan state had effectively defined wishing or praying for someone's death as a supernatural crime. The Jenks case can only have increased the government's sense of insecurity, especially since medieval witch-hunting manuals like the *Malleus maleficarum* ('Hammer of Witches') promised that witches and sorcerers could not harm their captors or judges.

CONCLUSION

The early years of Elizabeth's reign were far from secure, and the apparent proliferation of acts of magical treason in this period was as much an indication of the regime's fragility as the reality of actual threats. However, there can be no doubt that magicians with treasonous intent did practise against Elizabeth, the clearest example being John Prestall. The political significance of the act of 1563 (misnamed the 'Witchcraft Act' by many historians) should not be exaggerated, since the law of treason already covered the most serious magical cases dealt with in the 1560s. The revival of Henry VIII's statute should instead be seen as a combined attempt by church and state to introduce harsher penalties for superstitious practices, and it is a strange accident of history that the 1563 act was eventually deployed primarily against socially marginalised women accused of witchcraft. Specific legislation against magical treason would not come until the 1580s, as a result of the most significant magical scandal in English history.

CHAPTER 4

'A Traitorous Heart to the Queen': Effigies and Witch-Hunts, 1578–1603

In August 1578, a labourer made a disturbing chance discovery in a pile of animal dung inside a stable at Islington (some accounts say Lincoln's Inn Fields), then a village several miles outside London. Delving into the dunghill, he drew out three figures made of wax, about sixty centimetres tall. According to the Spanish ambassador, Bernardino Mendoza, 'The centre figure had the word Elizabeth written on the forehead and the side figures were dressed like her councillors, and were covered over with a great variety of different signs, the left side of the images being transfixed with a large quantity of pig's bristles, as if it were some sort of witchcraft'.[1] The figures were initially handed to a local magistrate, who passed them to the Lord Mayor and the bishop of London, who in turn sent to the Privy Council on 15 August 'a box fast-sealed, wherein were contained three pictures of wax and certain examinations taken by them touching the manner of finding the said pictures'. The Lord Mayor and bishop were necessary as intermediaries because that summer Elizabeth, with her Privy Councillors in tow, was on progress in East Anglia.

On 15 August Elizabeth was staying in the humble surroundings of Mergate Hall, in the tiny Norfolk village of Bracon Ash.[2] The following morning she and the rest of the court rode in magnificent procession into Norwich, the second largest city in England, where the hub of the court was established in the Bishop's Palace around the person of the queen. Publicly, the progress was a celebration of the queen's rule and a chance for the landowners and corporations whose estates and towns she passed through to ingratiate themselves with the monarch and entertain her with elaborate masques and other performances. Behind the glamour, however, the progress had a definite political purpose. Mendoza described the other side of the pageantry:

> During her progress in the north the Queen has met with more Catholics than she expected, and in one of the houses they found a great many images which were ordered to be dragged round and burnt. When she entered Norwich large crowds of people came out to receive her, and one company of children knelt as she passed and said, as usual, 'God save the Queen'. She turned to them and said, 'Speak up; I know you do not love me here'.[3]

Elizabeth was referring to an attempted rebellion in Norfolk that had been triggered nine years earlier in 1569, when the duke of Norfolk attempted to capitalise on the rebellion of the Northern Earls by trying to marry Mary, Queen of Scots. His plan was discovered and Norfolk fled to his manor at Kenninghall in Norfolk. A few months later Sir John Appleyard, a former Sheriff of Norfolk in Mary's reign, began whipping up popular hostility in Norwich against 'strangers', Protestant refugees fleeing the religious war in the Netherlands, in the hope of raising a rebellion against Elizabeth and marching on London. The attempt was a complete failure, but 32 people were questioned and tried for treason at the Norwich assizes in July and August 1570.[4] In 1578 the queen was going to meet the notoriously Catholic gentry of East Anglia in their stronghold.[5]

At the same time, Elizabeth's councillors had international affairs on their minds. While some were pressing for the queen to marry the French king's brother, the duke of Anjou, others, led by the earl of Leicester, were anxious about contracting an alliance with a Catholic power, and were doing their utmost to persuade Elizabeth to authorise an armed intervention in the Netherlands to support the Protestant rebellion against Spanish rule being led by the prince of Orange, William the Silent. This political background, combined

Effigies and Witch-Hunts, 1578–1603 121

with a period of illness for Elizabeth, contributed to the government treating the three wax effigies discovered at Islington in 1578 more seriously than any case of magical treason before or since. The later exposure of the effigies as a case of mistaken identity – they were made for use in love magic and had nothing to do with politics or Elizabeth – does not in any way diminish the significance that these effigies carried while they were the subject of intense official fear and investigation.

EFFIGY MAGIC

A few years after the Islington effigies scandal, in 1584, Reginald Scot described the sort of effigy magic deployed by Tudor necromancers to hurt or kill:

> Make an image in his name, whom [you] would hurt or kill, of new virgin wax; under the right arm-poke [armpit] whereof place a swallow's heart, and the liver under the left; then hang about the neck thereof a new thread in a new needle pricked into the member which you would have hurt, with the rehearsal of certain words ... Otherwise, sometimes these images are made of brass, and then the hand is placed where the foot should be, and the foot where the hand, and the face downward. Otherwise, for a greater mischief, the like image is made in the form of a man or woman, upon whose head is written the certain name of the party; and on his or her ribs these words, *Ailif, casyl, zaze, hit, mel meltat*; then the same must be buried.[6]

There were probably as many different spells used in effigy magic as there were magicians, but to a certain extent such magic took a basic common form. The fifteenth-century spell known as the 'Trojan Revenge' seems to have been typical of most early modern astrological image magic in use in England. Scot's reference to the reversal of hands and feet and the ceremonial burial of the image recalls the formula in the *Liber de angelis*. By the mid-sixteenth century the 'Trojan Revenge' was appearing in a slightly different but still recognisable form:

> If you want to harm a man or woman, take some earth from one recently dead and a pound and a half of virgin wax; and make from it an image as long as the palm of the hand, made of earth from the belly upwards and of wax from the belly downwards. And write on the top of

the head 'Dathyn: Maby: Chayl', on the front of the image the name of the person for whom the work is being done, and around the surface let these names be written: 'Xethenata: Martha: Xatenosate: Sathan'. On the breast write: 'Strayl: Chayl'. On the belly write 'Xathagundus'; on the sole of the right foot 'Baxtrala'. And with these have parts of the shroud of some dead person and bind whichever part of the body you want to carry off, invoking the aforesaid names on the image, saying what you are doing concerning this image and those persons N and N, making three defects and three dark spots. Let the image be pierced with a needle when it is the hour of Saturn, and pierce it in whatever part of the body you want, invoking the aforesaid and saying what you are doing concerning this image and those persons N and N. Let the image be buried in whatever place you want; and if you want to heal him, remove the needle and the shroud and wash the part of the body with sweet milk and he will be healed at once. Note that this image should be made in the hour of Saturn with the Moon being in Capricorn or in Virgo.[7]

The magical tradition was one that existed almost exclusively in manuscript form, even after the invention of printing, and authors of magical books often transcribed variant forms of the same spell. Thus the author of Cambridge University Library MS Additional 3544 offered an alternative 'which I have found in another book' (*in alio libro inveni*):

... make an image in the likeness of a man, or thereabouts, from virgin wax, and make everything of a filthy nature, with finger and joint anywhere you like; hold it fast in a hot bath for linens and afterwards offer it like an infant, by name [i.e. baptise it], and pierce it in whatever part of the body you want to make sick, then after those hot baths bend excrement into that part of the body of him or her for whom the image was intended. But beware lest the part of the body should perish or burn.[8]

However, in keeping with medieval traditions of ritual magic, neither operation for causing harm was intended to kill; rather, they were supposed to inflict harm on a particular part of the body. Not only that, but the author of the Cambridge manuscript provided rituals even more elaborate than the original one to ensure that the magician's victim recovered. The clear intent of rituals of this kind was to torment someone so that he or she would give in to the magician's will. Indeed, straightforward killing rituals are not found in surviving books of magic, and these seem to have existed largely in the imaginations of worried courtiers and princes.

We have no record of what was written on the wax images, other than the name 'Elizabeth', but this and the fact that the effigies had been buried was enough to make it certain that their purpose was magical. The Cambridge manuscript contains details and even drawings of the magic circles to be drawn on the effigy in the 'Trojan Revenge' spell. However, as we have seen, magic intended to harm and kill was by no means the only form of magic that employed wax effigies, and anyone with a knowledge of magical traditions would have been able to tell the difference. Neither the London magistrates nor the Privy Council possessed these skills, and when the box containing the wax images arrived in Norwich (probably on 18 August) the anxious councillors wrote to the one man loyal to Elizabeth who could certainly be trusted to know how to deal with this kind of supernatural threat.

JOHN DEE AND THE WAX EFFIGIES

In 1578 John Dee was living at Mortlake on the Thames, close to the court at Richmond Palace, where he was engaged in various projects under Leicester's patronage. In particular, Leicester was using Dee as a tool to persuade Elizabeth to adopt a more aggressive foreign policy that would see England compete with Spain for the New World and support the Protestant rebellion against Spain in the Netherlands. To this end, he commissioned Dee to write a book entitled *The Limits of the British Empire*, in which Dee attempted to prove that King Arthur (from whom Elizabeth claimed descent through her Welsh Tudor ancestors) had ruled over a vast European and American empire.[9] On a single morning (probably Wednesday 20 August) Dee received a whole series of letters about the wax effigies from the councillors, one after another. He set out at once from Mortlake, riding through torrential rain to meet the court.[10]

On the morning of 20 August the queen assembled with eight members of the Privy Council in the bishop of Norwich's Palace to view the effigies sent from London and discuss the potential threat. According to Mendoza, Elizabeth was concerned: 'When it reached the Queen's ears she was disturbed, as it was looked upon as an augury'.[11] However, the ambassador is a better source for contemporary gossip than the actual contents of the queen's mind, and it is impossible to know whether Elizabeth really took the threat seriously. The Council wrote a letter acknowledging receipt of the images to the Lord Mayor and bishop of London, instructing them and Sir William Cordell, Master of the Rolls, 'that it should be well if they could learn by some secret means where any persons are to be found that be delighted or thought to be favourers of such magical devices'.[12]

The queen had left Norwich by the time Dee arrived; it would have taken him at least forty hours of hard riding to catch up with the progress. He may have arrived in Norwich on the evening of 22 August. As Dee remembered many years later, 'My careful and faithful endeavour was most speedily required (as by divers messages sent to me one after another in one morning) to prevent the mischief, which divers of her Majesty's Privy Council suspected to be intended against her Majesty's person, by means of a certain image of wax, with a great pin stuck into it about the breast of it'.[13] Dee did not remember the affair with quite the same details as the Spanish ambassador, Bernardino de Mendoza; Dee mentioned only one image, transfixed with a pin, as opposed to the three stuck with pig's bristles, and Dee reported that the image had been found at Lincoln's Inn Fields rather than Islington. It is possible that Dee was shown only one of the images, and if so this may explain the mistake he made in identifying it as an instance of attempted magical treason.

Although the queen had by this time moved on to Kimberley Tower, between Norwich and Wymondham, the Council remained behind in Norwich to interrogate Catholic recusants who had been arrested during the course of the progress.[14] On the morning of Saturday 23 August, perhaps in the bishop of Norwich's Palace, Dee performed some sort of counter-magic to neutralise the threat posed by the effigy magic uncovered at Islington. As he later wrote, 'I did satisfy her Majesty's desire, and the Lords of the honourable Privy Council, within [a] few hours, in godly and artificial [i.e. skilful] manner: as the honourable Mr Secretary Wilson whom, at the least, I required to have by me a witness to the proceedings'. Dee left the 'proceedings' themselves obscure, but there are at least two possibilities. One is that Dee used some simple counter-magic against witchcraft, similar to rituals in the manuscripts later collected by Elias Ashmole. One of these, 'An experiment to discover witches', turns the effigy magic against the sorcerer or witch and involves the combination of astrological and image magic:

> Take a piece of parchment, and write thereon the similitude of the party suspected; write in his forehead the name of the person, and on his breast [the signs of Aquarius and Capricorn]; then take a sharp bodkin, and prick the picture's head and breast, say *ut sequitur* [as follows]. I command and conjure you witch or witches, by the living God, the true God, the holy God, and by all the patriarchs, prophets, martyrs and confessors, and by all holy people who follow the Lamb of God, and by all angels and archangels, thrones, dominations, princes, powers, cherubins and seraphins ... I conjure thee with or without whatsoever you be, that are within 7 miles of this place, no rest to have, nor out of pricking pains sleeping nor waking until you do come hither with speed into this pool of water, and therein to confess to me some part of the worked deeds you have done to [bewitch] a person N. By the virtue of the Holy Trinity: *Fiat fiat fiat* [let it so be]. Amen.[15]

A procedure of this kind certainly required 'artifice', although whether it was 'godly' was a matter of opinion. In fact, this procedure combined traditional sympathetic magic, compelling the author of the sorcery to reveal him or herself, with the ancient Catholic tradition of exorcism. However, it is unlikely that Dee used a spell exactly like this, given that he seems to have intended to defuse the potential magical threat to the queen rather than to discover the identity of the sorcerer responsible. Furthermore, if Dee spent several hours on the 'proceedings', as he said he did, it seems likely that he attempted a rite more extensive than the one collected by Ashmole.

Dee had been ordained a Catholic priest during Mary's reign and, although he was committed to the Protestant cause, he remained interested in Catholic spirituality.[16] Stephen Bowd has recently documented Dee's interest in exorcism. In 1590 he anointed with holy oil a serving maid who seemed to be possessed (a distinctively Catholic gesture), and he owned manuscript prayers of exorcism. In 1596, he acted as a consultant in the long-running exorcism of the children of Nicholas Starkey in Lancashire. Dee consulted a range of demonological literature for the case, borrowing Johann Weyer's sceptical *De praestigiis daemonum* ('On the Wonders of Demons') as well as Girolamo Menghi's *Fustis daemonum* ('Club of Demons') and *Flagellum daemonum* ('The Scourge of Demons') in March and April 1597.[17]

However, it seems unlikely that Dee's interest in exorcism developed only in the late 1590s. As early as 1590, an inventory of Dee's library at Mortlake reveals that he owned a copy of the 1589 edition of Menghi's *Flagellum*.[18] The Italian Franciscan friar Girolamo Menghi (1529–1609) was the most prolific writer on exorcism of the early modern period, and his *Flagellum* was first published in 1577.[19] Until 1604 the Church of England had no official policy on exorcism, while the Roman Catholic church had no centrally approved rite until 1614. Menghi pioneered a new style of 'hands on' exorcism that did not merely involve a verbal attack on the devil but also the use of herbs, incenses and other materials to drive away demons. Crucially, Menghi also responded to the threat of witchcraft which, by the 1570s, was regarded as a much more pressing problem than traditional demonic possession. Accordingly, Menghi provided rites in *Flagellum* for the destruction of *maleficalia*, instruments of witchcraft or sorcery. Menghi never addressed effigy magic directly, as it seems to have been less of a problem in Italy than curses involving the tying of magical knots. Knots in ribbons or locks of hair were believed to be concealed in the vicinity of the person about to be bewitched, and the destruction of these material 'fetishes' was therefore necessary to free a person from the influence of evil magic.

In 1578 Dee would have required a rite that allowed him either to destroy the wax images without injuring the queen and her councillors or to empty them of their power to cause harm. The easiest way to do this would have been to exorcise them. Since at least the third century, the church had been exorcising various substances including water, salt and oil for use in ceremonies, the idea being that any material thing employed in the service of God needed to be rid of any possible evil spiritual influence.[20] An exorcism restored the thing to its pristine condition, as God had created it. One option for Dee, therefore, would have been to exorcise the wax the images were made of and thereby neutralise the evil astrological influences that the 'figures' drawn on the surface of the wax might bring down on the queen and her councillors.

If Dee did have access to Menghi's *Flagellum* in August 1578, he would have found two rites that could have been adapted to suit his purposes. The first was a 'blessing of a fire to burn instruments of witchcraft' (*Benedictio ignis ad comburenda instrumenta maleficialia*):

> May he bless you, creature of fire, who created you; who appeared to his servant Moses in a red flame of fire; who went before his people in a pillar of fire through the darkness of the night in the desert; he who will judge the world will command you to go before the face of the Judge; he who chose you as an instrument of his justice against the contumacious spirits, just as in his majesty he preserved the three young men, his worshippers, unharmed in you, so he will torment and explode by means of you all apostate spirits.[21]

The blessing then turned into an exorcism, freeing the fire from any evil influence so it could be a divine fire that, by sympathetic magic, would torment the demons whose power made the instruments of sorcery effective. Some more prayers followed, after which the exorcist cast the instruments of sorcery into the fire while reciting Psalm 67. There was nothing necessarily offensive to a Protestant in the multiple biblical allusions in this exorcism, although many Protestants rejected the idea of blessing and exorcism altogether. Dee was certainly not one of them, and he took care to ritually consecrate his magical paraphernalia and fast before attempting to contact angels.

The second rite that Dee could have used or adapted from Menghi's book was more complex. This was the 'Conjuration of fire for burning an image of a demon drawn on paper' (*Coniuratio ignis ad comburendum imaginem Daemonis pictam in carta*). According to Menghi, the exorcist should ask a possessed person for the name of the demon tormenting him; the exorcist then drew an image of the demon, writing its name above it. When the picture was burned with the appropriate rites, the spirit would be tormented and forced to leave the possessed person. Clearly, this did not correspond to the situation in August 1578, where instruments of sorcery (the wax images) had been made but not yet deployed to cause demons to attack Elizabeth and her ministers. Nevertheless, a skilful practitioner like Dee could easily have adapted the rite to the occasion. He also possessed the knowledge to have found out the names of the demons invoked by the original magician. If the figures drawn on the wax images corresponded to astrological signs, an astrologer of Dee's calibre would have been able to calculate exactly when the effigies had been manufactured. Agrippa's *De caerimoniis magicis* provided the necessary information on how to calculate the name of the evil spirit associated with that day or hour.[22]

Menghi's rite for 'conjuration of fire' began with an exorcism (or conjuration) of the fire, similar to the one for burning instruments of sorcery but much more lengthy. Menghi's conjurations proceeded by means of constant, cumulative reiteration of the majesty of God and his saints, using numerous Greek and Hebrew names of God to increase the power of the conjuration. Had he used this rite, Dee could have inserted Elizabeth's name in the demand to the demon that 'having been most strictly forced, he should draw back from this creature of God N. at once, not to return to her, without injury to the body of the same, and all harm'.[23] The next part of the rite was a blessing of the fire, during which the priest sprinkled the fire with holy water. The exorcist then took a collection of foul smelling substances – sulphur, asafoetida, marigold and rue – and threw them into the fire, holding the image of the demon threateningly over the flames with the words: 'Hear, hear, hear, N. a spirit cursed by God, and fall forever into eternal punishment, most unspeakable and most iniquitous one, rebel against God, father of lies, betrayer of all, root of all evil ...'[24] Menghi piled insult upon insult against the demon for several pages, until finally the exorcist cast the image into the fire. At this point the exorcist was supposed to turn to the possessed person and pray over and exorcise her.[25] The whole procedure would have taken at least a couple of hours to set up and execute. There is no evidence, of course, that Dee actually did use any of these rites; all that can be said is that Dee performed some kind of counter-magical ritual, that he believed in the power of exorcism and that he had access to Menghi's newly published book.

On 4 September, evidently dissatisfied with the progress of the investigation, the Privy Council wrote to the Lord Mayor and the bishop of London, the Master of the Rolls, the Lieutenant of the

Tower and the Recorder of London 'touching the better examination of the finding of the pictures of wax', and then again on 18 September 'touching their remiss dealings in the proclamation and matter of the wax pictures'.[26] Finally, Dee was ordered back to London to help with the apprehension of the culprits,[27] and on 25 September the court returned to Richmond Palace. On 28 September Dee was invited to an audience with the queen, where Wilson 'declared to her Majesty, then sitting without the Privy Park by the landing place at Richmond, the honourable Earl of Leicester being also by' what Dee had done.[28] The queen was not in good health; her face was swollen and she was suffering the effects of an infection in her gums caused by her rotting teeth. To her physicians, however, the cause of her illness was unknown, and it may have been this that continued to worry her Councillors. Dee performed some sort of astrological magic in an attempt to cure the queen on 8 October.

LEICESTER'S WITCH-HUNT

The queen's ill-health gave Leicester the ammunition he needed to turn the search for the sorcerer responsible for the wax images into a witch-hunt (in the literal sense) against Catholics.[29] In Peter Elmer's view, 'The ... investigation in 1578 had clearly begun as an attempt by Leicester to discredit English Catholics through the taint of using sorcery to commit high treason against the Queen and so push religious moderates towards his own more militant brand of Protestantism'.[30] In one way, the investigation into the Islington effigies was just a continuation of a process that had begun during Elizabeth's East Anglian progress. On leaving Bury St Edmunds on 9 August, Elizabeth had stopped at Euston Hall on the border of Suffolk and Norfolk, where she was entertained by Edward Rookwood. The Rookwoods were an ancient Suffolk family who had been recusants, refusing to go to church because they were Catholics, since the very beginning of Elizabeth's reign. Patrick Collinson suggested that Elizabeth's visit to Euston was planned in advance as a means of entrapping her known recusant host.[31] The queen was accompanied by Richard Topcliffe, her enforcer of religious conformity who was notorious for his cruelty towards Catholics. On the queen's arrival,

Rookwood was presented to the monarch, but as he was about to kiss Elizabeth's hand he was pulled away by the Lord Chamberlain, who asked him how he dared approach his sovereign when he had been excommunicated (barred from attending church for disobedience).

On the evening of 10 August a piece of silver plate that belonged to the court mysteriously disappeared, and as a result Rookwood's outbuildings were searched. Topcliffe described what happened next:

> ... in the hayrick such an image of Our Lady was there found, as for greatness, for gayness and workmanship, I did never see a match; and after a sort of country dances ended, in Her Majesty's sight the idol was set behind the people who avoided ... Her Majesty commanded it to the fire, which, in her sight, by the country folks, was quickly done, to her content, and unspeakable joy of every one but some one or two who had sucked of the idol's poisoned milk.[32]

Rookwood was publicly humiliated in front of the queen. The episode is highly suspicious; why, for instance, did the servants think that they might find a piece of plate in a hayrick? It seems likely that the 'disappearance' of the plate was an excuse to conduct a thorough search of the premises, where Topcliffe knew the searchers were likely to find something incriminating, given Rookwood's Catholicism. It is even possible that the statue itself was planted.

Protestants such as Topcliffe considered Catholics guilty of the sin of idolatry, but 'idols' such as the image of the Virgin Mary discovered at Euston were to be treated as objects of contempt rather than feared; yet we are told that the people present 'avoided'. This seems to be a reference to the phrase 'Avoid, Satan', uttered as an impromptu spiritual protection against evil, usually accompanied by an apotropaic gesture of protection. The setting up of the statue in front of the queen and court at Euston appears to have taken on the significance of a ritual act designating it an evil image.

According to Mendoza, during the queen's progress 'in one of the houses they found a great many images which were ordered to be dragged round and burnt'.[33] This may be a reference to the Euston case, and again suggests ritual humiliation of Catholic images. Although the official justification of Protestant iconoclasm was that religious images were superstitious and diverted the faithful from the true worship of God, the ways in which images were destroyed confirmed that they remained potential sources of magical power. Iconoclasts did not just destroy images, they defaced them in specific ways to render them powerless and neutralise possibly threatening supernatural forces.[34] These included decapitation and public burning, sometimes with a 'mock trial' as if the image were a person guilty of heresy.

If religious images were idolatrous, and magic was a form of idolatry, then the difference between Catholic veneration of images and effigy magic was slight; or at least this was what the government wanted people to think. The equation of Catholic idolatry with magic was made clear in the Privy Council's promise of 29 January 1579 to give the bishop of Norwich 'the names of certain persons in his diocese that are privy to the secret keeping of certain images which are reserved to some ill purpose of sorcery or idolatry'. The councillors added that 'Their Lordships do understand that in Thetford and other places thereabouts ... there hath been seen, not long since, in some men's houses certain images which are either reserved to the private use of them that keep them for idolatry or for some other dangerous purpose of sorcery and witchcraft'.[35] This was surely an allusion to the events at Euston in August 1578 (Euston is just two miles south of Thetford). It seems unlikely that the councillors themselves, many of whom must have remembered Catholic worship from Mary's reign, literally believed that the veneration of images and effigy magic were one and the same thing. Instead, the conflation of religious images and magical effigies was a convenient way of smearing Catholics, and may explain why the discovery of the Islington images apparently speeded up proceedings against Catholics during the Norfolk progress.[36]

Shortly after Dee returned to London, a young Catholic named Henry Blower was arrested for alleged involvement in the Islington conspiracy, and on 10 September Blower's father was also arrested. Henry Blower confessed, under interrogation in the Tower, that the vicar of Islington, Thomas Harding, had made the wax effigies. Harding had been suspected of conjuration in April 1577, and thus was a plausible candidate, but the commissioners charged with getting to the bottom of the conspiracy were determined to force Harding to admit to Catholic sympathies. He was arrested on 18 September, but even under torture he failed to satisfy the commissioners that the wax effigies were part of a Catholic plot. In early October the commissioners decided to try an alternative method of getting the results the government needed: they arrested the veteran magician John Prestall.

It is possible that Dee himself suggested this, as a means of 'settling old scores' in his long-running rivalry with Prestall. The Catholic Prestall was like a dark twin to the Protestant Dee, matching Dee's enthusiasm for Elizabeth with hatred of everything the queen stood for. Against Dee's reformed prophetic magic, Prestall pitted the old 'superstitious' magic of the Catholic world, and Prestall's cynical cunning contrasted with Dee's innocent (sometimes naïve) piety. The two men first ran into each other in 1563, when Prestall made use of a rather unsavoury sorcerer, his brother-in-law Vincent Murphyn, to discredit Dee. He may have been motivated to do so by astrological rivalry: Dee cast a positive horoscope for Elizabeth's coronation on 15 January 1559, where Prestall had prophesied disaster.[37]

Murphyn was a low-grade cunning man who cast horoscopes and performed basic magic with hair and nail clippings, but he also had a talent for forgery. He used Dee's name to endorse his own magical practice, which Dee certainly did not approve of, and persuaded John Foxe to publish a document in his *Actes and Monuments* which painted Dee as a conjurer, an accusation Dee fiercely repudiated but which stained his reputation for life.[38] It is all the more ironic that Prestall and Murphyn recruited the great Protestant martyrologist Foxe to their cause, given their own Catholic sympathies. Dee had another run-in with Prestall in 1567, when Prestall successfully convinced Cecil that he, rather than Dee, could transmute silver into gold.

The circumstantial evidence that Dee may have been responsible for Prestall's arrest in 1578 is the fact that he had a personal audience with Elizabeth on 13 October, shortly before the Council remembered Prestall's track-record for treason and started running him to ground. Not long afterwards Murphyn, another of Dee's old enemies, was rounded up as well.[39] On 13 November Wilson reported to Leicester and Warwick the arrest of 'lewd and evil-disposed persons', noting that 'Our Murphyn brother-in-law and Prestall is sent for by a messenger, by whom it is thought some news will be dispensed when he is come. ... Yorkson called Endsby is also sent for, that had such great credit with Prestall'.[40] Leicester personally supervised the torture of Prestall and Murphyn, and early in 1579 Harding and Prestall were condemned to death. By this time, however, the political winds were changing. Elizabeth was pursuing the idea of a marriage to the duke of Anjou with renewed interest, pushing Leicester and his plans for a Protestant intervention in the Netherlands out of the picture.

The real story behind the Islington effigies finally emerged in the spring of 1579. Far from a sinister conspiracy against the queen and her Council, the incident turned out to be nothing more than a sordid case of love magic. A young man admitted that he had paid a known magician, Thomas Elkes, to make the images. Reginald Scot later told the real story in his *Discoverie of Witchcraft*:

> ... one old cozener wanting money, devised or rather practised (for it is a stale device) to supply his want, by promising a young gentleman, whose humour he thought would that way be well served, that for the sum of forty pounds he would not fail by his cunning in that art of witchcraft, to procure unto him the love of any three women whom he would name, and of whom he should make choice at his pleasure. The young gentleman being abused with his cunning devices, and too hastily yielding to that motion, satisfied this cunning man's demand of money. Which, because he had it not presently to disburse, provided for him at the hands of a friend of his. Finally, this cunning man made the three puppets of wax. &c. leaving nothing undone that appertained to the cozenage, until he had buried them, as you have heard.[41]

The best-recorded case of magical treason in English history, which had obsessed the Privy Council for months, turned out to be nothing but a tawdry case of magical fraud:

> But the young gentleman, who for a little space remained in hope mixed with joy and love, now through tract of time hath those his felicities powdered with doubt and despair. For instead of achieving his love, he would gladly have obtained his money. But because he could by no means get either the one or the other (his money being in hucksters handling, and his suit in no better forwardness) he revealed the whole matter, hoping by that means to recover his money; which he neither can yet get again, nor hath paid it where he borrowed. But till trial was had of his simplicity, or rather folly herein, he received some trouble himself hereabout, though now dismissed.[42]

The revelation was an embarrassment to Leicester, who quietly set Murphyn and the young Henry Blower free from the Tower. The death sentence against Prestall was not carried out. Elkes was sentenced to death in November 1580, but this was for repeated offences against the 1563 act (which prescribed the death penalty for a second offence), not magical treason.[43] If nothing else, Elkes was guilty of wasting an inordinate amount of the government's time. Nevertheless, Leicester had done all he could to publicise the 'conjured images' of Catholics, and it was probably through one of Leicester's ballads and pamphlets that the story of the Islington effigies reached the French demonologist Jean Bodin, who published a version of the story in 1580:

> [A story] is also newly arrived concerning an English magician priest, and the vicar of a village, which is called Istincton [sic.], who was found in September 1578 in the possession of three magical wax images, in order to bring about the death of the queen of England, and two others close to her person.[44]

Bodin's use of the term 'priest' was unfortunate. Even though his description of the magician as 'vicar of a village' ought to have made it clear that Harding was a clergyman of the established church, not a Catholic priest, the idea that Catholics were responsible took root. In 1668 Meric Casaubon confidently asserted that the wax effigies had been found 'in the house of a Priest'.[45]

The embarrassment of the Islington incident had propaganda value for hostile Catholics, and Leicester may have pushed too far in his campaign to discredit English Catholics as sorcerers, since 'he seems to have accidentally stirred a hornet's nest by uncovering activity of an equally dubious nature closer to home'.[46] Years later, in the aftermath of the defeat of the Spanish Armada in 1588, the Catholic printer and publisher Richard Verstegan, writing in the persona of a recently released Spanish prisoner, acknowledged that the failure of the invasion had been God's punishment of Spain for worldly presumption. Yet he also turned this argument against England, arguing that if God could cut Spain down to size, he might very well do the same to England as well:

> [The English] have made a resolution to run on in all impiety, and to try to the uttermost, whether God's puissance or their ungodly practices

can most prevail: wherein they shall well find, that he can many ways confound the wicked, when themselves shall no way prevent it. Meanwhile, their outward courage is mixed with inward care, and their feigned joy with restless jealousy: who in seeming to fear nothing, are seen to start at their own shadows.[47]

Verstegan's argument showed that the complexity and success of Elizabeth's intelligence service was a weakness in its own right, since it left her government open to the accusation of paranoia: 'intolerable fear is more manifested in your English government, than in any state else in the whole world: ... spyings abroad, and inquisitions at home: searchings of houses more at midnight than at noondays, apprehensions, examinations, and such daily exercise, and practise of the rack, as never the like was heard of'. Here was the dark side of the Elizabethan 'golden age', as many Catholics perceived and experienced it. Verstegan was keen to revive memories of Leicester's campaign to label Catholics as conjurers in 1578–81: the wrongful arrest of Thomas Harding, the vicar of Islington, was a notable instance of the government acting without proper evidence or process:

> You have heard of images of wax hidden in the earth, whereof both books and ballads were spread about the country, that this was done by Catholics, to consume the Queen, and some other: for the which cause, one Harding a Protestant minister of Islington was apprehended, charged that he was a papist, most cruelly racked, and unjustly condemned to death. And you have understood afterward, that one Elkes another Protestant, confessed himself to have been the doer thereof: yet not to destroy the Queen, but to obtain the love of some Londoner's wife.[48]

Leicester's failed campaign to smear Catholics as witches was another instance of a general failure by Protestant propagandists to make this connection convincingly.[49] Scot used the Islington case to support his slightly more subtle anti-Catholic argument that belief in magic and witchcraft was a superstition *as bad as* being a witch or magician: 'who will maintain, that common witchcrafts are not cozenages, when the great and famous witchcrafts, which had stolen credit not only from all the common people, but from men of great wisdom and authority, are discovered to be beggarly sleights of cozening varlets[?]' For Scot, all magic was fraud, and the 'great and famous witchcraft' he had in mind was the Islington case.[50]

In spite of his scepticism about the efficacy of magic and witchcraft, Scot was still adamant that magicians should be punished. Belief in magic and witchcraft made no sense because it called God's omnipotence into question, but magic and witchcraft were still offensive, and offenders needed to be punished for the impiety and presumption of believing they could perform magic:

> The words and other the illusions of witches, charmers, and conjurers, though they be not such in operation and effect, as they are commonly taken to be: yet they are offensive to the majesty and name of God ... For if God only give life and being to all creatures, who can put any such virtue or lively feeling into a body of gold, silver, bread, or wax, as is imagined? If either priests, devils, or witches could so do, the Divine Power should be cheeked and outfaced by magical cunning, and God's creatures made servile to a witch's pleasure.[51]

Scot reserved his strongest words for those who attempted magical treason. God would preserve the queen, he believed, from any attempts against her, and no magical attempt could work; but the fact that people believed in the efficacy of magical treason made it necessary to punish them anyway:

> But if the Lord preserve those persons (whose destruction was doubted to have been intended thereby) from all other the lewd practices and attempts of their enemies, I fear not, but they shall easily withstand these and such like devices, although they should indeed be practised against them. But no doubt, if such baubles could have brought those matters of mischief to pass, by the hands of traitors, witches, and papists, we should long since have been deprived of the most excellent jewel and comfort that we enjoy in this world. Howbeit, I confess, that the fear, conceit, and doubt of such mischievous pretences may breed inconvenience to them that stand in awe of the same. And I wish, that even for such practices, though they never can or do take effect, the practisers be punished with all extremity; because therein is manifested a traitorous heart to the Queen, and a presumption against God.[52]

For Scot, the fact that magical attempts to kill Elizabeth revealed 'a traitorous heart to the Queen' was enough to make them treason, and indeed this was true in law as well. There was no need for a court to prove that a magical attempt on the queen's life had any chance of working – only that a person had intended it. Thus the government could treat magicians as contemptible, deluded individuals but still punish them with the full force of the law. Scot was in a minority, and few shared his confidence that magic was impossible, but no-one in Elizabeth's government would have disagreed with his rationale for the punishment of treasonous acts of magic.

Paranoia continued to reign amongst Elizabeth's officials into the new year. In January 1579 a group of people from Windsor were accused of making effigies of the queen's person.[53] On 28 October 1580 Lord Rich wrote to the Council to report an allegation by a John Lee that Nicholas Johnson, rector of Woodham Mortimer in Essex had made 'Her Majesty's picture in wax' at the Saracen's Head tavern in Maldon.[54] The Council declined to pursue the matter but instructed Rich 'to examine the conversation of the said Johnson, and whether he hath heretofore been a dealer in sorcery and suchlike lewd practices'.[55] Around this time Stephen and Jane Kylden, late of Southwark, were indicted for making wooden images of both Cecil and Leicester, with the intention of using them to make wax images to harm the courtiers.[56]

Elmer has argued that the origins of one of the first true witch-hunts in English history, the Puritan magistrate Brian Darcy's campaign of prosecutions in Essex in 1582, lay in the Islington effigies scandal. Ten accused witches were arraigned in that year at St Osyth and elsewhere, a tiny number in comparison with the vast scale of Continental witch-hunts, but the largest number yet to be tried as a result of a determined campaign to seek out witches in England. Elmer noted that, after the execution of Elkes, the search for treasonous magicians widened to include witches more generally and was focused on Essex and south Suffolk. William Randall, who had been tried and executed alongside Elkes in 1580, was from Ipswich and Nicholas Johnson was an Essex man; three others tried alongside Randall came from Dedham, Chelmsford and Southminster. Randall informed the authorities that his conspiracy had been linked to a man who had been convicted of pretending to be Edward VI in 1578 but had subsequently escaped, Robert Mantell. In 1581 another Essex man, John Browning of Peldon, Essex was accused of making effigies to kill Burghley and Leicester.[57] In Elmer's view, Brian Darcy's witch-hunt probably drew its authority from Leicester's original commission to seek out treasonous magicians in the aftermath of the

Islington scandal, but it was also 'an attempt by Leicester to shift the focus of attention away from ... treasonous sorcerers and conjurers'.[58]

The climate of fear engendered by the Islington case resulted in a rare example in English legal history of the conflation of treason with witchcraft, as opposed to magic. In December 1583 a woman from Ripon was accused by William Beckwith of 'witchcraft and high treason touching the supremacy', a unique charge. Whether this meant that the woman was inclined towards Catholicism or was a religious dissenter is unclear, but the case produced a conflict between the archbishop and the mayor of York. Beckwith approached the Council of York with his accusation, who appointed a commission to investigate. The archbishop, presumably on the grounds that a matter of witchcraft fell under his jurisdiction, objected and eventually pardoned the woman, although the commissioners proceeded anyway and the woman was condemned at the 1584 Lent assizes.[59] As a convicted traitor, she was one of the very few English witches to suffer the penalty of burning.

In the same year, a list was drawn up in Wiltshire of 'confederates against Her Majesty who have diverse and sundry times conspired her life and do daily confederate against her'. These included 'Old Birtles the great devil, Darnally the sorcerer, Maude Twogoode enchantress, the old witch of Ramsbury, several other old witches, [and] Gregson the north tale teller, who was one them three that stole away the Earl of Northumberland's head from one [of] the turrets in York'.[60] The impression created by this list, of magicians in league with witches, recalls the accusations against Lord Hungerford as well as Shakespeare's later representation of Margery Jourdemayne in *Henry VI Part Two* (1594). It seems to have been characteristic of periods of extreme political stress that 'old witches', the sort of women who ran the risk of being prosecuted under the 1563 act, were lumped together with male magicians and their high status clients engaged in magical treason. However, the most interesting names in the list are those of nobles: Lord Paget, Sir Thomas Hanmer and Sir George Hastings. The inclusion of the name of Sir George Hastings, a member of the Hastings family (descended from the Plantagenets), was a clear indication that memories of the magical conspiracies of the 1560s still lingered.

VINCENT MURPHYN'S CONSPIRACY

The Council's fears of magical treason were not altogether without foundation. Perhaps under instructions from his brother-in-law John Prestall, in late 1579 Vincent Murphyn (recently released from prison) met with Sir George Hastings and his brother Walter, younger brothers of the earl of Huntingdon and Lord Hastings – and therefore cousins to Arthur Pole – along with the earls of Desmond and Westmoreland. A lengthy document survives giving Murphyn's own account of what happened next,[61] although the Privy Council labeled it 'an accusation false, foolish, improbable and impossible considering the circumstances'.[62] Murphyn was perhaps fortunate that he was regarded as a fantasist, given the treasonable import of his confession. However, Murphyn had a definite agenda in revealing the supposed plot, since he was trying to win a civil action against John Dee for slander.[63] According to Murphyn, the plotters first of all agreed to make use of Murphyn's skill in alchemy to raise money:

> He confirmeth the manner of executing thereof to have been agreed, that Murphyn should have been conveyed into Ireland to make dallers and Portuguese [i.e. silver thalers and Portuguese reals] to bear the charges of an army, and to make poisoned balls of fire to burn stones, and to kill with canon... That Sir George Hastings used conjurations with Murphyn and other to know whether Sir George should overlive his brother the Earl and be king and to the same intent had some old prophecies.

The conspirators then swore an oath in a suitably diabolical manner: 'Sir George Hastings, Walter Hastings and Ayard did swear to Murphyn, and caused Murphyn mutually to swear to them faithfully to execute, and truly to keep fast the promises, and for assurance of their oaths did drink together wine mingled with their own blood'. As proof of his story, Murphyn offered 'certain papers indented, one under his own hand containing his own oath to the effect abovesaid, and one under the hands and the parts of Sir George Hastings, Walter Hastings, and Ayard, all sealed with strange seals like crosses', and signed in the conspirators' own blood.

Sir George Hastings then proceeded to produce prophecies from 'an old book containing horrible treason', relating 'the setting up of the House of Pole, the crowning of the Scottish queen, marrying her to Sir George Hastings, crowning Sir George, the defaming of the queen's councillors by special names of murderers, usurers, extortioners, thieves, cutpurses, bawds, etc. and many other abominable slanderous matter'.[64] Terrified, Murphyn claimed that he had a change of heart and ran away to London, pursued by the plotters and their agents. Here he met two apparently friendly alchemists who later turned out to be part of the Hastings conspiracy. According to Murphyn's account, John Dee (who was secretly another of the Hastings plotters) then launched a prosecution against Murphyn for slander as a way to silence him. In reality, Dee brought the case because Murphyn had accused Dee of plotting the queen's death by magic.[65]

Murphyn's case was suspiciously well-supported by documents (what modern detectives would call 'an orgy of evidence'), and he seems to have been a compulsive forger. In the climate of fear that followed the Islington case, Burghley was forced to listen to Murphyn and he may even have suspected Dee for a while. However, the Council quickly concluded that the documents were forged, and that Murphyn's accusations were 'horrible, abominable, incredible, and setteth out in form of murdering and mischief that cannot have truth'.[66] However, the full extent of Murphyn's real treasonable activities only came to light when he was subjected to detailed questioning in August 1582. However, Prestall managed to engineer Murphyn's release from the Tower by making friends with another prisoner called Davison, who 'reconciled' him with Leicester. Davison or Leicester then arranged for the earls of Warwick and Ormond to post bail for Prestall, who escaped justice once again.[67]

THE 1580 ACT FOR SUPPRESSING SEDITIOUS WORDS AND RUMOURS

Neither the 1542 nor 1563 acts had been directed against magical traitors because the law of treason was perfectly adequate for dealing with them. However, the Islington affair and subsequent magical treason scares highlighted some potential ambiguities in the application of 'compassing and imagining' the queen's death. The Parliament of 1580–81 felt the need to classify the making of the queen's image for

Effigies and Witch-Hunts, 1578–1603

magical purposes, casting the queen's horoscope without authorization and prophesying the queen's future as explicitly treasonable acts. These provisions were included in the final section of 'An act for suppressing seditious words and rumours':

> Be it also enacted ... that if any person ... shall by setting or erecting of any figure or figures or by casting of nativities or by calculation or by any prophesying, witchcraft, conjurations or other like unlawful means whatsoever seek to know and shall set forth by express words, deeds or writings how long Her Majesty shall live or continue or who shall reign as King or Queen of this realm of England after Her Highness's decease or else shall advisedly and with a malicious intent against Her Highness utter any manner of direct prophecies to any such intent or purpose or shall maliciously by any words, writing or printing wish, will or desire the death or any deprivation of our sovereign lady the Queen's Majesty that now is or anything directly to the same effect, that then every offence shall be felony and every offender ... therein ... shall be judged as felons and shall suffer pains of deaths and forfeit as in case of felony is used without any benefit of clergy or sanctuary.[68]

The wording of the act was probably deliberately ambiguous; the 'figure or figures' mentioned could mean astrological diagrams or wax effigies, and the mention of 'witchcraft' and 'conjurations' confirms this. This clause was an addendum, almost an afterthought, to a law whose primary purpose was to prevent seditious rumours. The law was arguably unnecessary, as previous experience proved that the law of treason was adequate, but by exempting offenders from benefit of clergy and sanctuary the new law implied that such acts were treason – traitors were likewise exempt from such privileges. The new law did add something, however, since it concentrated on the attempt to gain *knowledge* of how long the monarch would live; at no point does it imply that a magical attempt on the monarch's life might work. In this sense the law was needed; its purpose was to curtail curiosity rather than to introduce a law that explicitly outlawed magical treason, which was already illegal.

'ANABAPTISTICAL WIZARDS'

As Elizabeth's reign entered its final decade, the government began to face magical threats from individuals who did not conform to the old stereotype of discontented Catholics. Slowly but surely, by the 1580s and 1590s, England as a whole was becoming decidedly Protestant. With cultural acceptance of Protestantism came an increasing diversity of Protestant interpretations of the Bible and the proper relationship between religion and the state. The state religion sponsored by the Elizabethan religious settlement had little deep theological underpinning other than the cautiously worded Thirty-Nine Articles. There was no English Luther, Calvin or John Knox to spearhead the Reformation, which was a centralised affair enforced by monarchs, legislators and magistrates. As a result, the soul of the English Reformation was not to be found in official policy but in the religious practices that grew up in parallel with, or outside, Protestant conformity.

Most Elizabethan Protestants were Calvinists, which created an immediate paradox since Calvin's church in Geneva was presbyterian in government, led not by bishops but by a conference of ministers. Elizabeth preferred episcopal government, however, because bishops were appointees of the crown. Protestant purists (Puritans) chafed under the government of bishops who were often more concerned with their secular power and landholdings than they were with the preaching of the Gospel, and some went so far as to dissent from the Church of England altogether. The Brownists attempted to establish independent congregations, while the Family of Love (to which Reginald Scot may have belonged) was a clandestine association of radical believers who outwardly conformed, a little like the Lollards in the fifteenth century.

It was perhaps inevitable, in the fervid religious environment of the Reformation, that a 'lunatic fringe' of belief would develop: at least this was how the authorities regarded independent radical interpreters of scripture. In this religious subculture, mystical visions, fundamentalist belief, confidence tricks and magic all merged together. For instance, on 19 August 1585 two informants, Owen Oglethorpe and Roderick Warcop, wrote to Cecil about a man called William Awder, who was causing trouble in Hertfordshire. Sometimes Awder impersonated a schoolmaster, sometimes a minister, and sometimes a physician or surgeon. Although Awder was an impersonator in the eyes of the authorities, in his own eyes he may have considered himself qualified to teach, preach and heal by his prophetic calling. The clue that Awder was a radical Protestant is that he was encouraging others to stop going to church. He could have been a Catholic recusant, of course, but this seems unlikely if he was pretending to be a Protestant minister. Awder also practised magic; Andrew Hawe, a wheelwright from Pirton in Hertfordshire, with whom Awder had stayed for a while, revealed that 'in private conference with me, he signified unto me how he could make the portrait of any man or woman in wax, and by art either preserve or kill the party'.[69]

The case of William Awder was reported to Cecil when the government was still concerned about magical attempts to kill the queen. That concern continued unabated into the 1590s, and on 28 July 1591 an illiterate maltmaker from Northamptonshire named William Hacket was hanged in Cheapside, having been convicted of compassing and imagining the death of the queen. Hacket's disciples proclaimed him as the Messiah who had come to overthrow Elizabeth and the religious settlement, and when Hacket caught sight of a picture of the queen in the house of a man called Kaye, 'with an iron instrument, [he did] villainously and traitorously deface the said picture, and especially that part of the picture which represented Her Majesty's heart, railing most traitorously against Her Majesty's person'.[70] Hacket did not fit the profile of the 'normal' magical traitor. He was neither a Catholic nor a religious conservative, but rather a religious radical who regarded himself as a prophet and advocated presbyterian church government. Indeed, to the archbishop of Canterbury, William Whitgift, Hacket's defiance of the religious settlement was more serious than the possibility that he was involved in magical treason.[71]

Like John Dee, Hacket claimed to be able to call angels into a crystal and exorcise evil spirits, and Dee's reputation suffered as a consequence of the propaganda campaign organised by Whitgift and his supporters against Hacket and other sectaries.[72] In September 1591 one of Whitgift's protégés, Richard Cosin, published an exposé of Hacket and his followers, which accused 'anabaptistical wizards' of seeking 'the overthrow of states'.[73] Cosin's book established a new government rhetoric, in which radical Protestants were portrayed as dangerous magical traitors. For Whitgift and Elizabeth, the single imperative in religious policy in the 1590s was the enforcement of conformity to the Church of England. Whitgift pursued this objective so relentlessly that he alienated many pious Protestants, who regarded conformity as conditional on their consciences and the continued reform of Elizabeth's church. Hacket, like those Gospellers who prayed for Queen Mary's death in the 1550s, straddled the boundary between magical treason and religious deviance. Although Hacket probably did not think of his own activities as magical, they certainly appeared so to the authorities, especially in the light of the panic of 1578–81.

ELIZABETH'S LAST YEARS

Whereas radical Protestants were being tempted to treasonable practices that straddled the boundary between religion and magic, the Elizabethan government's old Catholic foe, Robert Parsons, resorted to an opposite rhetorical strategy by accusing Elizabeth's courtiers of involvement in necromancy. In 1592 Parsons made a famous accusation against Sir Walter Raleigh, claiming that he and other members of the court had been involved in a 'school of atheism', directed by a necromancer, that taught young men to mock all authority:

> For such a thing is said to be known and public, that in their houses they had as a teacher a certain astronomer, once a necromancer; so that they might teach the small groups of noble youth to make as much fun of the old law of Moses as the new law of Christ our Lord with ingenious jokes and remarks, and to laugh at their own circles.[74]

Raleigh's necromancer was traditionally identified as the mathematician Thomas Harriot, although John Dee was convinced that the slur was aimed against him.[75] Parsons's attempts to smear Protestants as the only ones consorting with magicians were not altogether successful, however. The veteran Catholic magical traitor John Prestall, who seems to have been released from the Tower at some point after 1582, still had one more trick up his sleeve, at least according to the testimony of William Kinnevsley, who was examined by government servants on 8 March 1592. Kinnevsley claimed that he heard Prestall complaining bitterly about the wrongs done against him in England, saying that he was held in high esteem in Spain (perhaps as a result of his ability to make alchemical wildfire). He had only returned to England on Elizabeth's promise that he should want for nothing, and said that the queen 'has broken the faith of a prince with regard to him'.[76] Kinnevsley pointed out to Prestall that he had been saved from the rope more than once, but Prestall replied that he would have killed himself before he was hanged, 'for 500 gentlemen would have lain in the way to his execution to give him a sword, and he would have told at the gallows such a tale as was never told in England'.

Prestall claimed that the government had been weak since Leicester's death (in September 1588). According to Prestall, Cecil 'was the wizard of England, a worldling to fill his own purse, and good for nobody, and so hated that he would not live long, if anything happened [to] the Queen'. Prestall blamed Cecil for preventing him becoming Chancellor of the Duchy of Lancaster. He called the Lord Chamberlain, Lord Hunsdon, 'a testy fool and a hairbrain, and said, in an affair about a servant, that he would take no ill words from him, for he was as good a gentleman as any, and had beaten the old Earl of Arundel into his gates'. Kinnevsley said that he had approached Cecil with information against Prestall a year earlier, but Cecil had been sick. Kinnevsley testified that Prestall 'practises sorcery, witchcraft, or magic, to draw the affections of men and women'. He claimed that three other witnesses, a servant of Prestall's named Thomas Vaughan, Richard Pothay and Edmund Calton could also testify against the magician.[77] No record exists of the government's response. These were hardly unexpected accusations, given Prestall's black reputation, but it seems remarkable that Prestall ever thought he would be Chancellor of the Duchy of Lancaster. If true, then Prestall may have been close to Leicester in his last years and expected to receive preferment from him. Prestall must have been an old man by the time Kinnevsley gave his evidence, and it proved to be one of the notorious magician's last appearances in the historical record before his death in 1606.

On 30 November 1594 the magistrate Richard Young wrote to the queen to inform her that a number of sorcerers, witches and charmers had been examined, who had been employed by Jane Shelley, a prisoner in the Fleet, to discover the time of the queen's death and discover what would happen to the crown.[78] The question that Shelley sought to answer by magical means was a very good one, and one that was much on the minds of Elizabeth's counsellors (even if they refused to admit it), since the old queen consistently refused to settle or give her opinion on the question of the succession. The resurgence of worries about the time of the queen's death in the mid-1590s may have been one reason why the themes of magical treason emerged in Shakespeare's writing at this time.

In 1598 Elizabeth's reign produced one final case of *veneficium*, which was an apparent plot by two Catholics, Edward Squier and Richard Walpole, to poison the queen by smearing a sticky substance on the pommel of her saddle, which it was hoped her hands would transfer to her mouth, resulting in her death. Under torture, Squier admitted that he had been approached by Richard Walpole at the English College in Seville (a theological college for training Catholic priests to be sent to England), who asked him about his knowledge of the art of perfuming. Walpole instructed him that 'certain poisoning drugs wherewith opium was one were to be compounded and beaten together and steeped in white mercury water, and put in an earthen pot'. The pot was then to be left in the sun for a month. A double bladder, pierced with holes, was to be pressed down on the queen's saddle pommel. Squier acquired the ingredients from five different apothecaries in order to avoid suspicion, and actually carried out the act, but Elizabeth suffered no ill effects.[79]

The poison created by Squier calls to mind the poison carried to England by Bernard de Vignolles in 1494, which was also mixed together with mercury (an ingredient much used by alchemists). However, the fact that Walpole approached Squier as a perfumer rather than a necromancer or alchemist demonstrates that there was no automatic association between poison and magic by the end of Elizabeth's reign. As Francis Edwards pointed out, perfumes and cosmetics were becoming more widely available and more commonly used at this period, and many of them were actually poisons.[80] One effect of the greater availability and prevalence of poisons in apothecaries' shops may have been a gradual demystification of poison, which led ultimately to the demise of *veneficium* in its original, occult sense.

MAGICAL TREASON IN SHAKESPEARE'S *HENRY VI PART TWO*

The prominence of magical treason in the plays of William Shakespeare was first observed by Deborah Willis, who noted that it was

> ... a type of politically motivated charge of witchcraft which seems to have especially interested William Shakespeare. Typically in such cases, a charge of witchcraft is made against someone believed to have designs on the monarch or some highly placed official. The charge is frequently combined with accusations of treason or conspiracy against the state. In fact, the charge – and perhaps also the actual practice of witchcraft – may emerge from factional struggle, may be part of one aristocratic group's attempt to displace its rivals and remove them from power.[81]

Willis cited Joan of Arc, Eleanor Cobham, Jane Shore and Elizabeth Woodville as characters in the history plays embroiled in 'the intersection of witchcraft, treason and ambition' that reaches its culmination in *Macbeth*. However, it was in Shakespeare's early play *The First Part of the Contention of the Two Famous Houses of York and Lancaster with the Death of the Good Duke Humphrey*, first performed at some point in the period 1592–94,[82] that themes of magical treason in English history were treated most explicitly. This play would later form the basis for *Henry VI Part Two*, part of the cycle of history plays that begins with *Richard II* and ends with *Richard III*. The early version of the play was published in 1594 as the so-called 'Quarto Text', while the play in its final form did not appear until the publication of the First Folio of Shakespeare's complete plays in 1623.

Eleanor Cobham, duchess of Gloucester is a major character in the play. In Act 1, Scene 2, Eleanor asks her chaplain, Sir John Hum, 'Hast thou as yet conferred / With Margery Jourdayne, the cunning witch, / With Roger Bolingbroke, the conjuror?' (ll. 74–6). Hum explains (ll. 78–81),

> This they have promisèd to show your highness:
> A spirit raised from depth of underground
> That shall make answer to such questions
> As by your grace shall be propounded him.

The Duchess thanks Hum, and presents him with a gift of gold with the words 'Make merry, man, / With thy confederates in this weighty cause' (ll. 84–6). In an aside to the audience, Hum draws attention to the irony of his being rewarded for what is, in fact, a betrayal of his mistress (ll. 91–5, 97–9):

> Dame Eleanor gives gold to bring the witch;
> Gold cannot come amiss were she a devil.
> Yet I have gold flies from another coast:
> I dare not say from the rich Cardinal
> And from the great and new-made Duke of Suffolk,
> ...
> They, knowing Dame Eleanor's aspiring humour,
> Have hired me to undermine the Duchess,
> And buzz these conjurations in her brain.

The conjuration itself takes place in Scene 4, when the conjurers, Bolingbroke and Southwell, arrive at a location (usually identified as Eleanor's garden) with the witch Margery Jourdayne. Bolingbroke tells Eleanor and Hum to stand on a balcony, and instructs Jourdayne 'be you prostrate and grovel on the earth' (ll. 11–12). Eleanor is impatient, but Bolingbroke cautions her (ll. 15–19),

> ... wizards know their times.
> Deep night, dark night, the silent of the night,
> The time of night when Troy was set on fire;
> The time when screech-owls cry and bandogs howl,
> And spirits walk, and ghosts break up their graves:

Bolingbroke's reference to 'The time of night when Troy was set on fire' is suggestive of the 'Trojan Revenge' spell, and indeed the corresponding lines in the 1594 version of the play contain a direct reference to the Classical spirits of revenge, the Furies: 'Dark night, dread night, the silence of the night, / Wherein the Furies march in hellish troops'.[83] By assimilating the night of the conjuration to the night on which Troy was set on fire by the Greeks, Shakespeare seems to be highlighting the fact that Eleanor is seeking revenge on the members of the court who have ostracised her. Stage directions instruct the actors playing Bolingbroke and Southwell to improvise exorcisms, 'Conjuro te, etc.' Then 'it thunders and lightens terribly', and the spirit appears. He is addressed by Margery first, and then by

Bolingbroke, who enquires about the fates of the king, the duke of Suffolk and the duke of Somerset, receiving ambiguous answers. Bolingbroke then exorcises the spirit, which has scarcely disappeared 'with thunder and lightning' when the dukes of York and Buckingham break onto the stage with Sir Humphrey Stafford, arresting the whole group.

This theatrical scene bears little or no relation to the accounts of Eleanor's activities in the chronicles Shakespeare usually relied upon. The playwright may have felt the need to compete with the high-profile and shocking stage magic in another recent play, Christopher Marlowe's *Doctor Faustus*.[84] However, Shakespeare also seems to have had one eye on more recent cases of magical treason. A witch and two priest-conjurers are involved, just as in another case involving an ambitious and ungrateful peer, Lord Hungerford. Shakespeare had good dramatic precedents for women's involvement in necromancy, such as Medea in Greek and Roman drama,[85] but there is little evidence that women were involved in ritual magic in the sixteenth century. Medieval necromancy was the preserve of a 'clerical underworld',[86] and it continued to be a largely male preserve after the Reformation. Unlike witches, necromancers regarded ritual purity as necessary to magical success, and the widespread late medieval view that women's bodies were more susceptible to unwelcome spiritual influences may have rendered the idea of involving a woman inconceivable to most early modern magicians. Unless Shakespeare was alluding to the Hungerford case, there seems little reason for him to have placed Margery at the heart of the scene.

Shakespeare's assimilation of Eleanor's crime to sixteenth-century cases of 'magical treason' is most evident, however, in the scene of Eleanor's trial. Whereas in reality Eleanor appeared before an ecclesiastical court, in Shakespeare's fiction she is confronted by Henry himself, as if being punished as a traitor, or a witch under the 1563 act. In Act 2, Scene 1, Buckingham informs Henry that Eleanor has been 'Raising up wicked spirits from under ground, / Demanding of King Henry's life and death, / And other of your highness' Privy Council' (ll. 169–71). The idea of someone practising magic against the monarch and two Privy Councillors recalls the events of 1578. Furthermore, when Eleanor is brought to trial she is condemned by

Henry VI in person (Act 2, Scene 3), just as in 1591 James VI of Scotland had insisted that the North Berwick witches should be examined in his presence (see Chapter 5 below). Henry's mention of 'Such as by God's book are adjudged to death' (l. 4) is clearly an allusion to Exodus 22:18, 'Thou shalt not suffer a witch to live'. Shakespeare's Henry VI, relying for his judgements on 'God's book', is a Protestant prince on a mission to root out witches, a mirror image of James VI.

The correct name of the spirit raised by the conjurers in *Henry VI Part Two* has been a subject of debate, with some scholars reading 'Asmath', others 'Asnath' and others 'Asmode'.[87] In the 1594 version of the play, the demon's name is 'Askalon', and it seems most likely that this was inspired by Torquato Tasso's *Gerusalemme liberata* (1581). This poem did not appear in English translation until 1594, but since the 1580s it had been popular among the small number of cultivated Englishmen who could read Italian.[88] One character in the poem is the unnamed 'mago d'Ascalona' (mage of Ascalon), and it is possible that a vague association between magic and this exotic name already existed by the early 1590s, prompting Shakespeare's choice.

Supporters of the 'Asnath' reading maintain that the name is an anagram of 'Sathan', which might seem a lazy choice on the part of the dramatist. However, by using an anagram of 'Sathan', Shakespeare may have been making the point that England's overthrow by civil war, which comes about ultimately as a result of this scene, is being masterminded by the prince of darkness himself. The appearance of 'Sathan' thus gives an extra political edge to the conjuration, and *Henry VI Part Two* demonstrates the cultural impact that the perceived threat of magical treason, coupled with the steadily intensifying focus on female witches, was having in England by the end of the sixteenth century.

CONCLUSION

The affair of the wax images in 1578 was the most high-profile of its kind in English history and had lasting legal and judicial repercussions. In spite of the mundane explanation that eventually emerged for the effigies in the dunghill, the investigations triggered by them turned into a true 'witch-hunt', which went on for around five years. The fact that the discovery of the wax images coincided with Elizabeth's progress to East Anglia, where superstitious images were discovered, allowed her government to make anti-Catholic capital out of the affair, and the subsequent paranoia of the early 1580s gave rise to a new law and provided the background for Reginald Scot's composition of his *Discoverie of Witchcraft* (1584). Finally, there are good reasons to suspect that Shakespeare's portrayal of Eleanor Cobham's magical treason in his historical play *Henry VI Part Two* was influenced by the heightened awareness of magical treason, by Catholics and Puritans alike, in the second half of Elizabeth's reign.

CHAPTER 5

'A Breach in Nature': Magic as a Political Crime in Early Stuart England, 1603–42

In March 1603 Queen Elizabeth was dying, having stubbornly refused to the last to name anyone as her heir. There is little agreement among historians as to why Elizabeth decided not to marry. Early in her reign, rumours circulated that she was infertile. Retha Warnicke has speculated that Elizabeth half believed the accusations against her mother, Anne Boleyn, and feared that she had been cursed with barrenness by her mother's witchcraft.[1] Elizabeth's virginity elevated her above ordinary people – and ordinary monarchs – to the status of a living icon, Gloriana. 'Virgin Queen' propaganda offended Catholics by its blasphemous subversion of the image of the Virgin Mary, but for some Protestants as well, Elizabeth's perpetual virginity and her decision to rule without the guidance of a husband put her in rebellion against nature.

Robert Parsons, her old Jesuit adversary, was convinced that Elizabeth was a witch. Ten years after her death, he claimed that one of Elizabeth's ladies-in-waiting discovered a playing card, the Queen of Hearts, lying pierced with a nail beneath the old queen's chair. This was suggestive of Elizabeth deploying effigy magic against one of her enemies; an ironic allegation, given the number of accusations of effigy magic made against Catholics during her reign. Another lady, Parsons reported, saw an apparition of Elizabeth walk through a wall and then disappear, projected by demonic agency.[2] It seems unlikely that many people in England, even Catholics, believed these rumours; Parsons was particularly embittered against Elizabeth's regime. However, it was commonplace for Continental Catholics to portray Elizabeth as the very embodiment of the whore of Babylon, and where this kind of apocalyptic imagery appeared, suspicions of witchcraft were never far behind.

William Cecil's son, Robert Cecil, succeeded his father as Elizabeth's chief minister in 1598 and set about arranging the succession to the crown, communicating in secret with James VI of Scotland. James had a stronger claim than anyone else to the throne, and in spite of the fact that Elizabeth had authorised the execution of his Catholic mother in 1587, James was both a Protestant and friendly towards the queen. Although Henry VIII had bypassed the Scottish line descending from his sister Margaret Tudor in his will, by 1603 it was recognised that a union of the English and Scottish crowns would be beneficial to both kingdoms and provide a guarantee of stability. However, James brought with him a great deal of baggage when it came to magical treason, since he had been the object of repeated magical attacks in his homeland. The magical attacks James experienced in Scotland are important to the story of magic as a political crime in England not only because they were directed against a future English king, but also because they were widely publicised in England at the time.

JAMES VI AND MAGICAL TREASON

Scotland experienced considerable political instability following the death of King James V in 1542, just days after the birth of his only legitimate daughter, Mary. That instability haunted the kingdom until at least 1583, when James VI assumed the reins of government. The young Queen Mary was married to the dauphin of France in 1548, and Scotland was governed by regents until Mary's return from France in 1561. James Hamilton, earl of Arran, who favoured religious reform, was succeeded in 1554 by the queen's mother, Mary of Guise, who supported Catholicism and tried to reverse the forces of religious change unleashed by the murder of Cardinal Beaton, archbishop of St Andrews, in 1546. On her return to Scotland, the queen found it almost impossible to assert her authority over a profoundly fractured and fractious kingdom. She married her cousin Henry Stewart, Lord Darnley (the father of James VI), and shortly after he was murdered in 1567 she married for a third time James Hepburn, earl of Bothwell, who was widely suspected of having orchestrated Darnley's murder. Mary was deposed and imprisoned, but escaped to England in 1568, where she became a focus for the various Catholic plots described in Chapters 3 and 4 above. Once more, Scotland's monarch was an infant, and a succession of regents governed the country on behalf of James VI in the 1570s.

In Scotland, popular magic of any kind was seen as a menace to the state and was associated with treason. An act against witchcraft passed by the Scottish parliament in the same year as the English act of 1563 was much broader in scope as well as harsher in the penalties it appointed.[3] Scottish Protestant authors claimed that the mother of the earl of Moray had used witchcraft to seduce King James V, and that the earl of Bothwell, Mary's third husband, used magic to seduce the queen. Mary herself was seen as unreliable when it came to magic and, while she was giving birth to the future James VI in June 1566, the countess of Atholl attempted to use sympathetic magic to transfer Mary's labour pangs to someone else.[4] There were also treasonous attempts on the lives of the regents; Violat Mar confessed at her trial for witchcraft in 1577 to trying to kill the earl of Morton by magic.[5]

The most celebrated case of magical treason in Scottish history, which was to mark James VI for the rest of his life, came to light in November 1590, when David Seton, the baillie depute of Tranent in East Lothian, became suspicious about the night-time journeys of one of his servants, Geillis Duncan. Seton discovered the 'devil's mark' on Geillis and tortured her, after which she revealed that she belonged to a group of witches that included John Fian, the schoolmaster of Prestonpans, a sea-captain named Robert Grierson, and a number of women including Agnes Sampson, Agnes Thompson and Janet Sandilands. Other arrests soon followed, and the accused witches began to give evidence that a year earlier, when the king had been hampered by storms in his efforts to reach Denmark, it was their witchcraft that had been responsible. James's visit to Denmark was of crucial importance, because his purpose was to marry Princess Anne, daughter of Frederick II of Denmark, and thus secure the future of the House of Stewart.

According to Agnes Thompson, in 1589 the witches 'took a cat and christened it, and afterward bound to each part of that cat, the chiefest parts of a dead man, and several joints of his body'.[6] Then, Fian, Sampson and Grierson put out in a boat into the North Sea, just in front of the port of Leith, 'where Satan delivered a cat out of his hand to Robert Grierson, giving the word to "Cast the same in the sea, hola!"'. The sacrifice of the cat raised a storm that sank a boat on its way to Leith to deliver jewels for the new queen's arrival there. The witches delayed James's return to Scotland with his bride, giving his ship a contrary wind in the hope of shipwrecking him on the English coast. In addition to their attempt to hamper and possibly kill the king at sea, the witches gathered at Acheson's Haven on the coast one evening, where they handed a portrait of James wrapped in a long piece of cloth from hand to hand, saying the king's name as they did so. When the devil appeared in the circle 'as a man', the portrait was handed to him as well.

There was also more traditional effigy magic; one of the witches confessed that on 31 August 1590 around sixty witches assembled at Prestonpans 'to cumber and enchant a piece of wax which Agnes Sampson brought with her'. The effigy was passed anti-clockwise around the circle of witches and into the hands of the devil, who was 'standing in the likeness of a black priest with black clothes like a hair mantle', with the words 'Take there the picture of James Stewart, Prince of Scotland, and I ask of you, Master Mahoun, that I may have this turn wrought and done to wreck him for my Lord Bothwell's sake'.[7] 'My Lord Bothwell' was James's cousin Francis Stewart, nephew of James Hepburn, earl of Bothwell who had been the third husband of Queen Mary. Francis, earl of Bothwell was already in custody for treason in 1590 for attempting an armed rebellion against James, and the testimony of the East Lothian witches added magical treason to the charges. One of the witches, Agnes Thompson, explained the manner in which they had planned to kill the king:

> She confessed that she took a black toad, and did hang the same up by the heels three days, and collected and gathered the venom as it

dropped and fell from it in an oyster shell, and kept the same venom close covered, until she should obtain any part or piece of foul linen cloth, that had appertained to the King's Majesty, as shirt, handkerchief, napkin or any other thing which she practised to obtain by means of one John Kers, who being attendant in His Majesty's chamber, desired him for old acquaintance between them, to help her to one or a piece of such a cloth.

Lord Burgh, the English ambassador to Scotland, wrote a similar account to Cecil on 12 August 1593, reporting that the witches had planned:

> ... to hang, roast and drop a toad, and to lay the drops of the toad, mixed with strang wash (stale urine), an adder-skin, and the thing in the forehead of a new-foaled foal, in His Highness's way, where His Majesty would go in or out, or in any passage where it might drop upon His Highness's head or body, for His Highness's destruction, that another might have ruled in His Majesty's place, and the ward (government) might have gone to the devil.[8]

In the event, Kers refused to co-operate, but Agnes Sampson declared that if she had got hold of a piece of James's clothing, 'she had bewitched him to death, and put him to such extraordinary pains, as if he had been lying upon sharp thorns and ends of needles'.[9]

Geillis Duncan confessed to attending a gathering of witches at the kirk of North Berwick, at which point James became interested in the case and ordered her to be brought before him, since 'in respect of the strangeness of these matters, [James] took great delight to be present at their examinations'.[10] James would have been encouraged to hear that when the devil appeared in the pulpit of North Berwick kirk to address the assembled witches, he declared that 'the King is the greatest enemy he hath in the world'; this was confirmation of James's godliness and election. However, James was not entirely convinced that the witches were telling the truth, until Agnes Sampson took him aside and told him the exact words that he and the queen spoke to each other the night after their marriage at Uppsala.[11]

It soon emerged that a known magician, Richard Graham, was involved in the plot and had apparently been engaged by Bothwell, who had heard in Italy that his life would be in danger from the king and wanted Graham to protect him. The Italian connection and the magical method chosen to kill the king (a potion to touch him while moving from one room to another) make the affair strangely reminiscent of the attempt to kill Henry VII by magic in 1494. However, James was by no means sure that the evidence against Bothwell was sufficient to guarantee a conviction for treason, a worry that may have sprung from the fact that Bothwell was not the only Scottish nobleman to be involved with witches. Bothwell would, after all, be tried by his peers. Pressure was applied to James to have Bothwell tortured, and there was even a note to this effect pinned to the door of the king's chamber in May 1591.[12] On 9 May Bothwell was imprisoned in Edinburgh Castle and on 14 June new evidence emerged, in the form of testimony from another witch, who confirmed Bothwell's guilt and claimed to have been present when the king's image was being bewitched. However, Bothwell escaped on 21 June and remained a fugitive until he was finally brought to trial on 10 August 1593.

Meanwhile, news of the plot against James's life reached England, where accounts of the testimonies of the original witches were published by William Wright as a pamphlet entitled *Newes from Scotland*. Apart from the fact that there was always an appetite for sensational tracts about witches, English people were naturally interested in what happened to the man who would be their next king. *Newes from Scotland*, which was a translation of an original Scots pamphlet, spoke reverentially of James and emphasised his bravery in having the witches examined in his presence. However, the author explained that it was not possible for them to harm the king:

> It is well known that the King is the child and servant of God, and [witches] but servants to the devil; he is the Lord's anointed, and they but vessels of God's wrath; he is a true Christian, and trusteth in God, they worse than infidels, for they only trust in the devil, who daily serves them till he have brought them to utter destruction. But hereby it seemeth that His Highness carried a magnanimous and undaunted mind, not feared with their enchantments, but resolute in this, that so long as God is with him, he feareth not who is against him. And truly the whole scope of this treason doth so plainly lay open the wonderful providence of the Almighty, that if he had not been defended by his omnipotency and power, His Highness had never returned alive in his voyage from Denmark, so that there is no doubt but God would as well

defend him on the land as on the sea, where they pretended their damnable practice.[13]

According to James's elevated understanding of monarchy, the king was answerable to God alone and therefore enjoyed his direct protection. Yet in spite of the fact that witchcraft fascinated James, his preoccupation with magical threats was rather different from that of previous monarchs. James manifested intellectual curiosity concerning the marvellous and unusual. He never displayed anxiety that magic could harm him, in contrast to previous monarchs (or their ministers), who were genuinely concerned about magical threats. James's insistence that the witches who had wanted to harm him should appear in his presence is testament to his fearless approach. From James's point of view, the monarch was above the dealings of witches. Although he described witchcraft as 'so odious a treason against God',[14] his very curiosity about witchcraft and theoretical knowledge about it, combined with his very high estimation of his own office, may have led James to fear witchcraft *less* than any other monarch, in spite of his firm belief in its reality.

Although Bothwell was acquitted, as James had feared, the king had the earl banished and he died in poverty in Naples in 1612. Whether or not Bothwell was genuinely guilty of involvement in the magical conspiracy,[15] the profound effect that the case had on James was undeniable. It was not to be the last incident of magical treason against him. In the summer of 1597 the king attended a general assembly of the kirk at Dundee in an effort to suppress, once again, the kirk's hostility to the idea of bishops. The English ambassador, Robert Bowes, reported to Robert Cecil on 15 August that a man named McKolme Anderson had confessed to trying to raise a storm to drown the king on his way back from Dundee, 'and the life of the Prince [Henry] has likewise been sought by the witches, as is acknowledged by some of them'.[16]

Later that year, James arranged the publication of an imaginary dialogue on witchcraft and other related matters that he may have begun writing after the trials of 1591, entitled *Daemonologie*, which has become one of the most famous works on witchcraft in British history. James intended his book as a riposte to the scepticism of Reginald Scot's *Discoverie of Witchcraft* (1584), as well as the ideas of the Continental demonologist Johann Weyer who inspired Scot. James defended, amongst other things, the idea that wax images could be used to kill:

> They can bewitch and take the life of men and women, by roasting of the pictures ... which likewise is very possible to their master [the devil] to perform, for although ... that instrument of wax have no virtue in that turn doing, yet may he not very well even by that same measure that his conjured slaves melts that wax at the fire, may he not I say at these same times, subtly as a spirit so weaken and scatter the spirits of life of the patient, as may make him on the one part, for faintness to sweat out the humour of his body. And on the other part, for the not concurrence of these spirits ... he at last shall vanish away, even as his picture will do at the fire. And that knavish and cunning workman, by troubling him only at some times, makes a proportion so near betwixt the working of the one and the other, that both shall end as it were at one time.[17]

James's argument denied the idea that harmful effigy magic was a kind of natural magic; rather, it was an invitation to the devil to destroy a person. James seemed to imply that the devil ensured his attacks on the victim coincided with the magician's operations on the effigy, so as to deceive the magician into an inflated belief in his own powers. James had a clear idea about what necromancers were like, which was very probably formed from his encounter with Bothwell: 'such as though rich, yet burns with a desperate desire of revenge'.[18]

In *Daemonologie*, James alluded to the gravity of the crime of magical treason when he suggested that 'in a matter of treason against the prince' even witches themselves and children could be called upon to give evidence.[19] According to James's political theology of divine right, the king was 'a mortal God on earth' and, like God, was bound never to forgive certain crimes which showed an inherent contempt for the king's and God's dignity. As James advised his son in 1599, 'So is there some horrible crimes which you are bound in conscience never to forgive, such as witchcraft, wilful murder, incest ... sodomy, poisoning, and false coin'.[20] Murder, incest and sodomy violated nature; poisoning and witchcraft violated the laws of God; and counterfeiting of currency defaced and violated the image of the king. Furthermore, James considered it 'monstrous and unnatural' for a king's subjects to rise up against him,[21] thereby placing rebellion and treason in the category of unnatural acts along with incest, sodomy and witchcraft.

Maxwell-Stuart has argued that James's *Daemonologie* was a text directed as much at England as at Scotland. *Daemonologie* was not a partisan text designed to come down on one side or the other of the witchcraft debate; rather, it was proof that:

> ... [James] had investigated the subject thoroughly and could now be counted an authority on it. Hence he was at once an exemplar of a godly magistrate against whom the gates of Hell had not prevailed and would not prevail in future, and an authoritative arbiter of disputes regarding Satan, his minions, and the other world.[22]

However, James's battle with magical treason in Scotland was not yet over. In August 1600, during a hunting expedition, James was apparently lured to Gowrie House in Perth, where (according to the official account) John Ruthven, earl of Gowrie, threatened the king's life. James managed to recruit the aid of a servant who opened the windows, allowing James to shout 'Treason!' to his retainers below. The 'Gowrie Conspiracy' remains very murky indeed, and there was a strong suspicion from the start that James fabricated the whole affair in order to remove the earl. James's followers rushed up a small staircase into the Tower where James was struggling with Gowrie, and in the ensuing fight the earl was killed. A notebook was found on Gowrie's body which was later interpreted as a book of magic, and James's official propagandists made strenuous efforts to portray the earl as a necromancer;[23] in this way he fitted into the mould of the earl of Bothwell and was further discredited.

JAMES'S ENGLISH REIGN

Elizabeth finally died on 24 March 1603, and James arrived in London on 7 May as the monarch of three kingdoms (England, Scotland and Ireland). There seems to have been considerable popular interest in witchcraft at the time, perhaps partly inspired by James's own writings on the subject and the well-publicised attacks he had suffered from witches. Two new editions of James's *Daemonologie* were published in London that summer, and other works such as

George Giffard's *Dialogue concerning Witches and Witchcrafts* were reprinted as well. Even the playhouses were full of performances on magical themes, including Christopher Marlowe's *Doctor Faustus*, *The Merry Devil of Edmonton* and Thomas Heywood's *Wise Woman of Hogsdon*.[24] The government seems to have been concerned at this time about the proliferation of the use of parts of dead bodies in necromancy,[25] but the most prominent supernatural scandal of the time was a case of demonic possession. Mary Glover, the daughter of a London merchant, showed signs of possession in December 1602, and her case ignited a medical debate.[26] The mainstream interpretation of her affliction, however, was that she was a victim of bewitchment.

James's first English Parliament met between March and July 1604, and produced the most important of all the English acts against magic and witchcraft, because it remained in force the longest (until 1735). However, there is no evidence that Parliament's renewed emphasis on witchcraft was directly inspired by James himself. It may have been partly a form of flattery, a way for Members of Parliament to send a message that they shared the same concerns as the king, but the act did not draw on ideas from James's *Daemonologie* and it does not seem to have been personally orchestrated by the king in any way.[27] Maxwell-Stuart suggested that Edmund Anderson, Chief Justice of the Court of Common Pleas, may have been the moving spirit behind the act.[28] Nevertheless, the 1604 act was much more explicit than what had gone before, because it condemned behaviour specifically associated with malefic witchcraft:

> If any person or persons ... shall use, practise or exercise any invocation or conjuration of any evil and wicked spirit, or shall consult, covenant with, entertain, employ, feed, or reward any evil and wicked spirit to or for any intent or purpose; or take up any dead man, woman, or child out of his, her, or their grave, or any other place where the dead body resteth, or the skin, bone, or any other part of any dead person, to be employed or used in any manner of witchcraft, sorcery, charm, or enchantment; or shall use, practise or exercise any witchcraft, enchantment, charm, or sorcery, whereby any person shall be killed, destroyed, wasted, consumed, pined, or lamed in his or her body, or any part thereof; that then every such offender and offenders ... shall suffer pains of death as a felon or felons.[29]

The act also made attempted harmful magic an offence, imposing imprisonment for one year, with quarterly appearances in the pillory, on anyone who tried 'to hurt or destroy any person in his or her body, although the same be not effected and done'. The penalty for a second offence of attempted harmful magic was death and attainder.

The primary way in which the 1604 act differed from the act of 1563 was by specifically criminalising the magician or witch who consulted, made a covenant with, entertained, employed, fed or rewarded an evil spirit. The prohibition against feeding an evil spirit might seem, in hindsight, to refer to the idea that witches suckled the devil on their own blood, but this accusation only appeared in pamphlet literature and witchcraft trials in the middle of the seventeenth century. Instead, the primary targets of the 1604 act at the time were necromancers who made use of human body parts. The elderly John Dee became convinced that the act was intended as a personal attack against him, and thought that John Prestall and Vincent Murphyn's original libel against him was being revived.[30]

In the provinces the old Tudor problem of political prophecy allied with magical treason had not gone away. In January 1605 William Morton was examined by magistrates at Hinchinbrook in Huntingdonshire. He reported that as he rode between St Ives and Somersham in September 1604, a man called Butler, from Elm near Wisbech, 'a labourer, yet a practitioner in physic', had told him that England could expect great troubles and rebellion. Butler knew this because 'there was one in Norfolk ... that had the judgments of 26 ancient writers therein'. Furthermore, Butler himself was involved in practices that hinted at magic: Morton's daughter was ill with smallpox, 'for which Butler sent her a medicine and a prayer out of Mr. Johnson's little prayer book' and the magistrates noted that 'Some report this Butler to deal miraculously in his cures'.[31] At the very end of his examination, Morton revealed evidence of necromancy when he reported that 'the said Norfolk man had obtained by prayer a true angelical spirit that would tell the truth'. This, then, was more than astrological prognostication and the reading of almanacks – more even than the reading of illicit prophecies. The mysterious Norfolk man had crossed the line between prophecy and magic by claiming to be in regular communication with a spirit; whether it was a good or evil angel, his activities sounded suspiciously like necromancy directed against the king and the good government of the realm.

In spite of such incidents, like its predecessor from 1563 the 1604 act would primarily be deployed against witches rather than magicians, and has likewise become known as the 'Witchcraft Act'. In August 1612 the witch trials took place in Lancaster Castle of groups of women from two Lancashire villages, Pendle and Samlesbury, that have become known collectively as the trials of the 'Lancashire Witches'. These trials are well known, partly because they were recorded and published in great detail by the clerk of the court, Thomas Potts, and partly because they introduced new ideas into English witch trials. Although in both cases the import of the charges was familiar – supernatural harm caused by ill-wishing – at the Pendle trial the court took pains to ensure that the witches were exposed as devotees of traditional Catholicism.[32] 'Old Chattox' and Jennet Device admitted to using half-remembered fragments of Catholic liturgy as charms, rather like Agnes Waterhouse's confession in 1566 that her familiar would only let her pray in Latin.

However, the English courts were never successful in linking witchcraft to Catholicism in the way that the Scottish courts managed, and the second of the Lancashire trials, that of the Samlesbury witches, ended with the acquittal of the suspects on the grounds that the informant, a fourteen-year-old girl called Grace Sowerbutts, had been put up to it by a seminary priest. The judge concluded that Christopher Southworth, a priest who was passing himself off as a schoolmaster, had told Grace to accuse her grandmother and others of witchcraft because they had started attending the Protestant services at the local parish church. Lancashire was a deeply Catholic part of England where the Reformation was meeting stiff resistance, and Southworth had apparently taken ideas about the abominations committed by witches from a recently published account of a French witch trial and put them in the young girl's mind. The judge ended up attacking the priest Southworth as a 'bloody butcher' for trying to get the accused women hanged.[33]

The trials of the Lancashire Witches were a turning point in English witch prosecutions because they established that seventeenth-century witch-hunting was not going to be a sectarian affair.

Catholics in England would not be labelled as witches, as they had often been in Scotland. Because religion and politics were virtually one and the same thing in the seventeenth century, the effect of this was that persecution of witches in England on a national scale became a largely apolitical business. This is not to say that *local* politics did not play a part in witch-hunting; there is much evidence that it did, and for many Puritans the campaign against witches was a mark of religious fervour, but witches were not accused of trying to kill the king or overthrow the government.

James's own interest in witchcraft seems to have waned at the time he came to the throne in England, and he started to adopt a more sceptical attitude to supernatural phenomena in general. In the summer of 1605 James visited Oxford, where the academics of the university presented him with a supposed demoniac, Anne Gunter. James was unconvinced by her performance, and instructed the archbishop of Canterbury, Richard Bancroft, to investigate the case.[34] The reason for James's scepticism was primarily political. English Protestantism was in a dangerously divided state, and James was determined to maintain the authority of the crown and bishops against the Puritans. The preservation of religious conformity required the suppression of 'enthusiastic' practices, such as exorcism, which empowered Puritan ministers and created a cult of personality around prominent exorcists like the preacher John Darrell.[35] In 1604 Canon 72 prohibited prayer and fasting to dispossess demoniacs without a licence from the bishop, but the Latin text of the canon referred to *exorcismos*, thereby prohibiting liturgical exorcisms as well.[36] However, Archbishop Bancroft's attack on exorcism concentrated on portraying it as a form of fraud rather than harmful magic.

The defining moment of James's reign came on 5 November 1605 when, on the eve of the state opening of Parliament, the Catholic extremist Guido Fawkes was discovered with barrels of gunpowder in the cellars under the Palace of Westminster. The discovery of the 'Gunpowder Plot' was a propaganda coup for the English Protestant establishment whose significance was to be exploited for centuries to come, but many of the early reactions to the Plot likened Fawkes to a devil and portrayed his plot as a plan to recreate hell on earth, quite literally. The Gunpowder Plot was, if not magical treason, certainly diabolical treason that violated nature just as dramatically as effigy magic. Like traditional effigy magic, the plot was an attempt to kill the king remotely, using technology – albeit this time everyone can agree that the technology would have worked. Fawkes was widely described as 'The Devil of the Vault', and a pamphlet that appeared early in 1606 entitled *The Arraignment and Execution of the Late Traitors* referred to the 'bewitched wit' of one of the conspirators, Everard Digby.[37] As Maxwell-Stuart has noted,

> The Gunpowder Plot had the devastating effect of turning, even more than may have been the case previously, common perception of English Catholics into "enemies within", people naturally and confessionally allied with Satan and therefore peculiarly susceptible to the seductions and allurement of witchcraft which might be, so it seemed, at once an ally of witchcraft and a victim of it.[38]

In November 2014 it was reported that apotropaic 'witch marks' (ritual protection marks) were found scratched on underfloor joists of a room at Knole House in Kent. The joists were dated by dendrochronology to 1606, when there had been a plan for James I to visit Knole House.[39] The marks were arranged to form a box or 'demon trap' around the hearth, and the discovery led to much speculation by archaeologists and historians that James may have felt vulnerable to supernatural attack in the aftermath of the Gunpowder Plot. It is certainly true that James's reign saw the triumph of a religious rhetoric that equated treason with witchcraft, as the ultimate rebellion against nature. However, it is ironic that suspected cases of magical treason in England almost entirely vanish from the historical record during this period, and it is important not to exaggerate the political ramifications of witchcraft in Jacobean England. Decades of Shakespeare criticism, along with an unsupported assumption that James's interest in witchcraft continued after his accession to the English throne, have created the impression that witchcraft and magic were much more significant to matters of state during James's reign than is borne out by the evidence. That being said, it possible that it was the owners of Knole rather than the king himself who worried that he might be subjected to magical attack.

There is some evidence that potential traitors still felt the need for magical aid to support their efforts in James's reign. In the spring and summer of 1607 a rural revolt broke out in Northamptonshire, Leicestershire and Warwickshire, stimulated by James's grants of vast tracts of land to the nobility to enclose as pasture, forcing the local population off the land. One of the leaders of the revolt, John Reynoldes, was known as 'Captain Pouch',

> ... because of a great leather pouch which he wore by his side, in which purse he affirmed to his company, that there was sufficient matter to defend them against all comers, but afterward when he was apprehended, his pouch was searched and therein was only a piece of green cheese. He told them also, that he had authority from His Majesty to throw down enclosures, and that he was sent of God to satisfy all degrees whatsoever, and that in this present work, he was directed by the Lord of Heaven.[40]

Reynoldes, like Hacket a few years earlier, straddled the boundary between prophecy and magic. His claims of having received authority from God and the king, combined with his belief in his own invulnerability guaranteed by magical means, amounted to something very close to treason.

THE CASE OF SIR THOMAS LAKE

A more threatening case of magical treason, because its author was closer to the person of the king, emerged early in 1619. Sir Thomas Lake was an ambitious and successful civil servant who had been close to James since he rode to Scotland to inform the king about the state of England in 1603. By 1609, Lake had been appointed the king's Latin Secretary and Robert Cecil had begun to resent his influence. When Cecil died in 1612 he left his seal as First Secretary in Lake's hands, but James refused to allow Lake to be more than acting First Secretary, probably because he was known to be a secret Catholic, giving the post instead to Sir Ralph Winwood. However, as James gravitated towards the idea of an alliance with Spain, he became more sympathetic to Lake and appointed him Secretary for Home Affairs in January 1616. At the zenith of his fortunes, Lake married his daughter Anne to the Catholic Lord Ros, the grandson of the earl of Exeter.

Unfortunately, Lake's fortunes began to unravel at this point because the marriage failed. Lord and Lady Ros were soon living apart, and Lady Ros demanded that her husband should pay for her upkeep. Thomas Cecil, earl of Exeter, considered this a slight to his family and intervened, at which point Lady Ros and her mother targeted Cecil's wife, the countess of Exeter, accusing her of trying to poison Lady Ros. They even forged a document in which the countess confessed her guilt. The countess protested, and Lake's wife and daughter found themselves on trial for slander in the Court of Star Chamber. Lake appealed for assistance to James's favourite, the duke of Buckingham, but was refused. The duke's mother, Mary Villiers, was more accommodating, but in February 1619 Lake's wife and daughter were found guilty of slander, and Lake himself was found guilty of unlawfully imprisoning two servants of Lord Ros and the earl of Exeter who refused to give evidence against the countess. The Lake family were sent to the Tower.[41]

Matters were made worse for Lake when a former minister and schoolmaster named Peacock was arrested on suspicion of trying to influence the king's judgement by magic. On 2 February the Lord Chancellor, Francis Bacon, wrote to Sir George Calvert (Lake's replacement), promising to take 'special care' with Peacock's examination, presumably because it touched the matter of treason.[42] Five days later Bacon wrote to the king, informing him that:

> Sir Edward Coke is now afoot, and according to your command, signified by Mr Secretary Calvert, we proceed in Peacock's examinations; for although there have been very good diligence used, yet certainly we are not at the bottom; and he that would not use the utmost of his line to sound such a business as this, should not have due regard neither to your Majesty's honour nor safety.

Sir Edward Coke was Chief Justice of the King's Bench and England's foremost jurist, and the 'good diligence' Bacon referred to was intensive questioning. Coke's appearance was a prelude to the next stage of interrogation: torture. 'If it may not be done otherwise', Bacon declared, 'it is fit Peacock be put to torture'.[43] Bacon's cold assurance is a reminder that, although this was the first alleged direct magical attack in England on the person of the monarch since the 1580s, magical treason had lost none of its seriousness and required the full attention of the highest officers of state. Indeed, Bacon compared Peacock to another traitor, Thomas Peacham, who had been tortured after he wrote a sermon calling for the king's death.

It was only at the end of the month, after Peacock had been tortured, that the court gossip John Chamberlain reported that there was a magical element to the case:

> One Peacock, sometime a schoolmaster and minister (but a very busy brained fellow) was the last week committed to the Tower for practising to infatuate the King's judgement by sorcery (they say) in the business of Sir Thomas Lake and the Lady of Exeter. He hath been strictly examined by the Lord Chancellor, the Lord Coke, the Lord Chief Justice, the Attorney, Solicitor, and others; and on Tuesday was hanged up by the wrists; and though he were very impatient of the torture and swooned once or twice, yet I cannot learn that they have wrung very great matter out of him. Sir Thomas Lake was confronted with him at the Lord Chancellor's; whereon a suspicion arises that the matter may reach to him or his Lady.[44]

The way in which Lake was confronted with Peacock is reminiscent of a similar tactic tried on the earl of Bothwell in 1593. Lake, like Bothwell, was being presented as the treacherous mastermind behind a magical conspiracy. Rumours also circulated that Lake had committed incest with his daughter. The court was certainly ready for more stories of magical conspiracy. Just three years earlier, in 1616, a woman named Anne Turner had been executed for murder by poisoning of the courtier Sir Thomas Overbury. The murder was supposedly arranged by Frances Howard, countess of Essex, who was concerned that Overbury opposed her affair with Viscount Rochester, and Anne received assistance from the notorious astrologer Simon Forman. This magical scandal at the heart of the court may have lingered in the minds of Peacock's interrogators.[45]

Peacock, the 'busy brained fellow' who had been both a minister and a schoolmaster, comes across as a figure similar to William Awder, who impersonated figures of learning and authority in the 1580s; he was a man of some learning who clung to the fringes of the religious establishment and was prepared to dabble in the underworld of magic and radical prophecy. There is no further evidence of Peacock's fate, and none at all to give an indication of the kind of 'sorcery' that he was supposed to have been using against James. However, there was one feature of the case of Lake and Peacock that anticipated future events: the involvement of the countess of Buckingham, Mary Villiers. The countess interceded with the king on Lake's behalf, but just a few years later, Mary herself would be implicated in an alleged plot to kill James by poisoning.

MAGICAL TREASON IN THE PLAYS OF SHAKESPEARE

Magical treason is a prominent theme in the plays of William Shakespeare. Quite apart from the centrality of magical treason to his earliest history play (*Henry VI Part Two*), the plots of two of his best-known tragedies, *Hamlet* (c. 1602) and *Macbeth* (c. 1606), arguably hang on acts of magical treason as well. The ghost of Hamlet's father reveals in Act 1, Scene 5 that he was killed by his brother Claudius 'with witchcraft of his wits, with traitorous gifts', and the magical nature of Claudius's treason is laid bare in the ghost's description of the king's manner of death (ll. 61–7):

> Upon my secure hour thy uncle stole,
> With juice of cursed hebona in a vial,
> And in the porches of my ears did pour
> The leperous distilment; whose effect
> Holds such an enmity with blood of man
> That swift as quicksilver it courses through
> The natural gates and alleys of the body.

To a contemporary audience, the murder of Hamlet's father is a simple poisoning couched in evocative language. To a seventeenth-century audience, this was plainly a case of *veneficium*, the supernatural composition of substances that had the power to dissolve the natural constitution of the human body (and in this case, the natural constitution of Denmark as well) in occult, mysterious ways. Hebona was a plant specifically associated with witchcraft, and the comparison of the poison with quicksilver (mercury) brings alchemy to mind, while the poison's 'enmity with blood of man' is a reference to the idea that certain substances possessed natural affinities or enmities with the body, drawn from astrological medicine. In Act 3, Scene 2 the magical character of Claudius's treason is made still more explicit in the words placed in the mouth of Lucianus, the king's nephew in the 'play within a play' performed in front of Hamlet's uncle (ll. 249–54):

> Thoughts black, hands apt, drugs fit, and time agreeing;
> Confederate season, else no creature seeing;
> Thou mixture rank, of midnight weeds collected,
> With Hecat's ban thrice blasted, thrice infected,
> Thy natural magic and dire property
> On wholesome life usurps immediately.

The words chosen make clear that Claudius has made use of his knowledge of 'natural magic' to kill the king; 'time agreeing', 'confederate season' and 'midnight weeds' all point to the involvement of astrological magic. Hecate, in addition to being the goddess of witchcraft, was also the goddess of the moon, so 'Hecat's ban' may refer to the gathering of plants at a full moon.

Magical treason is even more deeply woven into the fabric of the plot of *Macbeth*. Encountering three witches on a 'blasted heath', Macbeth is told that he will be 'king hereafter', and the prophecy plants the seeds of the treason that Macbeth plans with his wife: the murder of King Duncan. Macbeth himself describes the murder of Duncan in Act 2, Scene 3 as 'like a breach in nature'; the unnatural act of treason is motivated by the unnatural prophecy of the witches, just as prophecies had been a driver behind magical treasons in Elizabeth's reign. It would not be true to say that either *Hamlet* or *Macbeth* is a play about magical treason; both plays are tragedies in which the outworking of character-flaws in their protagonists reveals timeless truths about human nature. Nevertheless, in both plays the character-flaws only begin to assert themselves after a supernatural event: in *Hamlet*, the revelation of Claudius's magical *veneficium* and, in *Macbeth*, the witches' malicious prophecy.

Even in Shakespeare's history play *Richard III* the influence of recent instances of magical treason is apparent, albeit turned on its head. Shakespeare's Richard is destroyed by the curses of those he has wronged, such as Jane Shore and Margaret Beaufort. Mary Steible has argued that the 1580 'Act against seditious words and rumours', which outlawed curses against the monarch's person, aided in the political assassination of the memory of Richard III and contributed to Shakespeare's negative portrayal of the monarch. The act made it possible for Tudor and Jacobean historians and playwrights to impose a meaning on curses (and attribute an effectiveness to them) that people may not necessarily have accepted in the fifteenth century.[46]

One possible interpretation of Shakespeare's play *The Tempest*, advanced by G. J. Guenther, is that it was a critical reply to the 1604 act and an attempt to present magic as harmless. The play was first performed in 1610 or 1611. At the beginning of the play Prospero appears amidst thunder and lightning in the guise of a sinister magician, apparently trying to kill the king of Naples and his companions in the same way that Bothwell's witches tried to kill James in 1589: by shipwreck. This is 'the diabolical magic of illegitimate politics'.[47] However, it soon becomes clear that Prospero instructed his spirit Ariel not to harm the castaways, and the magician emerges as an increasingly fatherly, unthreatening character until he finally agrees to marry his daughter Miranda to the king's son. By the end of the play, Shakespeare successfully 'evacuates the charged content of magic',[48] and presents Prospero as a master illusionist rather than an evil necromancer. In Vaughan Hart's view, by contrast, *The Tempest* presented a tame view of magic as the restoration of the natural order (returning Prospero to his duchy) rather than as a challenge to monarchical authority.[49]

The character of Prospero may simply have been a tribute to a king who lived at the centre of a court that constructed itself through Neoplatonic and Hermetic symbolism. Masques portrayed James as a natural magus controlling the forces of nature, and *The Tempest* was performed in his presence on 1 November 1611. Ben Jonson's *Masque of Queens* (1609) depicted twelve witches dancing and boasting about their evil-doing, before they were banished by the twelve virtues of the House of Fame.[50] In one performance Queen Anne of Denmark herself released knights imprisoned in pillars of gold by dark enchantments. As Vaughan Hart has argued, 'The white powers of the king and his perfect emblem, the Court, here banished black magic identified with the imperfect country at large as the harbinger of witchcraft and, later, the dark forces of revolution'.[51]

THE 'POISONING' OF JAMES I

James I's health began to deteriorate in 1624, and in March 1625 he suffered a stroke from which he died at his favourite house, Theobalds in Hertfordshire. James's ill-health meant that he had been increasingly absent from London, and this gave his favourite, the duke of Buckingham, the opportunity to seize the reins of power and ensure that James's son and heir, Prince Charles, came under his control. Charles was James's second son and, like Henry VIII, had not initially expected to rule, but the death of Henry, prince of Wales, in 1612 catapulted the stuttering Charles into the position of king-in-waiting. The early years of Charles's reign saw the world of the court diverge further and further from the concerns of many people in seventeenth-century England. Although Charles claimed to be loyal to the Protestant Reformation, his wife was a French Catholic and he gave preferment to Buckingham's Catholic relatives. Not only that, but his decision to rule without Parliament silenced the voice of an increasingly Puritan-dominated Protestant establishment. Slowly but surely, dissent was gathering against Charles's rule.

The magical treason scandal of the 1620s differed from what had gone before, because popular opinion was aligning itself against Buckingham (and, implicitly, against King Charles himself). The allegations of magical treason against Buckingham's family and servants were attacks on the court from the outside, in contrast to the Tudor period when accusations of magical treason often emanated from – or were encouraged by – the monarch's own ministers. This was one of many signs that the centralised systems of government established by Henry VIII and Elizabeth were beginning to unravel in Charles's reign. For many ordinary English people, and even for Members of Parliament, the court itself had become the enemy. Buckingham ruled the king and, it was widely believed, the duke was ruled by his mother. The countess's conversion to Catholicism under the influence of the Jesuit John Percy, coupled with the dark reputation of the Jesuits, produced the inevitable belief that England was being indirectly governed by the Jesuits and moving ever closer to the Catholic powers.

Rumours circulated soon after James's death that the king's demise had been hastened by a plaster and treacle posset, made by the countess of Buckingham and administered by her son with the aid of a Catholic physician who was not one of the king's personal doctors. The fact that the countess had been supportive of Sir Thomas Lake did not help her public image. The story was reported by the Venetian ambassador and made public in 1626 in a pamphlet, *The Forerunner of Revenge*, by James's personal physician, Dr George Eglisham.[52] Eglisham did not explicitly accuse Buckingham and his mother of using magic, but referred to the 'subtill' craft of a foreign mountebank hired by them to kill the king, thereby playing into a longstanding cultural association between poisoning and magic. As Alastair Bellany and Thomas Cogswell note, 'Readers may thus have assumed that Buckingham's mountebank was not merely a poison artist but a witch, wielding demonic power to devise poisons that violated nature's laws'.[53]

Parliament began proceedings to impeach Buckingham, but Charles dissolved Parliament, effectively putting an end to the process, on 12 June 1626. Later that same day an enormous thunderstorm broke over London, followed by 'a tempest whirling and ghoulish' that caused a wall to fall down in the churchyard of St Andrew's, Holborn, thereby opening the graves of some recent plague victims. This ominous event was widely attributed to Buckingham, perhaps acting through the agency of his 'wizard', the self-styled 'Doctor' John Lambe, especially since the storm seemed to centre on Buckingham's house:

> Upon the Thames arose a mist in the form of a round circle above the waters; the fierceness of the storm bent itself against York House, the habitation of the Duke of Buckingham; the round circle dispersed itself like smoke issuing out of a furnace, and then vanished away; the vulgar attributed it to Dr Lambe's art of conjuring, he then appearing upon the Thames.[54]

Lambe was an unsavoury character who practised as an astrological physician but had no medical training, and combined his 'medical' advice with magical services. This was a typical career for an early modern 'cunning-man', and there may have been hundreds of men like Lambe. Lambe, however, was unique in having attracted preferment from the duke of Buckingham.

Lambe had been tried in 1608 under the 1604 act at the Worcester assizes for using magic to sap the strength of Lord Windsor and raising evil spirits.[55] Thereafter he was imprisoned in Worcester Castle and, later, at the King's Bench Prison in London. According to the author of an account of Lambe's life, who was perhaps drawing upon the myth of Rowland Jenks, the justices, sheriff and foreman of the jury mysteriously died shortly after Lambe's Worcester trial.[56] Lambe was able to afford comfortable conditions in captivity, and capitalised on his notorious reputation by receiving numerous guests, including Buckingham. In 1623 Lambe was tried and convicted of the rape of an eleven year-old girl, but pardoned and released from prison in 1623, perhaps because he was now under Buckingham's protection. Lambe moved into a house near the Palace of Westminster where he was able to practise magic freely.[57]

Allegations that Lambe was involved in magical treason emerged only after his death: he was beaten to death by a mob in a London street in 1628. In 1653 a cunning-woman named Anne Bodenham was tried for witchcraft at Salisbury,[58] and a pamphleteer of the time made much of the fact that Anne claimed to have been a servant of Lambe's. She told a grocer who visited her in prison:

> ... that she lived with Dr Lambe, and he taught her to raise spirits, and she told him how people came to learn it. If those that have a desire to it, do read in books, and when they come to read further then they can understand, then the Devil will appear to them, and show them what they would know; and they doing what he would have them, they may learn to do what they desired to do, and he would teach them.[59]

On another occasion, Bodenham explained why she had originally gone into Lambe's service, and claimed he had calculated King James's death:

> ... the occasion she came to live with [Dr Lambe], she said was, that she lived with a lady in London, who was a patient many times to him, and sent her often in business to him, and in particular, she went to know what death King James should die; and the Doctor told her what death, and withal said that none of his children should come to a natural death; and she said she then saw so many curious sights, and pleasant things, that she had a mind to be his servant, and learn some of the art; and Dr Lambe seeing her very docile, took her to be his servant; and she reading in some of his books, with his help learnt her art, by which she said she had gotten many a penny, and done hundreds of people good.[60]

Buckingham's 'well-known relationships with occult practitioners operating in the ambiguous zones between illicit demonic magic and licit natural medicine' were undoubtedly a contributory factor to the accusations of treason by *veneficium* levelled against him by Eglisham, whose pamphlet wove insinuations of actual magic together with assertions that Buckingham had metaphorically 'bewitched' James (an accusation often made against royal favourites). Whether Eglisham intended to accuse Buckingham of magic or not, this was certainly how the pamphlet was interpreted by Catholics such as Gabriel Browne,[61] and in 1628 a satirical poem had Buckingham openly boast, 'Nor shall you ever prove, by Magick Charmes / I wrought the Kings Affection, or his harmes'.[62]

TOWARDS CIVIL WAR

The cranks and fanatics, in the mould of Hacket and Peacock, persisted into the seventeenth century. In 1639 a man named John Hammond claimed that he had the power, at a moment's notice, to take away the king's power by magic.[63] However, there were no other accusations of magic as a political crime made during Charles's personal reign (1629–40), when Charles managed to rule without summoning Parliament. One possible reason for this was that Charles's opponents were Puritans who, although they sometimes embraced millenarian prophecy, rejected magic as popish superstition. Catholics, accused of superstitious practices in earlier reigns, generally supported Charles's regime because he made exceptions to the penal laws for Catholic favourites and their families, and Catholics cherished hopes of wider toleration.

In the event, magic would not be required to take away the king's power. In 1641 a disastrous defeat in his war against the Covenanters in Scotland compelled Charles to recall Parliament, and once assembled, the 'Long Parliament' was determined not to be dissolved. Parliament impeached Charles's hated favourite, Thomas Wentworth, earl of Strafford. The Strafford case served to re-define treason, in fact if not in law, as a crime to be construed by Parliament rather than by the king's ministers or the Privy Council. The traditional definition of treason as a personal attack on the monarch or his ministers was beginning to break down, as Parliament claimed the right to indict the king's favourites, against his wishes, as traitors. What Londoners had wished to do to Buckingham in 1626 was now accomplished in Strafford. Charles's attempt to arrest the Puritan ringleaders of the Parliamentarian revolt in 1642 disastrously backfired, and, having slipped away from London, Charles chose to recover his royal authority by force, raising the royal standard at Nottingham in August 1642 and inaugurating the first English Civil War.

CHAPTER 6

The Decline of Magic as a Political Crime, 1642–1700

The conspiracy theories surrounding the death of James I in 1625 turned out to be the last major accusation of treason to be tinged with suspicions of occult machinations, but accusations and insinuations that traitors and enemies of government were allied with supernatural power nevertheless continued into the 1670s. However, in the second half of the seventeenth century interest in magic as a means of advancement tailed off decisively amongst England's courtly elite. Even when a huge and largely fabricated treason panic swept England in 1678–81, and even when that panic targeted 'superstitious' Catholics as scapegoats, accusations of magical treason were absent. In this respect, England stood in stark contrast to France, whose own treason panic between 1676 and 1682 uncovered the most lurid accusations of ritual magic and diabolism. However, the involvement of some English actors in France's 'affair of the poisons', together with the fact that England was the refuge of choice for fleeing suspects of Louis XIV's investigation, suggest that events in France and England may have been more closely interconnected than hitherto imagined.

Nevertheless, although accusations of non-magical poisoning periodically resurfaced in England, by the 1690s the association of treason with magic and witchcraft was the subject of satire rather than a matter of serious concern to governments. The early and conspicuous adoption of mechanical and Newtonian views of the universe by England's ruling elite, compared with other European nations, is one possible reason for the decline of treasonous magic. Another may be that the slow cultural 'Protestantisation' of England begun by Elizabeth was finally accomplished by the reign of Charles II, leaving little room for 'Catholic' ideas of manipulating the political process by means of magical rituals. Related to the 'Protestantisation' of England may have been the increasing tendency, from the 1640s onwards, to reduce all supernatural crime to malefic witchcraft (disregarding ritual magic). Since England had no tradition of political witchcraft, the triumph of witchcraft as a catch-all category may have played a role in eliminating the longstanding tradition of political magic.

POLITICAL MAGIC IN THE ENGLISH CIVIL WARS

Accusations of treason were emptied of much of their former meaning in the England of 1642, divided against itself by competing models of sovereignty and the relationship between king and parliament. Ironically, in spite of the fact that they were making war on the king, old anxieties about magical threats to government emerged most obviously on the Parliamentarian side. Before the Civil Wars, Archbishop Laud was subjected to frequent accusations of 'necromancy' and in 1645 the Scottish Presbyterian Robert Baillie claimed that Laudianism had 'bewitched the Court and Country' when it was really 'a Schoole of ... Treacherie'.[1] Parliament might have removed the king as the object of magical treason, but the suspicions that had inspired earlier panics remained. This is not surprising, given that the last major magical treason scare – surrounding the duke of Buckingham's involvement in the death of James I – had emerged among the gossip-mongers of Puritan London. Furthermore, the disruption of law and order occasioned by the Civil Wars seems to have made English people more, not less, determined to accuse and punish wrongdoers; one way to interpret the East Anglian witch-hunt of 1644–7 is that people craved the punishment of infringements against the local order all the more because the national order had been 'turned upside down'. It might have been impossible to say who was and was not a traitor but, reassuringly, it was still possible to identify malefice at the local level.

On 9 September 1645 Mary Lakeland of Ipswich was burned to death for petty treason, the murder of her husband by witchcraft. As Malcolm Gaskill has observed, 'Disobedience in one form could set off a chain reaction in people's minds' and 'a homicidal wife was a symbolic attack on the authority of the state'.[2] Petty and high treason were not unrelated crimes in the minds of seventeenth-century judges.

However, there were also reports that witchcraft was being used as a weapon in the war itself. A Parliamentarian newssheet, the *Scotish Dove*, confidently reported that witches convicted at Bury St Edmunds on 27 August 1645 'confessed they had been in the King's army, and have sent out their hags to serve them ... His Majesty's army it seems is beholding to the devil'.[3] In what Alex Stoyle has described as 'the single worst atrocity of the Civil War in England', around a hundred female camp followers of the Royalist army were massacred by victorious Parliamentarians after the battle of Naseby in June 1645, and many of those who were not killed had their faces mutilated. Parliamentarian literature later claimed the women were witches, 'which many of Colonel Cromwell's souldiers did plainly perceive to fly swiftly from one side of the king's army to the other'.[4] It was also claimed that the women were Irish, although it is possible the women were Welsh and their language was mistaken for Irish.[5] Stoyle interpreted the massacre as revenge for the massacres of Protestant settlers in Ireland in 1641, and the mutilation as revenge for Royalist atrocities committed after the battle of Lostwithiel in August 1644, but there was a long tradition in English witchcraft belief of 'scoring above the breath' (i.e. cutting the witch's face somewhere above the mouth) in order to neutralise witchcraft, so it is also possible that the facial mutilation of the women had ritual significance.[6] Perhaps the best known Parliamentarian allegation of witchcraft against the Royalists was the claim that Charles's nephew Prince Rupert of the Rhine was invulnerable to bullets because his dog 'Boy' was a familiar spirit. When Boy was shot at the battle of Marston Moor in 1644, the Parliamentarian soldier responsible was thought to have been able to do so only because he was 'skilled in necromancy'.[7]

Richard Weisman has argued that the 'covenant theology' adopted by Puritans in the Massachusetts colony meant that they identified witchcraft as a form of treason,[8] and it is possible that similar ideas were also in circulation in East Anglia (where many of the Massachusetts colonists came from) in the mid-seventeenth century. No English document of the period explicitly associates witchcraft and treason, but the witch-trial of John Lowes, the vicar of Brandeston, in July 1645 had overtones of treason. Although the clergy had long been associated with criminal magic, it was highly unusual for a clergyman to be accused of witchcraft (Lowes was the only one during Matthew Hopkins's and John Stearne's East Anglian campaign). Lowes was accused of commanding his imps to sink ships setting sail from the port of Ipswich, an allegation that recalled the treasonable activities of the North Berwick witches against James VI of Scotland in Leith harbour in 1589. Attacks on shipping went beyond the usual locally based activities of witches and had a potential impact on the wellbeing of the nation at large, especially during time of war.[9]

It is harder to locate accusations of diabolism and witchcraft against Parliamentarians in Royalist propaganda. In the aftermath of Charles's execution in January 1649, Royalist newssheets declared that the regicides were planning to establish an alternative calendar to that of the church, which would celebrate famous traitors in a parody of the Christian faith.[10] Lurid tales circulated amongst Royalists about the providential fates of those involved in Charles's execution, and when in January 1650 all adult males were to be compelled to swear loyalty to the Commonwealth in the Engagement Oath, the Royalist *Man in the Moon* declared that to do so would be equivalent to making a pact with the devil.[11] However, Parliamentarian and Royalist propaganda differed in that, whereas many Parliamentarians took allegations of diabolism literally, Royalists were interested in rhetoric that *metaphorically* portrayed rebellion as a sin as bad as witchcraft.

INTERREGNUM AND RESTORATION: THE DECLINE OF MAGICAL TREASON

Magic thrives on inaccessibility, complexity and mystique, and trades on the exclusivity of magical knowledge. Once that exclusivity disappears, magic inevitably appears less threatening. The Printing Act of 1649 allowed limited freedom of the press because the Parliamentarian government did not have the right to decide directly what could and could not be printed; this was left to a group of licensers who authorised a wide range of material, including radical literature. The Printing Act expired in 1651, leading to a period of unrestricted freedom, but was revived in 1653.[12] Nevertheless, the climate of the Interregnum was more conducive to the publication of previously unacceptable literature than any that had gone before. When he assumed the title of Lord Protector in 1655, Oliver Cromwell took direct control of printing once more, and religious freedom was progressively restricted as more radical voices were suppressed, but the extent of censorship under Cromwell still compared favourably to that under Charles II.

In 1655 the translator Robert Turner took advantage of press freedom to publish a translation of one of the most notorious of all early modern magical books, Heinrich Cornelius Agrippa's *Three Books of Occult Philosophy*.[13] Agrippa's *Three Books* were first published in 1533, and hardly deserved their dark reputation, which probably arose because they were almost the only works on magic to exist in print. The *Three Books* were a theoretical and philosophical discussion of natural magic and contained no information on magical operations. However, in 1560 the Béringer brothers at Lyons printed an edition of Agrippa's works that included the *Fourth Book*, which may or may not have been written by Agrippa himself.[14] Entitled *De caerimoniis magicis* ('Of Magical Ceremonies'), it purported to be a grimoire or magical instruction manual embodying the occult doctrine set forth in the *Three Books*. This was a work that had probably been circulating in manuscript for decades, since even the Béringers described it as spurious. Whether or not it was written by Agrippa himself, the *Fourth Book* flourished in the dark light of Agrippa's reputation.

In the preface to his 1655 translation of the *Fourth Book*, Turner was careful to portray Agrippa as a sophisticated Renaissance magus, more philosopher than common magician. He insisted that magic in the true sense was an art to be learned, not a power to be gained by allying oneself with evil spirits, and was damning of those

> ... who without the art of magic do indeed use the help of the devil himself to do mischief; practising to mix the powder of dead bodies with other things by the help of the devil prepared; and at other times to make pictures of wax, clay; or otherwise (as it were *sacramentaliter*) to effect those things which the devil by other means bringeth to pass. Such were, and to this day partly, if not altogether, are the corruptions which have made odious the very name of Magic, having chiefly sought, as the manner of all impostures is, to counterfeit the highest and most noble part of it.[15]

The difficulty of this argument was that it relied on the idea that traditional effigy magic of the type used to harm or kill was not in any way an art and was directly sponsored by the devil. In reality, as we have seen, there existed no real distinction between effigy magic used to harm and other forms of magic, as the proliferation of variants on the 'Trojan Revenge' spell demonstrates. The author of the *Fourth Book* was careful to avoid any overt reference to harmful magic, but the procedures described to invoke evil spirits are clearly drawn from the same tradition of effigy magic that produced harmful spells:

> But when we do intend to execute any effect by evil Spirits ... then that is to be done, by making and forming that thing which is to be unto us as an instrument, or subject of the experiment itself; as, whether it be an Image, or a Ring, or a Writing, or any Character, Candle, or Sacrifice, or anything of the like sort; then the name of the Spirit is to be written therein, with his Character, according to the exigency of the experiment, either by writing it with some blood, or otherwise using a perfume agreeable to the Spirit.[16]

The *Fourth Book* remained a rare and sought-after book even after its appearance in print, especially by cunning-folk, who wanted to enhance their reputation by possessing a rare and dangerous book of magic. Ritual magic, in popular form, remained in demand amongst ordinary people into the early twentieth century, as Owen Davies has shown.[17] However, the democratisation of magic seems to have coincided with its demise as a serious method to be adopted by would-be traitors. From the second half of the seventeenth century onwards, magic would increasingly come to be associated with the ignorant, the marginalised and the ill-educated – and its abandonment by the political elite led to its elimination in large part from the sphere of politics.

After the Restoration of Charles II in 1660, Royalists were determined to demonise Cromwell's regime, and an attempt was also made to smear Cromwell with witchcraft by an anonymous Restoration pamphlet *The English Devil: or, Cromwel and his Monstrous Witch discover'd at White-Hall* (1660). The pamphleteer claimed that, in 1648, Cromwell had brought a 'prophetess' (described throughout the pamphlet as a 'witch') before key figures in the Parliamentarian government. The witch made the case for putting the king on trial:

> Cromwel ... had provided a Monstrous Witch full of all deceitful craft, who being put into brave cloaths, pretended she was a Lady come from a far Countrey, being sent by God to the Army with a Revelation, which she must make known to the Army, for necessity was laid upon her: This Witch had a fair Lodging prepared for her in White-hall. Now having had her Lesson taught her before by Cromwel and Ireton, by whose order she was entertained, desired to have audience at the Council of War, for to them (she said) she was sent.[18]

Cromwell and Henry Ireton, according to the pamphlet, portrayed the woman as a 'precious saint' and 'prophetess' as she came before the 'Council of War':

> By this time the Witch was come to the door, and forthwith had admittance; where all the Officers beheld her strange postures, expressing high Devotion: Cromwel and Ireton fixing their Eyes upon her in most solemn manner (to beget in the rest of the Officers (who were ready to laugh) an apprehension of some serious thing) fell both of them to weeping; the Witch looking in their Faces, and seeing them weep, fell to weeping likewise; and began to tell them what acquaintance she had with God by Revelation, and how such a Day, such an Hour, after such a manner she had a Revelation, which she was to reveal only to them; and that was, That the glorious time of setting up Christs Kingdom was near at hand, and that Anti-christ must be speedily thrown down, and that they were the Instruments that were by God ordained to throw him down, and how they were about that great work, and that if they would prosper in it, they must first remove the KING out of the way, which they must do first by proceeding to Try him, and then to Condemn him, and then to Depose him, but not to put him to Death.[19]

The pamphlet's author claimed that he had received this story 'from one that was strongly of the Armies party, but related this shamefull story with much indignation', and noted that 'A Lillonian [i.e. a follower of John Lilburn] was taught at this time with Bribes to Print his opinion, which was much according to the opinion of his Sister Witch'. The author's description of the prophetess as a witch recalls the accusations made against Elizabeth Barton, the 'holy maid of Kent', in the 1530s, who was likewise designated a witch for her prophecies against Henry VIII. However, the pamphlet's final comment, implying that followers of the Leveller leader John Lilburn were likewise 'witches', raises the question of how literally we should take the accusation of witchcraft presented here. Although apparently describing Cromwell's association with an actual witch, the pamphlet was really just echoing the conventional political trope that rebellion was *analogous* to witchcraft ('For rebellion is as the sin of witchcraft'). The prophetess metaphorically 'bewitches' the regicides with her words, and neither the traditional components of malefic witchcraft nor magical treason are present in this account.

WITCHCRAFT AND TREASON

The colourful rhetoric of Civil War and Restoration pamphleteers was not matched by legal proceedings against people accused of using magic or witchcraft against the government. The 'Witchcraft Act' of 1604 was seldom if ever used, after the Restoration, to prosecute conjuration, and magic ceased to be of much interest to the authorities except as a form of fraud and a public nuisance. Because there was no tradition in England of regarding witches as capable of treason, the continuing prominence of witchcraft as the supernatural crime *par excellence* in no way guaranteed the survival of the idea of supernatural treason. Judicially speaking, witchcraft became a 'greedy concept' that, in a Protestant England drifting away from its Catholic inheritance, swallowed ritual magic. Accusations of treasonable magic or witchcraft, even when they did arise, were not taken seriously by the authorities because they were confined to the same class of people usually accused of witchcraft – the poor and marginalised. The later Stuart monarchs had no particular interest in treasonable sorcery. Confident in their divine right, as James I and Charles I had been, Charles II and James II never betrayed any personal fear of magic, although this did not prevent people trying to use it against them.

In 1660 Henry Townshend reported that the eldest daughter of a certain Widow Robinson, who had been brought from Kidderminster to Worcester to be tried for witchcraft, 'was said to say that if they had not been taken the King should never have come into England, and though he now doth come yet he shall not live long, but shall die as ill a death as they'.[20] These words are suggestive of the accused witches' republican sympathies, and seem to imply that Robinson and her daughter believed they had been working to prevent Charles's return in May 1660.

One of the very last recorded cases of witchcraft directed against the king and government was reported by Thomas Holden, writing from Falmouth to the Under-Secretary of State, Sir Joseph Williamson, on 27 February 1672. Holden reported that a woman had been apprehended at Looe in Cornwall 'for a witch':

> I am informed she has discovered that she was in the fleet when the Duke of York was at sea, and hindered the prosecution of that victory against the Dutch, and that she has been the cause of the Queen's barrenness and several other things, and that she caused the bull to kill Col[onel] Robinson, an MP and JP, because he prosecuted the Nonconformists, she being one herself ... She was discovered by cats dancing in the air, and by inviting one of her neighbours to the same craft. Some say she is maze [mad] and saith and confesseth anything, but letters that come thence say she hath several marks about her where the devil has sucked her.[21]

The naval engagement that Holden referred to was the battle of Sole Bay, an indecisive confrontation off the coast of Suffolk during the Third Anglo-Dutch War in which both sides claimed victory. Charles II's brother and heir apparent, James, duke of York, was in command of the fleet as Lord High Admiral during the battle and narrowly escaped death. The woman's confession recalls the traditional belief in witches' power to sink ships at sea, although here the witch's activity was overtly treasonable because she was hindering the Royal Navy. The reference to the inability of Charles II's queen, Catherine of Braganza to bear children recalls another contemporary source of anxiety – witches' ability to compromise fertility – and suggests that the witch of Looe thought she was trying to cut off the royal succession by plotting the defeat and death of the king's brother

James as well as ensuring the queen's childlessness. Holden's identification of the woman as a dissenter explains her interest in killing a magistrate, since at this period Charles II's government was still attempting to prosecute members of illegal conventicles who refused to worship in the parish church according to the Prayer Book and worshipped illegally elsewhere.

There is no record of the trial or indictment of the witch of Looe. It would seem that Holden's view that she was 'maze' prevailed, perhaps because the woman's claims were so wide-ranging and touched matters of state. Had she confessed to harming her neighbours' children and animals, it is far more likely that her story would have been believed; but for a poor old woman to make wild claims about sinking ships and harming the queen was proof of madness rather than witchcraft in Restoration England. Indeed, it is likely that the very fact that claims touching the state were added to accusations of otherwise parochial and ordinary witchcrafts contributed to her never coming to trial. The potential embarrassment of an investigation and public trial to the king and duke may have dissuaded magistrates from prosecuting the woman.

ENGLAND AND THE 'AFFAIR OF THE POISONS'

The idea of magical treason virtually disappeared in England in the second half of the seventeenth century, but on the other side of the English Channel, the late 1670s saw the eruption of what was perhaps the most notorious case of magical treason in history, the 'affair of the poisons' (1676–82) at the court of Louis XIV. What began as a police investigation into the sordid underworld of Parisian poisoners, abortionists and procurers of love potions soon turned into an investigation of plots to kill or manipulate the Sun King which even threatened to implicate his mistress, Madame de Montespan. As Gabriel de la Reynie, Louis XIV's superintendent of police, delved deeper he uncovered seemingly endless and labyrinthine depravities and treasons, and a special tribunal, the so-called 'Chambre Ardente', was set up to deal with the cases. Many confessions were obtained under the torture of forcing suspects to drink gallons of water. The scale of this French witch-hunt against magical traitors far exceeded anything in English history, and it is necessary to return to the sixteenth century for even partial comparisons (Lynn Wood Mollenauer, for instance, noted the similarity of an alleged plot to poison the king and the duchesse de Fontanges uncovered in 1680 with the poisoned saddle-pommel plot against Elizabeth in 1598).[22]

Perhaps inevitably, given the great significance of Charles II's relationship with France in the 1670s, English actors – and actors connected to England – became involved in French events. Olympe Mancini, comtesse de Soissons, whom Louis XIV allowed to slip away into exile in 1680 for the suspected poisoning of her husband, was the sister of Charles II's mistress Hortense Mancini (1646–99), herself a fugitive from an unwanted marriage. Both women were nieces of the former chief minister Cardinal Mazarin (1602–61), who had been accused of involvement in magic in 1649.[23] When Olympe was eventually offered refuge at the Spanish Court, it was by Charles's niece, Marie-Louise d'Orléans, the daughter of his youngest sister Henrietta Anne Stuart, duchess of Orléans.[24] Indeed, the late 'Henriette d'Angleterre' was herself named by one witness as having engaged the services of a priest to celebrate a sacrilegious mass against her husband the duke of Orléans, presumably in the late 1660s.[25]

England's envoy extraordinary to France, the Restoration libertine Sir Henry Savile (1642–87) was ambivalent in his attitude to the accusations, reporting back that '*le monde* is inclined to think that there is something considerable against [all the suspects], because they are such a quality that they would not be treated so severely without reliable witnesses against them'.[26] Savile did not make clear whether or not he agreed with *le monde* – and, as a foreign diplomat, it was not his place to do so. However, Savile was inclined to be contemptuous of French credulity, remarking on one occasion that 'all their crime comes down, one thinks, to certain practices with fortune tellers regarding amorous intrigues'.[27] So great was the gulf between French and English court culture – and between French and English attitudes to *veneficium* by this date – that Savile was uncomprehending of the events unfolding in Paris.

Many of those implicated in the affair of the poisons seem to have regarded England as a safe destination for escape. The comte de Cessac, implicated along with the comtesse de Soissons, fled there in 1680,[28] and two of the most notorious female poisoners, La Trianon and La Voisin, discussed escaping to England in July.[29] However, the English government was also prepared to extradite accused individuals on request; hence the marquise de Brinvilliers, who had taken refuge in England in 1675, was forced to flee to a convent at Liège in the Spanish Low Countries when Louis XIV asked Charles II to extradite her.[30] Perhaps partly because she had sought refuge in England, the marquise's activities were well-publicised there.[31] The affair of the poisons was more than just a treason panic, however, and concern about poison and harmful magic seems to have filtered down to all levels of society, with Savile reporting in April 1679 that 'the least accidents are now attributed to poison and vast numbers of people are quaking with fear over it'.[32]

The most overt involvement of an English actor in the affair of the poisons was the alleged complicity of an unnamed English nobleman in abominable rites intended to help Madame de Montespan retain the king's affections and influence the affairs of the kingdom. The shocking details emerged in the testimony of a sacrilegious priest, Etienne Guibourg, who was almoner to the Franco-Scottish nobleman François, comte de Montgomery (a descendent of the first captain of Francis I's Scots Guards), but was known as 'the Prior'.[33] In October 1680 Guibourg confessed to having been an associate of the infamous Parisian poisoner, fortune teller and abortionist Catherine Deshayes (known as La Voisin), for whom he regularly said black masses in order to hasten people's deaths. When 'put to the question' by De la Reynie, Guibourg claimed that he was approached by a court functionary named Leroy, governor of the pages of the Petite Ecurie (little stable), who asked him to say a series of three black masses for the intentions of Madame de Montespan. He said all three masses over the body of the same naked woman whose face remained concealed from him, and each mass involved the sacrifice of a small child who was offered to the devil before its heart and entrails were used to make powders for Madame de Montespan to use on the king.

Guibourg was hazy about when he had said these masses, claiming at different times that it was seven, eight, nine, ten, thirteen or fourteen years previously (so between 1666 and 1673). However, he also claimed that in 1675 he had said another mass at La Voisin's house in Paris over the same woman, 'Whom he had always been told was Madame de Montespan'. A child was sacrificed as usual and, when he put his coat down on a chair after mass, Guibourg discovered a pact:

> I..., daughter of... ask the love of the king and of the dauphin, and that it should be continued toward me; that the queen should be barren; that the king should leave her bed and her table for me and that I should obtain from him all that I should ask of him for me and for my parents; that my servants and domestics should be agreeable to him; dear to and respected by great lords, that I should be called to the counsels of the king and know what is happening; and, with this love redoubling more than in the past, that the king should leave and no more regard La Vallière and that, the queen being repudiated, I might marry the king.[34]

On one occasion in 1675 or 1677, the Prior claimed that the naked woman was accompanied by a young 'milord anglais' (English nobleman) who was the lover of Claude de Vin des Œillets and declared his intention to marry her. The Englishman handed the text of the pact to the naked woman.

> One day the woman Des Œillets, with a foreigner who was said to be English, arrived at La Voisin's home where Guibourg, having vested in an alb, put on a stole and maniple; he took some menstrual blood of Des Œillets and some semen of the foreigner in the chalice, some blood of an infant killed by La Voisin, some powders, some bat's blood, [and] some flour to give form to the mixture; Guibourg said a mass, beginning at the *Te igitur*,[35] which he called a 'dry mass',[36] to which he added a conjuration which included the name of the king.

> The intention was to effect a charm against the king; this accursed man [Guibourg] explained that it was to bring about the king's death. This intention was in common between Des Œillets and the nobleman. Des Œillets spoke with anger, made complaints against the king, and testified that she had left the home of Madame de Montespan; the Englishman soothed her. They intended to put the mixture on the clothes of the king, or where he walked, which Des Œillets pretended she could do easily, having been at court, and that this would make the king die of a wasting disease (*en langueur*). It was a charm according to the method of the book of La Voisin.[37]

Guibourg put the mixture from the chalice 'in a little vessel which Des Œillets or the man carried'.[38] Guibourg's evidence, given under torture, can scarcely be regarded as reliable, but the involvement of the 'milord anglais' was confirmed by the independent and willing testimony of Marie Marguerite Deshayes, the daughter of La Voisin who had turned king's evidence (albeit two of La Voisin's female associates, Delaporte and Pelletier, had already denied Guibourg's story completely). Marie Marguerite confirmed Madame de Montespan's presence at the black masses, which she claimed lasted from ten o'clock until midnight. She spoke of:

> ... that which was done by Guibourg with Des Œillets and the English nobleman, the filthy things in the chalice, the powders; everything was put in a tin box with a separate packet of powder which Guibourg gave to the English nobleman. He was to take Guibourg and La Voisin to England. Since the capture of her mother, a man had been sent to Paris with a letter; but she, the daughter of La Voisin, had not wanted to go to England. She saw Des Œillets and the nobleman at her home.[39]

Des Œillets promised her accomplices the enormous sum of 100,000 écus and that she would secure their passage to England, which suggested to Petitfils that the plot against Louis XIV might have been orchestrated from England. He noted the ubiquitous presence of the 'milord' at the sacrilegious masses:

> It seems that this individual was not a mere occasional participant, thrown by his mistress [Des Œillets] into an affair that did not concern him. He took part in the conjurations and really sought the death of the king by the intermediaries of La Voisin and Guibourg. Monvoisin's daughter saw him arrive three or four times with her mother in the company of Des Œillets around five o'clock in the evening. 'Why him, why this foreigner?' La Reynie asked himself with anguish on several occasions. The key to the mystery seems to have escaped him.[40]

Unfortunately, neither Guibourg's nor Marie Marguerite Deshayes's testimonies offered any clues as to the identity of this mysterious 'milord' who became implicated in magical treason against Louis XIV.[41] Petitfils noted the existence of a violently anti-Catholic party in England at the time opposed to Louis XIV and speculated that Des Œillets might have been 'an instrument manipulated by foreign interests'. There was indeed great hostility in England in the 1670s to the secret Treaty of Dover (1670) between Louis XIV and Charles II, but by 1675 England and France had withdrawn from their formal military alliance against the Dutch Republic. Some English soldiers were still serving as mercenaries in the French army, however, and a number of aristocratic English émigrés, most of them Catholics, had settled in France on account of their association with the courts of the dowager queen Henrietta Maria (1609–69) at Saint-Germain-en-Laye and her daughter the duchess of Orléans, Henrietta Anne Stuart (1644–70) at Saint-Cloud. English Catholics were also regular visitors to Paris, where institutions for the education of English Catholics, such as the Priory of St Edmund and the College of St Gregory, acted as a hub for a shifting expatriate community.

Petitfils's suggestion that the 'milord' might have represented English anti-Catholic interests seems unlikely, given the end of England's involvement in the Third Dutch War and the overtly Catholic and ritualistic nature of the sacrilegious rites in which the 'milord' participated. So deeply entrenched was the English Protestant tradition of contempt for Catholic rites that it is very hard to imagine an English Protestant – even the most atheistic libertine of the Restoration court – participating in perverted Catholic rites of this kind. There is no evidence of elite interest in ritual magic at the court of Charles II, and libertines tended towards contemptuous rationalism rather than the diabolism of French courtiers. Instead, the anonymous nobleman's apparent belief in the magical efficacy of sacrilegious masses – and his active involvement in them – suggest that he could have been an English Catholic. Furthermore, his behaviour is suggestive of someone long immersed in French court culture and religion, perhaps at Saint-Germain or Saint-Cloud. This speculation does not shed any light on the nobleman's motives – why would an English Catholic have wanted to kill Louis XIV? – but it is more likely than Petitfils's suggestion of an English Protestant plot.

TREASON WITHOUT MAGIC: THE POPISH PLOT

Against the background of the extensive nature of the allegations of treasonous magic in France during the same period, and at a time when Charles II's court often took the lead of the French court, it is striking that accusations of magical treason did not surface during the

Popish Plot scare of 1678–80. England's treason panic began as a murder investigation into the mysterious death of a London magistrate, Sir Edmund Berry Godfrey. An ex-Catholic turned Protestant preacher, Titus Oates, managed to convince the Privy Council that Sir Edmund's death was part of a vast Catholic plot aimed at killing the king. Oates's accusations should be viewed in the context of Parliament's failed attempts earlier in the 1670s to exclude Charles's Catholic brother James from the throne, and it seems likely that James was Oates's ultimate target. However, in spite of Oates's penchant for the most lurid allegations against his victims, neither magic nor witchcraft made any appearance in the story of the Popish Plot. The decision of this most creative of perjurers to avoid insinuations of magic and witchcraft is a strong indicator that treason was by this time almost completely disentangled from magic, even when it came to poisoning. Allegations of poisoning did surface – directed against Sir George Wakeman, but without any of the occult connotations of *veneficium* that had accompanied conspiracy theories surrounding the death of James I.[42] This was in stark contrast to France, where Catherine Belleau's admission to De la Reynie on 27 May 1679 that she had obtained the technique of aborting foetuses with a special syringe from an English physician was treated as evidence of her involvement in occult *veneficium*.[43]

A comparison of the affair of the poisons with the Popish Plot reveals vast cultural differences between the courts of Louis XIV and Charles II, between Catholic Paris and Protestant London. Baroque Catholic piety (even in the form of perverted piety) prevailed in France against the kingdom's increasingly marginalised Huguenot Protestants, whereas in England the Catholic ideas of sacred power that underpinned ritual magic had been weakening, slowly but surely, ever since the abolition of the mass in 1559. The rural laity continued to cling to 'sub-Catholic' beliefs, such as an abiding belief that only a Catholic priest could perform an effective exorcism,[44] but the educated elite with the skills and knowledge to perform diabolical ritual magic showed little interest in such matters. In France, the accused traitors in the affair of the poisons hired disreputable priests to say sacrilegious masses or pass poisonous powders under the chalice during mass. In doing so, they exploited the specifically

Catholic theological belief that the priest's ordination and the words of the mass made his consecration of the elements automatically effective (*ex opere operato*). Priesthood was exploited by French magicians as an illicit conduit of divine power. Even when Louis XIV decriminalised witchcraft in 1682, the edict still referred to those who were 'convicted of poisoning by magical or natural means'.[45]

Although belief in the sacred power of Catholic priests lingered in some parts of England until the late seventeenth century in the form of ongoing demand for Catholic exorcisms,[46] it seems unlikely that the idea of ritual magic abusing the rites of the church would have occurred to educated English people in the 1670s, and certainly not to the ordained clergy of the Church of England, whose plain liturgy was enshrined in the Book of Common Prayer. Furthermore, English Catholics were hypersensitive to Protestant accusations of superstition directed against them,[47] downplaying practices that might be construed as magical,[48] and in the reign of James I anti-Catholic rhetoric had taken a decisive turn away from portraying Catholics as magicians and witches and instead portrayed them as fakers of supernatural phenomena.[49] To have accused Catholics of working magic or occult *veneficium* against Charles II would have been to unravel the longstanding anti-Catholic narrative that Catholic priests falsely pretended to be in possession of spiritual authority and sacramental power, and any such accusation would have been counterproductive to the anti-Catholic cause. Allegations of poisoning continued to be made against Catholics even after the Popish Plot scare; Gilbert Burnet, bishop of Salisbury, was convinced that Catholics had poisoned Charles II when he died in 1685 (in spite of the fact that Charles converted to Catholicism on his deathbed),[50] but Gilbert's imaginings contained no hint of magic or witchcraft.

MAGIC AND POLITICS PART COMPANY

Perhaps the last hint of an attempt to make use of magic in a treasonous enterprise in English history is to be found in a letter from Christopher Croft to Charles Bull of 18 July 1685, noting that after the execution of the duke of Monmouth for high treason his body was searched, and 'in his pocket was a manuscript of spells, charms and conjurations, songs, receipts, and prayers, all written with his own hand'.[51] Monmouth was the eldest illegitimate son of Charles II who, after the accession of Charles's Catholic brother James in 1685, invaded the West Country under a banner of Protestant rebellion, claiming that Charles had secretly been married to his mother and therefore he was the true king. Monmouth was defeated by government forces at the battle of Sedgemoor. His book of spells recalls both the magical pouch carried by the rebel 'Captain Pouch' in 1607 and the mysterious book found on the body of the earl of Gowrie in 1600. Whether Monmouth's 'conjurations' were intended to help overthrow James II, or were just charms to protect Monmouth in battle, prevent his execution or give himself a painless death, we can never know. However, there was a long tradition of soldiers carrying charms into battle and convicted felons bringing charms to the scaffold. The discovery was cause for ridicule rather than alarm from James's advisers, and further discredited the young upstart duke.

In the 1690s England, under the joint monarchy of William of Orange and Mary II, was again at war with France, and one of the principal commanders on the French side was the duc de Luxembourg, Marshal of France, who had briefly been implicated in the affair of the poisons in 1680.[52] The tradition of the English suspecting enemies of using magic against them in war went back to the accusations made against Joan of Arc in the fifteenth century (resurfacing in Parliamentarian attacks on Prince Rupert), and Luxembourg's involvement was exploited by a Catholic Jacobite propagandist to mock Protestant credulity (the Jacobites were the supporters of the James II, by then an exile in France). In 1695 the Catholic priest John Sergeant published a pamphlet entitled *A Letter from a Trooper in Flanders to his Comrade shewing that Luxemburg is a Witch, and deals with the Devil*, a mock missive whose true intention was to satirise English military blunders by recasting them all as setbacks caused by the devil.[53] It is by no means unlikely that Luxembourg's involvement in the poisons scandal meant that some English soldiers really did suspect him of witchcraft, and Sergeant seems to have been trading on this reputation. In another satire of 1694, Sergeant had William summon a comic witch who sent out spirits of rebellion, falsehood, folly and ingratitude to depose James II.[54]

The power of the biblical analogy, 'For rebellion is as the sin of witchcraft', remained undiminished – but no-one reading Sergeant's satire could possibly have believed he was really accusing William of Orange of being in league with dark powers.

ECHOES

In the early eighteenth century, most educated people in England stopped believing in witchcraft, at least publicly. The reasons behind this loss of belief are much disputed by scholars; available explanations include the idea that a mechanical, Newtonian conception of the universe made supernatural power irrelevant, increasing judicial dissatisfaction with the quality of evidence for witchcraft (making it impossible to prove witchcraft to a jury's satisfaction), reluctance to torture suspects (meaning that outlandish confessions could no longer be obtained), and growing willingness to attribute 'witchcraft' and its effects to mental illness.[55] In 1735 the 1604 'Witchcraft Act' was repealed and replaced by a new law that made it illegal to pretend to possess magical powers. Henceforth the law would not punish witches, but rather pretension to supernatural powers. Yet in spite of elite attitudes, belief in witchcraft remained commonplace in rural society, as well as the idea that witches might be in league with the enemies of the state. In 1751 a woman called Ruth Osborne, who died as a result of being 'swum' as a witch by a mob, was supposed to have spoken words in support of the Jacobite claimant to the thrones of England, Scotland and Ireland, Prince Charles Edward Stuart.[56]

Horace Walpole, the creator of the Gothic novel, was fascinated by magic and owned John Dee's obsidian scrying stone. He was also fascinated by treason in his own family: in the room next to his bedchamber at Strawberry Hill, his mock-gothic house at Twickenham, he kept 'the portrait of Henry Walpole the Jesuit, who was executed for attempting to poison queen Elizabeth'. Walpole reported that 'This picture came from Mr. Walpole's of Lincolnshire, the last of the Roman catholic branch of the family, who died about the year 1748'.[57] The notion that Henry Walpole tried to poison Elizabeth probably resulted from a confusion of the martyr with

Richard Walpole, one of the men who tried to poison Elizabeth's saddle pommel and kill the queen by *veneficium* in 1598. The proximity of this emblematic 'traitor' and 'poisoner' to the very room in which Walpole dreamt up his dark tale of dynastic doom, *The Castle of Otranto* (1764), is suggestive of an interest on Walpole's part in the imaginative possibilities of treason, and Henry Walpole – albeit undeservedly – joined the collection of gothic artefacts that fired Horace Walpole's imagination.

The demise of magical treason as a serious threat to monarchs did not mean that they were despised any less intensely by their enemies. Lady Charlotte Bury (née Campbell) claimed in 1814 that the unloved wife of the Prince Regent, Caroline of Brunswick, used to practise effigy magic against the prince as an after-dinner pastime:

> After dinner, her Royal Highness made a wax figure as usual, and gave it an amiable addition of large horns; then took three pins out of her garment, and stuck them through and through, and put the figure to roast and melt at the fire ... Lady — says the Princess indulges in this amusement whenever there are no strangers at table; and thinks her Royal Highness really has a superstitious belief that destroying this *effigy* of her husband will bring to pass the destruction of his royal person.[58]

That Caroline really believed that she could harm her husband by magic is doubtful, but magical acts against the powerful had always served a subsidiary purpose as a psychological relief for the powerless; the princess may simply have been channelling her rage and hatred in ritual form, even if unaccompanied by a literal belief in the agency of the ritual. The rise of Romanticism produced a revival of interest in and curiosity about magic, including the publication of Francis Barrett's latter-day grimoire *The Magus* (1801). Barrett distinguished witchcraft from 'Sorceries', which he regarded as 'those which kill only by poison, inasmuch as every common apothecary can imitate these things'. Witchcraft, in Barrett's view, was intimately tied to effigy magic, since a witch was primarily someone 'who can strongly torment an absent man by an image of wax'. Barrett insisted that witches were able to kill by this method, although he rejected the idea that Satan was responsible and argued that 'some other power, far superior to a corporeal attempt, yet natural to man' was responsible.[59] Barrett's argument that a witch harmed by sending out her 'vital spirit' echoed the Neoplatonic vitalism of the Renaissance, but also (and perhaps more immediately) the 'animal magnetism' of Franz Anton Mesmer (1734–1815); indeed, Barrett's observations on witchcraft formed part of a treatise on 'magnetism'. His grimoire was a strange mixture of the old and the decidedly new. Nevertheless, the apparent belief of Caroline of Brunswick and Francis Barrett in the effectiveness of effigy magic was exceptional and eccentric.

When the journalist William Godwin (1756–1836) published a collection of colourful anecdotes about magicians, *Lives of the Necromancers* (1834), he felt it necessary to include a digression on the law of treason,[60] since he believed that the terms 'compassing and imagining' referred directly to harmful witchcraft:

> ... the force and propriety of these terms [compassing and imagining] will strikingly appear, if we refer them to the popular ideas of witchcraft. Witches were understood to have the power of destroying life, without the necessity of approaching the person whose life was to be destroyed, or producing any consciousness in him of the crime about to be perpetrated. One method was by exposing an image of wax to the action of fire; while, in proportion as the image wasted away, the life of the individual who was the object contrived against, was undermined and destroyed. Another was by incantations and spells. Either of these might fitly be called 'compassing or imagining the death.'

Godwin argued that 'language which properly describes the secret practices of such persons, and is not appropriate to any other, ... insinuate[d] itself into the structure of the most solemn act of our legislature, that act which beyond all others was intended to narrow or shut out the subtle and dangerous inroads of arbitrary power!'[61] Although there is no direct evidence to show that the Statute of Treason was framed with the specific intention of incriminating magicians, Godwin's early analysis was essentially correct: the Statute of Treason was indeed framed in such a way that it made punishment of magical treason possible. However, Godwin's belief that the purpose of the Statute was to restrict arbitrary power shows how far he was from understanding the application of the law of treason in the medieval and Tudor eras.

The last person to be tried under the 1735 Witchcraft Act (often erroneously and misleadingly described as the last person tried for witchcraft) was put on trial because she was considered a potential threat to the state. The 1735 act made it illegal to pretend to supernatural powers, and in 1944 Helen Duncan was sentenced to nine months' imprisonment because her activities as a Spiritualist medium were thought to have revealed secrets about movements of British forces in World War Two.[62] For the authorities, Duncan was an 'inadvertent traitor', and prosecuting her for fraudulently claiming powers was simply the easiest way to silence her. In 1951 the 1735 act was finally repealed, meaning that it was no longer illegal to lay claim to any kind of supernatural powers; it was simply illegal to charge people money for spiritual services like mediumship.

The repeal of the 1735 act saw the appearance of individuals who openly defined themselves as witches, most notably the 'Bricket Wood coven' led by Gerald Gardner, the founder of the modern religion of Wicca, whose book *Witchcraft Today* (1954) built on ideas first developed by the Egyptologist Margaret Murray. Murray's book *The Witch Cult in Western Europe* (1921) argued that accused witches were members of a secret Neolithic fertility cult surviving into the early modern period. Gardner went a step further, and claimed that the witch-cult still existed in the twentieth century and that he had been initiated into it. In the 1950s Murray became preoccupied with the idea that leading members of society, including kings, had continued to practise 'the Old Religion' (witchcraft) alongside Christianity.[63] She argued that the origin of the seventeenth-century idea of the 'divine right of kings' lay in a 'royal coven' that existed in medieval England; it 'consisted of the king and his councillors, the king being regarded as the God Incarnate'.[64]

Because the king was also 'grandmaster of all the covens', the stability of his rule depended on the Old Religion, which demanded regular sacrifices disguised as judicial executions. At times, however, the king's own life was demanded as a voluntary sacrifice, and Murray attempted to argue, by a tortuous interpretation of English history, that every king who died violently from William Rufus to Charles I

The Decline of Magic as a Political Crime, 1642–1700 201

had in fact been sacrificed as part of the ritual demands of a coven of the 'Old Religion'. Murray's eccentric thesis completely contradicted Kittredge and Ewen's insistence that early modern English witches did not involve themselves in issues of national politics; she was claiming, in effect, that every successful act of treason had been an act of witchcraft. Yet unlike Kittredge and Ewen, Murray supported her claims with deeply contentious interpretations of existing historical evidence rather than detailed and comprehensive research into witchcraft trials. Murray's ideas were, in fact, little more than a detailed application to English history of the concept of royal sacrifice central to Sir James Frazer's immensely influential book *The Golden Bough*. Even in Murray's lifetime, however, her theories about English history were not taken particularly seriously – particularly her belief in the ritual killing of kings – even if scholars continued to accept her account of witchcraft as a surviving fertility religion into the 1970s.

In the 1960s and 1970s rumours circulated that a coven established to continue the magical work of the controversial pioneer of pagan witchcraft Robert Cochrane (1931–66), known as 'the Regency', had attracted attention from the security services. According to the apocryphal story – which cannot be authenticated – MI5 officers paid a visit to coven members because they were concerned that the claims of one of the witches, Ronald White, implied a potential threat to the monarchy. White claimed that he 'was to take the role of merlin … as a kingmaker and restore Arthur'.[65] This story, reminiscent of Thomas Hammond's claim in 1639 that he could take away the king's power by magic, may not be true, but the evidence presented by Tanya Luhrmann in her study of London witches and ritual magicians in the 1980s sets Ronald White's claims in their ritual and magical context. The groups described by Luhrmann took on the roles of historical figures (such as Merlin, Arthur, Sir Francis Drake, Queen Elizabeth and John Dee) in elaborate ritual tableaux, allowing themselves to be 'possessed' by these characters.[66] It is conceivable that over-zealous members of the security services misinterpreted such rituals, especially in the politically unstable and spiritually turbulent 1970s. In 1976 the leading Anglican exorcist Robert Petitpierre warned that:

The dangers inherent in these coven ... is not widely enough recognised. They constitute a very dangerous element in our social life because of this wish to impose their views and ideas ... [S]uch influences could be directed into social and political fields with incalculable consequences. I have been told that certain groups, indeed, are already carrying out experiments to see if they can influence political life.[67]

Such concerns may have been misplaced, however, if (as Ronald Hutton has argued), followers of modern pagan witchcraft were more likely to hold conservative rather than radical political views.[68]

CONCLUSION

It has been the argument of this book that, in the Middle Ages and the sixteenth century (and possibly beyond) magic was thoroughly intertwined with political crimes such as treason, sedition and *lèse majesté*. It is not enough merely to note that some would-be traitors expressed their dissatisfaction with the government through magic. Medieval and early modern conceptions of treason as imagining the death of the monarch, combined with the tendency to regard an attack on the monarch's image as an attack on his or her person, meant that directing harmful thoughts towards the monarch by means of a ritual abusing the monarch's image was high treason in its purest form. So deep was a traitor's hatred for the monarch, and so deep was a traitor's evil in the imaginations of justices and royal counsellors, that magical acts seemed to them the logical precursor to physical rebellion – for, after all, 'Rebellion is as the sin of witchcraft' (1 Samuel 15:23).

Traitors were, by definition, cowards in the minds of their accusers, and therefore they could be expected to use any means to harm that were occult, remote and involved the least exposure of themselves to physical danger. Not only that, but evidence of involvement in supernatural thought-crime was easily fabricated, shocking to the public, scandalising to the church, and served instantly to discredit and taint a person in a highly religious society. It is small wonder that allegations of magical involvement were so often part of cases of 'constructive treason'. Treason in the Middle Ages and early modern period cannot be properly understood without an acknowledgement of its intimate connection with supernatural crimes, especially poisoning (*veneficium*), which in England still implied magical knowledge as late as the 1620s.

The diminishing role of magic in allegations of political crime can be assigned partly to political causes; Charles I's unpopularity cast accusations of witchcraft back against the monarchy's defenders rather than its opponents, while Charles's execution and the chaos of the Civil Wars weakened the perceived sacrality of kingship. The causes were also religious; elite ritual magic directed against monarchs was an inheritance of the Middle Ages that gradually lost its relevance amongst educated people in a Protestant culture. Witchcraft, rather than elite magic, came to dominate the post-Reformation imagination, with accusations of witchcraft eventually subsuming many different supernatural crimes (a tendency only assisted by the catch-all nature of the 1604 'Witchcraft Act'). The dominance of witchcraft contributed to the declining connection between magic and crimes against the state, since England (unlike Scotland) had no tradition of political witchcraft. The rise of Enlightenment scepticism concerning both magic and witchcraft was the final nail in the coffin for accusations of magic as a political crime in England.

The lasting legacy of the intertwined relationship between treason and magic is to be found in the language, loaded with connotations of supernatural power, that we still use today to describe politics and politicians. Unscrupulous or secretive politicians are said to have mastered 'the dark arts'. The Conservative leader Michael Howard was said to have 'something of the night' about him, and the British press regularly portrayed Labour politician Peter Mandelson in the 1990s and 2000s as 'the Prince of Darkness', a sinister and manipulative, almost witch-like figure. Similarly, the death of Margaret Thatcher in 2013, renowned for her almost hypnotic control of her party and cabinet, was greeted with mass downloads of the song 'Ding dong! The witch is dead'. Calling a female politician a witch may be no more than a colourful expression of unpopularity, but it also captures the secretive, obscure and almost occult character of high politics. Yet it may be too early to write off attempts at actual magical operations against political leaders just yet. In February 2017 it was widely reported that American followers of Wicca were trying to 'bind' President Donald Trump by burning an orange candle supposed to represent the president, in a ritual somewhat reminiscent of medieval and early modern precedents.[69] It would seem that the history of magic as a political instrument in the western world is not quite over.

Notes

INTRODUCTION

1. G. de la Bédoyere, *Gods with Thunderbolts: Religion in Roman Britain* (Stroud: Tempus, 2007), pp. 77–9.
2. C. Larner, *Witchcraft and Religion: The Politics of Popular Belief* (Oxford: Blackwell, 1984), pp. 10, 69–78.
3. P. G. Maxwell-Stuart, *The British Witch: The Biography* (Stroud: Amberley, 2014), p. 37.
4. C. L. Ewen, *Witchcraft and Demonianism* (London: Heath Cranton, 1933), p. 70.
5. Ibid. p. 302.
6. K. Thomas, *Religion and the Decline of Magic*, 4th edn (London: Penguin, 1991), pp. 276–7, 612–13.
7. W. R. Jones, 'Political Uses of Sorcery in Medieval Europe', *The Historian* 34 (1972), pp. 670–87; H. A. Kelly, 'English Kings and the Fear of Sorcery', *Mediaeval Studies* 39 (1977), pp. 206–38; J. K. Van Patten, 'Magic, Prophecy, and the Law of Treason in Reformation England', *The American Journal of Legal History* 27 (1983), pp. 1–32.
8. R. A. Griffiths, 'The Trial of Eleanor Cobham: an episode in the fall of Duke Humphrey of Gloucester', in R. A. Griffiths (ed.), *King and Country: England and Wales in the Fifteenth Century* (London: Hambledon, 1991), pp. 233–52; J. Freeman, 'Sorcery at court and manor: Margery Jourdemayne, the witch of Eye next Westminster', *Journal of Medieval History* 30 (2004), pp. 343–57.
9. J. Leland, 'Witchcraft and the Woodvilles: a standard medieval smear?' in D. L. Biggs, S. D. Michalove and A. Compton Reeves (eds), *Reputation and Representation in Fifteenth-Century Europe* (Brill: Leiden, 2004), pp. 267–88.
10. R. M. Warnicke, 'Sexual Heresy at the Court of Henry VIII', *The Historical Journal* 30 (1987), pp. 247–68; R. M. Warnicke, *The Rise and Fall of Anne*

Boleyn: Family Politics at the Court of Henry VIII, 3rd edn (Cambridge: Cambridge University Press, 1991); R. M. Warnicke, *The Marrying of Anne of Cleves: Royal Protocol in Tudor England* (Cambridge: Cambridge University Press, 2000).
11. Kelly (1977), pp. 235–8.
12. L. Baldwin Smith, *Treason in Tudor England*, 2nd edn (London: Pimlico, 2006), pp. 59–66.
13. Ibid. pp. 36–40.
14. D. Cressy, *Dangerous Talk: Scandalous, Seditious and Treasonable Speech in Pre-Modern England* (Oxford: Oxford University Press, 2010).
15. N. Jones, 'Defining Superstitions: Treasonous Catholics and the Act against Witchcraft of 1563', in C. Carlton (ed.), *State, Sovereigns and Society in Early Modern England: Essays in Honour of A. J. Slavin* (Stroud: Sutton, 1998), pp. 187–204; M. Devine, 'Treasonous Catholic Magic and the 1563 Witchcraft Legislation: The English State's Response to Catholic Conjuring in the Early Years of Elizabeth I's Reign' in M. Harmes and V. Bladen (eds), *Supernatural and Secular Power in Early Modern England* (Farnham: Ashgate, 2015), pp. 67–94.
16. D. Underdown, *A Freeborn People: Politics and the Nation in Seventeenth-Century England* (Oxford: Oxford University Press, 1996), pp. 34–5; N. Johnstone, *The Devil and Demonism in Early Modern England* (Cambridge: Cambridge University Press, 2006), p. 197.
17. A. Bellany and T. Cogswell, *The Murder of King James I* (New Haven, CT: Yale University Press, 2015), pp. 185–6.
18. B. Copenhaver, *Magic in Western Culture: From Antiquity to the Enlightenment* (Cambridge: Cambridge University Press, 2015), p. 18.
19. R. Kieckhefer, *Forbidden Rites: A Necromancer's Manual of the Fifteenth Century* (Stroud: Sutton, 1997); R. Kieckhefer, *Magic in the Middle Ages*, 2nd edn (Cambridge: Cambridge University Press, 2000); F. Klaassen, 'English Manuscripts of Magic, 1300–1500: A Preliminary Survey' in C. Fanger (ed.), *Conjuring Spirits: Texts and Traditions of Medieval Ritual Magic* (Stroud: Sutton, 1998), pp. 3–31; F. Klaassen, 'Medieval Ritual Magic in the Renaissance', *Aries* 3 (2003), pp. 166–99; F. Klaassen, 'Learning and Masculinity in Manuscripts of Ritual Magic of the Later Middle Ages and Renaissance', *Sixteenth Century Journal* 38 (2007), pp. 49–76; F. Klaassen, 'Ritual Invocation and Early Modern Science: The Skrying Experiments of Humphrey Gilbert' in C. Fanger (ed.) *Invoking Angels: Theurgic Ideas and Practices, Thirteenth to Sixteenth Centuries* (University Park, PA: Pennsylvania State University Press, 2010), pp. 341–66; F. Klaassen, *The Transformations of Magic: Illicit Learned Magic in the Later Middle Ages and Renaissance* (University Park, PA: Pennsylvania State University Press, 2013); O. Davies, *Grimoires: A History of Magic Books* (Oxford University Press: Oxford, 2009).
20. R. Merrifield, *The Archaeology of Ritual and Magic* (London: Batsford, 1987), p. 36. The meaning of the term 'supernatural', which originally referred to divine agency, has evolved to encompass the occult and preternatural.

21. Klaassen (2013), pp. 81–156.
22. D. J. Collins, 'Introduction' in D. J. Collins (ed.), *The Cambridge History of Magic and Witchcraft in the West: From Antiquity to the Present* (Cambridge: Cambridge University Press, 2015), pp. 1–14, at p. 6.
23. E. E. Evans-Pritchard, *Witchcraft, Magic and Oracles among the Azande* (Oxford: Clarendon Press, 1937), pp. 8–11.
24. Copenhaver (2015), p. 439.
25. Collins (2015), p. 6.
26. B. Malinowski, 'Magic, Science and Religion' in B. Malinowski, *Magic, Science and Religion and Other Essays* (Glencoe, IL: Free Press, 1948), pp. 1–71.
27. For a discussion of this debate see H. Parish, 'Magic and Priestcraft: Reformers and Reformation' in D. J. Collins (ed.), *The Cambridge History of Magic and Witchcraft in the West: From Antiquity to the Present* (Cambridge: Cambridge University Press, 2015), pp. 393–425, at pp. 410–11.
28. S. Clark, *Thinking with Demons: The Idea of Witchcraft in Early Modern Europe* (Oxford: Clarendon, 1997), p. 552.
29. Parish (2015), pp. 393–425.
30. Kieckhefer (2000), p. 56.
31. C. Rider, 'Common Magic' in D. J. Collins (ed.), *The Cambridge History of Magic and Witchcraft in the West: From Antiquity to the Present* (Cambridge: Cambridge University Press, 2015), pp. 303–31, at p. 303.
32. D. J. Collins, 'Learned Magic' in D. J. Collins (ed.), *The Cambridge History of Magic and Witchcraft in the West: From Antiquity to the Present* (Cambridge: Cambridge University Press, 2015), pp. 332–60, at p. 333.
33. On poisoning as magic, see D. Paton, 'Witchcraft, Poison, Law, and Atlantic Slavery', *William and Mary Quarterly* 69 (2012), pp. 235–64, at pp. 239–43.
34. O. Davies, 'Magic in Common and Legal Perspectives' in D. J. Collins (ed.), *The Cambridge History of Magic and Witchcraft in the West: From Antiquity to the Present* (Cambridge: Cambridge University Press, 2015), pp. 521–46, at pp. 528–9.
35. Maxwell-Stuart (2014), pp. 13–14.
36. On magic in contemporary British society see V. K. Srivastava, 'Ethnographic Notebook: Modern Witchcraft and Occultism in Cambridge', *The Cambridge Journal of Anthropology* 13 (1988), pp. 50–71; T. Luhrmann, *Persuasions of the Witch's Craft: Ritual Magic in Contemporary England* (Oxford: Blackwell, 1989); R. Hutton, *The Triumph of the Moon: A History of Modern Pagan Witchcraft* (Oxford: Oxford University Press, 1999).
37. Collins (2015), p. 348.
38. M. D. Bailey, 'Diabolic Magic' in D. J. Collins (ed.), *The Cambridge History of Magic and Witchcraft in the West: From Antiquity to the Present* (Cambridge: Cambridge University Press, 2015), pp. 361–92, at p. 371.

39. Hutton (1999), pp. 98–100.
40. G. Bailey and J. Peoples, *Essentials of Cultural Anthropology*, 3rd edn (Stamford, CT: Wadsworth, 2013), pp. 265–6.
41. M. Gaskill, *Witchfinders: A Seventeenth-Century Tragedy* (London: John Murray, 2005), pp. 138–43.
42. O. Davies, *Popular Magic: Cunning-folk in English History*, 2nd edn (London: Continuum, 2007), pp. 29–65.
43. Maxwell-Stuart (2014), pp. 40, 58.
44. C.-R. Millar, 'Sleeping with Devils: The Sexual Witch in Seventeenth-century England' in M. Harmes and V. Bladen (eds), *Supernatural and Secular Power in Early Modern England* (Farnham: Ashgate, 2015), pp. 207–31.
45. Ibid. p. 211n.
46. *The Lawes against Witches and Conjuration* (London, 1645), pp. 6–7.
47. Ibid. p. 7.
48. W. Hawkins, *A Treatise of the Pleas of the Crown* (London, 1716), p. 5. The last witchcraft trial in England took place in 1717.
49. Davies (2007), pp. 70–1. On the meanings of the word 'witchcraft' see A. MacFarlane, *Witchcraft in Tudor and Stuart England: A Regional and Comparative Study* (London: Routledge and Kegan Paul, 1970), pp. 3–4.
50. 'Witches' in the fifteenth-century Peterborough Lapidary, for example, seem to be ill-intentioned people who are skilful in using the magical properties of stones; see F. Young (ed.), *A Medieval Book of Magical Stones: The Peterborough Lapidary* (Cambridge: Texts in Early Modern Magic, 2016a), p. xxxvii.
51. Cambridge University Library, MS EDR (Ely Diocesan Records) B/2/5. For a summary of the case see A. Gibbons (ed.), *Ely Episcopal Records: A Calendar and Concise View of the Episcopal Records Preserved in the Muniment Room of the Palace at Ely* (Lincoln: J. Williamson, 1891), p. 37.
52. Davies (2009), pp. 61–7.
53. Gaskill (2005), pp. 219–28.
54. R. Hutton, *The Pagan Religions of the Ancient British Isles: Their Nature and Legacy*, 2nd edn (Oxford: Blackwell, 1993), p. 291.
55. F. Heal, *Reformation in Britain and Ireland* (Oxford: Oxford University Press, 2003), pp. 101–2.
56. See F. Young, *A History of Exorcism in Catholic Christianity* (London: Palgrave MacMillan, 2016), pp. 16–19.
57. S. Page, *Magic in the Cloister: Pious Motives, Illicit Interests, and Occult Approaches to the Medieval Universe* (University Park, PA: Pennsylvania State University Press, 2013), pp. 49–72.
58. Davies (2009), pp. 25–6.
59. Kieckhefer (2000), p. 158.

CHAPTER 1 'COMPASSING AND IMAGINING': MAGIC AS A POLITICAL CRIME IN MEDIEVAL ENGLAND

1. For this argument see A. Boureau (trans. T. L. Fagan), *Satan the Heretic: The Birth of Demonology in the Medieval West* (Chicago, IL: University of Chicago Press, 2006), pp. 22–7; R. Kieckhefer, *European Witch Trials: Their Foundation in Popular and Learned Culture, 1300–1500* (Berkeley, CA: University of California Press, 1976), pp. 12–13; F. Chave-Mahir, *L'Exorcisme des Possédés dans l'Eglise d'Occident (Xe–XIVe siècle)* (Turnhout: Brepols, 2011), pp. 322–3; Maxwell-Stuart (2014), pp. 40–2; Young (2016), p. 66.
2. William was supposed to have declared that he put no faith in sorcery after his armour was put on back-to-front (a bad omen) before the Battle of Hastings (Kittredge (1928), p. 41).
3. *Gesta Herwardi incliti exulis et militis* in Geoffroy Gaimar, *Lestorie des Engles*, ed. T. D. Hardy and C. T. Martin (London: HMSO, 1888), vol. 1, p. 389: *Qua ascensa contra insulam et habitatores ejus diu sermocinata est, plurimas destructiones, similitudines, et figmenta subversionis faciens.*
4. *Liber Eliensis*, ed. E. O. Blake, Camden Third Series 92 (London: Royal Historical Society, 1962), p. 186: *Predicta quoque illa venefica super cunctos in loco eminentiore, ut liberius suis incantationibus vacaret, constituta, a timore velud a turbine percussa, de alto lapsum dedit. Sicque fracta cervice prior hec, que ad aliorum internicionem venerat, exanimata interiit.*
5. Parish (2015), pp. 401–2.
6. Ewen (1933), p. 27.
7. In 1320 a commission convened by Pope John XXII concluded that magic was heresy, but John's decree condemning magic, *Super illius specula* (1326) was not promulgated for fifty years in Europe and seems to have had little or no impact in England (Bailey (2015), p. 368).
8. H. S. Cronin, 'The Twelve Conclusions of the Lollards', *English Historical Review* 22 (1907), pp. 292–304, at p. 298.
9. Cambridge University Library, MS EDR (Ely Diocesan Records) G/I/5, fols 133r–v: *... ex causa vehementi suspicione heres[ie] & artis nigromantis.*
10. Ibid. fol. 133v: *superstitiosa sapientia idolatriam, et ex consequentia hereticam pravitatem.*
11. Kelly (1977), pp. 210–11.
12. Ewen (1933), p. 38.
13. H. A. Kelly, 'Canon Law and Chaucer on Licit and Illicit Magic', in R. M. Karras, J. Kaye and E. A. Matter (eds), *Law and the Illicit in Medieval Europe* (Philadelphia, PA: University of Pennsylvania Press, 2008), pp. 210–21, at p. 219.
14. Ibid. p. 210.
15. Quoted in Maxwell-Stuart (2014), p. 38.
16. Ibid. p. 41.

210   *Notes to Pages 27–32*

17. The thirteenth-century *Key of Solomon* advised that 'old and deserted houses, whither rarely and scarce ever men do come' were suitable for magical operations (E. M. Butler, *Ritual Magic* (Cambridge: Cambridge University Press, 1949), p. 52).
18. Kittredge (1928), p. 29.
19. D. Whitelock (ed.), *English Historical Documents, c. 500–1042* (London: Eyre and Spottiswoode, 1953), p. 519.
20. C. Hough, *'An Ald Reht': Essays on Anglo-Saxon Law* (Newcastle-upon-Tyne: Cambridge Scholars Publishing, 2014), p. 98; On this case see also A. Davies, 'Witches in Anglo-Saxon England: Five Case Histories' in D. G. Scragg (ed.), *Superstition and Popular Medicine in Anglo-Saxon England* (Manchester: Manchester University Press, 1989), pp. 41–56, at pp. 49–51.
21. BL MS Sloane 312 fols 136r–148v. On this and the other manuscripts of astrological magic in the British Library, see L. E. Voigts, 'The "Sloane Group": Related Scientific and Medical Manuscripts from the Fifteenth Century in the Sloane Collection', *British Library Journal* 16 (1990), pp. 26–57.
22. BL MS Sloane 312, fols 147r–148v: *Fac Imaginem Scorpionis ascendente Scorpione; luna sit idem [sub] infortunato domino et ... aspectu malevolenti. Inserabantur hoc nomina ascendenti & nomen lune. Quam id bonus quod inserebit, pone in antorso; idem malis in dorso. Sepeli Imaginem ipsum in medio loci loco ... & sepulta Scorpione ut recedat a loco isto & non redeat.*
23. Ibid.: *Ffortune caput in quo fundis Imaginem sculpe, sole ascendente, in quo sit caput domine ... sic boni esse corpus, sole ascendente, in quo sit luna accuta luna instantia fortune. Spatula & pectore sole ascendente in quo sit Inprime ventrem sole ascendente in quo sit venus [sol deleted] antefatus sol ascendente in quo sit sol. In aquam dimitte sua sine remora sole ascendente in quo sit iniuria nec retracta nec abstrahe sed in aquam dimitte. Sua pedes, sole ascendente, in quo sit luna veni foccata. Completa est.*
24. Kieckhefer (1997), p. 75.
25. A Norman-French exclamation of distress, still in use in the Channel Islands, where a subject of the duke of Normandy who feels that his or her land rights have been infringed can make the so-called *Clameur de Haro*.
26. Kieckhefer (1997), pp. 74–5.
27. Kittredge (1928), pp. 77–8; P. Doherty, *Isabella and the Strange Death of Edward II* (London: Constable, 2003), p. 81.
28. Ewen (1933), pp. 29–30.
29. Maxwell-Stuart (2014), p. 57.
30. J. Collyer (ed.), *The Criminal Statutes of England* (London: S. Sweet, 1832), p. 225.
31. There is no reason to suppose, as Maxwell Stuart (2014), p. 78 suggests, that 'imagine' here had the literal sense of making a physical image for magical purposes.
32. J. G. Bellamy, *The Tudor Law of Treason: An Introduction* (London: Routledge and Kegan Paul, 1979), pp. 10–11.

33. Van Patten (1983), p. 5.
34. Kelly (1977), p. 215.
35. *The St Albans Chronicle: The* Chronica Maiora *of Thomas Walsingham*, ed. J. Taylor (Oxford: Clarendon, 2003), vol. 1, pp. 822–3: ... *maleficiis cuiusdam fratris qui cum dicto Roberto fuit rex impeditus, nequaquam quod bonum est et honestum cernere uel sectari uolebat.*
36. H. M. Carey, *Courting Disaster: Astrology at the English Court and University in the Later Middle Ages* (Basingstoke: MacMillan, 1992), pp. 139–40; Maxwell-Stuart (2014), p. 83.
37. *Chronica Maiora*, vol. 1, pp. 46–9: ... *sed magus erat nequissimus maleficiis deditus, cuius experimentis eadem Alicia dominum regem allexerat in suum illicitum amorem.*
38. Ibid.: *Dicebatur enim eundem fratrem cereas fecisse effigies, regis uidelicet et eiusdem Alicie, quibus, per herbarum potentium succos et incantamina sua loquens ut quondam fecit ille magus famosissimus, rex Egipti Nectanabus, effecit ut dicta Alicia potuit a rege quicquid uoluit optinere. Anulos etiam, ut quondam Moyses fecerat, obliuionis et memorie, [et] ita iste frater ymaginauerat, quibus rex quamdiu uteretur predicte meretricis recordatione nunquam careret.* On the Perrers case see Kittredge (1928), p. 105; Kelly (1977), p. 217.
39. Kittredge (1928), p. 38.
40. M. Jones, 'Joan [Joan of Navarre]' in *ODNB*, vol. 30, pp. 139–42; Kelly (1977), pp. 218–19.
41. Kittredge (1928), pp. 79–80.
42. Maxwell-Stuart (2014), p. 69.
43. Kittredge (1928), p. 83.
44. Freeman (2004), p. 347.
45. R. A. Griffiths, 'The trial of Eleanor Cobham: an episode in the fall of Duke Humphrey of Gloucester', in R. A. Griffiths (ed.), *King and Country: England and Wales in the Fifteenth Century* (London: Hambledon, 1991), pp. 233–52, at p. 237.
46. Freeman (2004), p. 347.
47. Griffiths (1991), pp. 234–5.
48. C. L. Harris, 'Eleanor [née Eleanor Cobham], duchess of Gloucester' in *ODNB*, vol. 18, pp. 27–8; Carey (1992), p. 139.
49. M. Beard, J. North and S. Price, *Religions of Rome* (Cambridge: Cambridge University Press, 1998), vol. 1, pp. 231–2.
50. Griffiths (1991), pp. 238–9.
51. Kittredge (1928), p. 81.
52. J. Norden, *Speculum Britanniae* (London, 1593), p. 36.
53. Note, for instance, the apparent popularity of Holyrood Park just outside Edinburgh amongst Scottish witches (P. G. Maxwell-Stuart, *Satan's Conspiracy: Magic and Witchcraft in Sixteenth-Century Scotland* (East Linton: Tuckwell Press, 2001), p. 59).
54. Freeman (2004), p. 350.
55. Griffiths (1991), p. 240.

56. *An English Chronicle of the Reigns of Richard II, Henry IV, Henry V, and Henry VI written before the year 1471*, ed. J. S. Davies (London: Camden Society, 1856), p. 57.
57. Kittredge (1928), p. 82.
58. Cambridge University Library MS Dd.xi.45, fols 134v–139v. For an edited version of the text see J. Lidaka, '*The Book of Angels, Rings, Characters and Images of the Planets*: Attributed to Osbern Bokenham' in C. Fanger (ed.), *Conjuring Spirits: Texts and Traditions of Medieval Ritual Magic* (Stroud: Sutton, 1998), pp. 32–75, at pp. 44–75.
59. Ibid. p. 34.
60. Cambridge University Library MS Dd.xi.45, fol. 135v: *et cum ipsa ymagine quicquid uis potes destruere aut discerpere.*
61. Kieckhefer (1997), p. 78.
62. Cambridge University Library MS Dd.xi.45, fol. 136r.
63. Cambridge University Library MS Dd.xi.45, fol. 137v.
64. Ibid.: *Qua uero protracta viliore modo quo poteris ac turpiore, videlicet vultu tortuoso, manibus loco pedum positis & pedibus econtrario loco manuum.*
65. Ibid.: *Postea suffumigetur vngulis caballinis, soleis antiquis, stanno putrefacto, ossibus humanis atque capillis. Post ipsam, ymaginem inuolue panno funeris & in loco eciam subhumetur horribili, fetido, & inmundo, vultu versus terram.*
66. Ibid.: *... & si uis neci tradere, figas acum super spinam a capite usque ad cor [dem].*
67. For Aquinas's teaching on the effectiveness of sacraments, see *Summa Theologica*, III, qs 66–71.
68. Griffiths (1991), pp. 241–3.
69. Kelly (1977), p. 226.
70. Ibid. p. 228.
71. Kittredge (1928), p. 83.
72. Kelly (1977), pp. 220–1.
73. Freeman (2004), p. 356.
74. Maxwell-Stuart (2014), p. 71.
75. Freeman (2004), p. 357.
76. Kelly (1977), p. 224: *in occulto machinantes mortem regis.*
77. *Cobbett's Complete Collection of State Trials* (London, 1809), vol. 3, p. 360.
78. Cressy (2010), pp. 44–5.
79. Kieckhefer (1997), p. 72 compares the Eleanor Cobham case to that of Guichard, bishop of Troyes, who was accused in 1308 of having employed a friar and a female witch to kill the queen of France by a mixture of image magic and invocation of demons.
80. *Historical Manuscripts Commission, 5th Report* (London: HMSO, 1876), p. 455.
81. Maxwell-Stuart (2014), p. 78.
82. Kelly (1977), p. 233; Maxwell-Stuart (2014), pp. 76–8.
83. Carey (1992), p. 155.
84. Kelly (1977), pp. 232–3.

85. M. Hicks, 'George, duke of Clarence' in *ODNB*, vol. 21, pp. 792–5.
86. T. More, *The History of King Richard III*, ed. R. S. Sylvester, in *The Complete Works of St. Thomas More* (New Haven, CT: Yale University Press, 1963), vol. 2, pp. 47–48. See also M. Steible, 'Jane Shore and the Politics of Cursing', *Studies in English Literature, 1500–1900* 43 (2003), pp. 1–17.
87. J. Dover Wilson, 'A Note on *Richard III*: The Bishop of Ely's Strawberries', *Modern Language Review* 52 (1957), pp. 563–4.
88. T. B. Murray, *A Notice of Ely Chapel, Holborn* (London: John Parker, 1840), pp. 15–16.
89. Kittredge (1928), pp. 84–85.
90. Leland (2004), p. 275.
91. Ibid. pp. 268–70.
92. J. Hughes, *The Religious Life of Richard III: Piety and Prayer in the North of England* (Stroud: Sutton, 1997), p. 166.
93. Quoted in Leland (2004), p. 270.
94. Kelly (1977), pp. 234–5; Leland (2004), pp. 281–2.
95. Carey (1992), pp. 156–7.
96. Leland (2004), p. 285.
97. John Kendal was 'Turcopolier and Pillar of England' 1476–89 and Grand Prior of England 1489–1501 (E. J. King, *The Seals of the Order of St John of Jerusalem* (London: Taylor and Francis, 1932), pp. 109–11).
98. *Letters and Papers Illustrative of the Reigns of Richard III and Henry VII*, ed. J. Gairdner (London: Longman, 1863), vol. 2, pp. 318–20. An account of the plot can also be found in Maxwell-Stuart (2014), pp. 82–3.
99. Kittredge (1928), p. 50.

CHAPTER 2   TREASON, SORCERY AND PROPHECY IN THE EARLY ENGLISH REFORMATION, 1534–58

1. Baldwin Smith (2006), p. 186.
2. Ibid. p. 120.
3. Van Patten (1983), p. 13.
4. Ibid., p. 9.
5. *Life and Letters*, vol. 1, pp. 376–7.
6. Maxwell-Stuart (2014), pp. 102–3.
7. Van Patten (1983), pp. 10–11.
8. Ibid. pp. 14–15.
9. *Letters and Papers*, vol. 10, p. 164; Elton (1972), pp. 154–5.
10. *Letters and Papers*, vol. 13:1, p. 1150.
11. Maxwell-Stuart (2014), p. 102.
12. Parish (2015), pp. 400–402.
13. John Butler to Thomas Cranmer, 9 July 1537, *Letters and Papers*, vol. 12:2, 231.

14. W. H. Kelke, 'Master John Schorne', *Records of Buckinghamshire* 2 (1869), pp. 60–74; W. Sparrow Simpson, 'Master John Schorne', *Records of Buckinghamshire* 3 (1870), pp. 354–69.
15. *Letters and Papers*, vol. 13:1, 1383.
16. Cambridge University Library MS Add. 3544, fol. 85 (P. Foreman (trans. F. Young), *The Cambridge Book of Magic: A Tudor Necromancer's Manual* (Cambridge: Texts in Early Modern Magic, 2015), p. 86).
17. Wolsey was supposed to have inflicted a troublesome spirit on the duke of Norfolk by means of magic (Maxwell-Stuart (2014), pp. 99–100).
18. Elton (1972), pp. 50–5.
19. Kittredge (1928), p. 63.
20. Heal (2003), pp. 54–6.
21. On the legends surrounding Bacon see Davies (2009), pp. 37–8.
22. The Franciscans' 'magical' approach to exorcism proved a controversial element of the European Counter-Reformation, and Franciscan books of exorcism were eventually banned by Rome. See Young (2016), pp. 107–9, 162–5.
23. Both the Dominicans and Franciscans were at the forefront of Spanish and Portuguese missions to the New World and Asia.
24. *Letters and Papers*, vol. 9, 740.
25. Ibid. vol. 9, 846.
26. Ibid. vol. 13:1, 487.
27. Ibid.
28. On chantries and their suppression see A. Kreider, *English Chantries: The Road to Dissolution* (Cambridge, MA: Harvard University Press, 1979).
29. J. H. Lynch and P. C. Adamo, *The Medieval Church: A Brief History*, 2nd edn (London: Routledge, 2014), p. 306.
30. J. Bale (ed. J. Payne Collier), *King Johan: A Play in Two Acts* (London: Camden Society, 1838), vol. 2, p. 77.
31. John Foxe adopted Bale's king John into the proto-Protestant martyrology of his *Actes and monumentes* and Bale's narrative of the murder is illustrated comic-strip style in the 1570 edition (J. Foxe, *The first volume of the ecclesiasticall history contayning the actes and monumentes of thynges passed in euery kynges tyme in this realme, especially in the Church of England* (London, 1570), plate facing p. 290).
32. Warnicke (1987), p. 256.
33. Warnicke (1991), pp. 2–3.
34. *Life and Letters*, vol. 2, p. 12.
35. Warnicke (1991), p. 231.
36. Ibid. p. 216.
37. Warnicke (1987), p. 259.
38. N. Sander, *De origine et progressu schismatis Anglicani* (Cologne, 1585), p. 17: *In dextera manu sextus agnascebatur digitus, sub mento etiam succrescebat turgidum nescio quid*. For Sander's description of Anne's monstrous birth see pp. 85–6.

39. Warnicke (1991), pp. 245–6.
40. M. H. Dodds, *The Pilgrimage of Grace 1536–1537 and the Exeter Conspiracy 1538* (Cambridge: Cambridge University Press, 1915), vol. 1, p. 297; Kittredge (1928), p. 86; Elton (1972), p. 49.
41. Elton (1972), p. 57.
42. *Life and Letters*, vol. 2, p. 271.
43. Warnicke (2000), p. 205.
44. For the accusations against Hungerford see Kittredge (1928), p. 65; Warnicke (2000), pp. 226–8; D. J. Ashton, 'Hungerford, Walter' in *ODNB*, vol. 28, pp. 827–8.
45. See *Life and Letters*, vol. 2, pp. 35, 62, 160, 234.
46. Elton (1972), p. 340.
47. For the Act of Attainder against Hungerford see *Letters and Papers*, vol. 15, p. 498.
48. Warnicke (1987), p. 250. The crime was also occasionally coupled with magic, as in 1628 when John Hockenhull of Prenton was indicted 'p[ro] buggery and sorcery' (Ewen (1933), p. 415).
49. *Correspondance politique de MM. de Castillon et de Marillac, ambassadeurs de France en Angleterre (1537–1542)*, ed. J. Kaulek (Paris: Germer Baillière, 1885), p. 207: 'Avec lui a esté semblablement décollé le seigneur de Haigrefort, homme aigé d'ung quarente ans, attaint de sodomye, d'avoir forcé sa propre fille et d'avoir usé d'art magicque et invocation de dyables'.
50. Warnicke (2000), pp. 195, 228.
51. Baldwin Smith (2006), p. 121.
52. Warnicke (2000), p. 227.
53. M. Gaskill, 'Witchcraft and Evidence in Early Modern England', *Past and Present* 198 (2008), pp. 33–70, at p. 39.
54. The full text of the act may be found in B. Rosen (ed.), *Witchcraft in England, 1558–1618* (Amherst, MA: University of Massachusetts Press, 1991), pp. 53–4.
55. Maxwell-Stuart (2014), pp. 113–14.
56. Van Patten (1983), p. 20 n. 114.
57. Davies (2007), pp. 4–5.
58. Cressy (2010), pp. 54–5.
59. A. Ryrie, *The Sorcerer's Tale: Faith and Fraud in Tudor England* (Oxford: Oxford University Press, 2008), p. 27.
60. Davies (2003), pp. 4–6.
61. E. Underhill, *The Autobiography of Edward Underhill*, in *Narratives of the Days of the Reformation* (London: Camden Society, 1859), pp. 172–5.
62. *Reformatio Legum Ecclesiasticarum* (London, 1641), p. 32: *Magia pactum est, vel foedus cum demonio percussum, & ejus ministris, carminibus, precibus, characteribus, vel similibus impietatis instrumentis conflatum, quod vel ad futurorum casuum investigationem refertur, vel ad certarum rerum, quas expetimus, conquaestionem.*
63. Ibid. p. 33.

64. *Acts of the Privy Council*, vol. 4: 1552–54, p. 528.
65. Ryrie (2008), pp. 52–53.
66. Cressy (2010), p. 57.
67. F. Young, *English Catholics and the Supernatural, 1553–1829* (Farnham: Ashgate, 2013), p. 126; Maxwell-Stuart (2014), pp. 121–2.
68. For instance, in around 1558 the leading Suffolk Catholic Roger Martin of Long Melford deleted a passage from his transcription of a prayer book of Erasmus that equated the cults of St Roche and St Anthony with 'magical arts'; see F. Young, 'Early Modern English Catholic Piety in a Fifteenth-Century Book of Hours: Cambridge University Library MS Additional 10079', *Transactions of the Cambridge Bibliographical Society* 15 (2015), pp. 541–59, at p. 551.
69. Cressy (2010), p. 58.
70. *Johannis, confratris & monachi Glastoniensis, chronica sive historia de rebus Glastoniensibus*, ed. T. Hearne (Oxford, 1726), vol. 2, p. 520.
71. Parry (2011), pp. 31–7.

CHAPTER 3   ELIZABETH VERSUS THE 'POPISH CONJURERS', 1558–77

1. R. Parsons, *An Epistle of the Persecution of Catholickes in England* (Douai [Rouen], 1582), pp. 148–50.
2. F. Coxe, *A Short Treatise declaringe the detestable wickednesse, of magicall sciences, as Necromancie. Coniurations of spirites, Curioue Astrologie and suche lyke* (London, 1561). On the importance of prophecies at this time see Devine (2015), pp. 71–2.
3. Coxe (1561), unpaginated.
4. *Acts of the Privy Council*, vol. 7, pp. 5, 7, 22; Parry (2011), p. 48.
5. Quoted in Devine (2015), p. 70.
6. Jones (1998), p. 193. Also sent before the bishop were two men who had consulted the conjurers, John Thirkle and Richard Parlaben (Devine (2015), p. 71).
7. F. Peck, *Desiderata Curiosa* (London, 1779), vol. 1, p. 78.
8. T. F. Mayer, *Reginald Pole: Prince and Prophet* (Cambridge: Cambridge University Press, 2000), pp. 199–200; R. Beccatelli, *The Life of Cardinal Reginald Pole* (London, 1766), p. 142. This statement does not amount to an outright rejection of astrology in principle.
9. Henry Owyn's undated plea to William Cecil, entitled 'The brief content whereby John Prestall entrapped Henry Owyn', BL MS Lansdowne 87, fols 100r–101r. The document is accompanied by a list of debts owed by Prestall.
10. Devine (2015), pp. 83–4.
11. Jones (1998), p. 189.

Notes to Pages 94–99 217

12. Richard Cox to the Privy Council, undated, Gonville and Caius College MS 53/30, fol. 28r.
13. For an example of a prosecution of a woman in a church court for promoting magical girdles see Gibbons (1891), p. 37.
14. The quotations are taken from the Geneva Bible of 1576, which was essentially a translation of the Vulgate. 'Soothsayers' was replaced by 'wizards' in the Authorised Version of 1611.
15. The Latin verb *hariolor* is concerned exclusively with foretelling the future, and need have no connotations of witchcraft.
16. Devine (2015), p. 73.
17. Jones (1998), p. 79.
18. C. S. Knighton, 'Westminster Abbey Restored' in E. Duffy and D. Loades (eds), *The Church of Mary Tudor* (Farnham: Ashgate, 2006), pp. 77–123.
19. T. Cooper (revised D. D. Rees), 'Sayer, Robert [*name in religion* Gregory] (1560–1602)' in *ODNB*, vol. 49, p. 161.
20. BL MS Add. 48023, fol. 354v: 'The powers were appointed to enquire for mass mongers, and conjurers, whereupon the Lord of Loughborough, Sir Edward Waldegrave [and] Sir Thomas Wharton were apprehended and so confessed their massing, and divers others were condemned for it at Brentwood. The heir of Geoffrey Pole was imprisoned, and suspicion of some confederacy was, by reason of the enticement of my Lord of Loughborough, This Pole should have married the Earl of Northumberland's sister, for whose marriage new costly apparel was prepared ... and many were invited to the feast'.
21. J. E. Oxley, *The Reformation in Essex: To the Death of Mary* (Manchester: Manchester University Press, 1965), pp. 199, 208.
22. Knighton (2006), pp. 117 –18.
23. *The Correspondence of Reginald Pole*, ed. T. F. Mayer and C. B. Walters (Aldershot: Ashgate 2008), vol. 4, p. 260; C. Cross, 'Hastings, Henry, third earl of Huntingdon' in *ODNB*, vol. 25, pp. 756–9; H. Pierce, 'Pole, Arthur' in *ODNB*, vol. 44, pp. 691–2.
24. Alvaro de la Quadra to Count de Feria, 27 December 1559, *Calendar of Letters and State Papers relating to English Affairs: preserved principally in the Archives of Simancas*, ed. M. A. S. Hume (London: HMSO, 1892–9), vol. 1, 81.
25. BL MS Add. 48023, fol. 354v.
26. Alvaro de la Quadra to Cardinal Granvelle, 21 April 1561, in *Relations Politiques des Pays-Bas et de l'Angleterre, sous le règne de Philippe II*, ed. J. M. B. C. Kervyn de Lettenhove (Brussels: F. Hayez, 1883), vol. 2, p. 557: '... por la confession de un capellan del uno dellos, que yva a Flandres, han sin accusados de haver tenido missa en sus casas. Ellos fueron ayer traydos a Londres con gran guardia y luego embiados con gran escarnio por medio de Londres a otra carcel. Los que vinieron, destos dos tambien estan presas. Han prendido oy a Artur Polo, un moco sobrino del Cardenal Polo, poque dizen quo oyo missa, y mandado venir a Milord Asting, que era Cameraro

Mayor de la Reina Maria; creese que yra tambien a la Torre. Llaman a muchos otros y dizen que es gran numero de los nombrados en esta materia, y la reyna cree que sea conjura y conspiracion contra ella'. There is an ambiguity in translation here, because the Spanish word 'conjura' (like the Latin *coniuratio*) can mean 'plot' or 'conspiracy' as well as 'conjuration'.
27. Ibid. pp. 560–61: 'Tanbien han prendido a seis o ocho clerigos muy honrados y doctores de Oxonia los dos dellos, y publican que son nigromanticos y que conjuravan demonios para hacer morir a la Reyna, lo qual hacen por escarnio y para hacerlos mas odiosos del pueblo'.
28. Ibid. p. 561.
29. Richard Jones to Sir Nicholas Throckmorton, 6 May 1561, BL MS Add. 35830, fol. 107v.
30. Jones (1998), p. 195.
31. Maxwell-Stuart (2014), pp. 128–9.
32. Devine (2015), p. 83.
33. Parry (2011), pp. 61–2.
34. *Calendar of Patent Rolls preserved in the Public Record Office: Elizabeth I* (London: HMSO, 1964), vol. 4, pp. 63–4.
35. W. Camden, *Annals, or, The historie of the most renovvned and victorious princesse Elizabeth, late Queen of England* (London, 1635), p. 44.
36. Devine (2015), pp. 88–9.
37. Quoted in Jones (1998), p. 192.
38. BL MS Add. 48023, fol. 354v. The reference is probably to Sir Richard Cotton of Combermere, Shropshire (1539/40–1602) whose wife was Mary Mainwaring (1541–78).
39. Devine (2015), p. 78.
40. BL MS Add. 48023, fol. 354v.
41. Cambridge University Library MS Add. 3544, fol. 60: *Scribe in pomo in pane vel in casio: Honey: Baxuti: Tetragrammaton: & nome[n] tuu[m] et nome[n] mulieris.*
42. Ibid. fol. 62: *Accipe pomu[m] in die veneris luna crescente: & fac anulum in pomo & scribe in circuitu eius: Guel: Lucifer: Sathanas.* See also fol. 60: *Accipe tres crines de capite eius & cera virgineam & fac ymagine[m] & include illos in ymagine, & scribe in fronte ymaginis: Sathan: & in dextra brachio: Bellial: & in sinistro brachio: Brith: & in dextro pede: Belzebub:* For another example of a sixteenth-century love spell see R. Scot, *The Discoverie of Witchcraft* (London, 1665), p. 145.
43. Cambridge University Library MS Add. 3544, fol. 63: *Accipe talpam & pone in ollo ben[edic]te multa foramina postea claude os illius olli & pone in loco ubi sunt multe formice per decem dies, postea accipe ossa illius talpe & pone in aqua currente & tene ossa que vertent contra aqua[m] & tange muliere[m] in facie vel in manu & statim amabit te.*
44. Ibid. fol. 63: *Accipe virgam coryli uniq[ue] anni crescentis serite cum sanguine albe columbe sup[er] virgam Arax: Apeaxy: Lepeary: femani: & tange mulierem & segnatur te.*

45. Jones (1998), p. 193.
46. Devine (2015), p. 81.
47. Coxe (1561), unpaginated.
48. Ibid.
49. Ryrie (2008), p. 117.
50. [J. Morwen], *An Apologie to the Causes of the Brinnynge of Paule's Church* (London, 1561). On Morwen see A. Walsham, *Providence in Early Modern England* (Oxford: Oxford University Press, 2001), p. 233; Ryrie (2008), p. 66.
51. Walsham (2001), pp. 232–3. On the black dog of Bungay, see pp. 192–4.
52. Devine (2015), p. 82.
53. Parsons (1582), pp. 148–9.
54. Jones (1998), pp. 197–8; Parry (2011), p. 63; Maxwell-Stuart (2014), pp. 132–6; Devine (2015), pp. 67–8.
55. Devine (2015), p. 68.
56. Gaskill (2008), pp. 33–70, at pp. 38–9.
57. For the text of the act see Rosen (1991), pp. 54–6.
58. Devine (2015), p. 86.
59. Ibid. p. 89.
60. Jones (1998), p. 199.
61. Devine (2015), p. 79. The exiled bishop of St Asaph, Thomas Goldwell, participated anyway.
62. Ibid. p. 91.
63. *The Examination and Confession of Certain Wytches at Chensford in the Countie of Essex ... Anno 1566*, reprinted in Ewen (1933), p. 324.
64. Walsham (2001), p. 82.
65. BL MS Add. 70984, fol. 256r.
66. J. Lock, 'Story, John' in *ODNB*, vol. 52, pp. 955–8.
67. Camden (1635), p. 147.
68. *A Copie of a Letter lately sent by a Gentleman, Student in the Lawes of the Realme, to a Frende of his concernyng. D. Story* (London, 1571), Sigs. A2–A3.
69. Parry (2011), pp. 63, 78–9.
70. Ibid. pp. 81–3.
71. *Copie of a Letter*, Sig. A4r.
72. Ibid.
73. Camden (1635), pp. 146–7.
74. John Lee to William Cecil, 23 March 1572, in *Calendar of State Papers, Foreign Series, of the Reign of Elizabeth*, ed. A. J. Crosby (London: HMSO, 1876), vol. 10 (1572–74), 690.
75. Parry (2011), pp. 92, 223.
76. *Acts of the Privy Council*, vol. 8, p. 31.
77. Baldwin Smith (2006), p. 122.
78. J. Leslie, *A Treatise of Treasons against Q. Elizabeth, and the Crown of England* (London, 1572), fol. 134v. The word 'coven' had no specific association with witches at this time and meant simply 'a gathering'.

79. Ibid. fol. 158v.
80. Ibid. fol. 166v.
81. Parsons (1582), p. 150. On the Jenks case see Walsham (2001), pp. 234–5.
82. J. Stowe, *The Annales of England* (London, 1592), p. 1165.
83. *Calendar of State Papers (Domestic Series) of The Reign of Elizabeth, 1581–1590*, ed. R. Lemon (London: HMSO, 1865), p. 391; Kittredge (1928), p. 89. On the Dewse case see W. H. Hart, 'Observations on some Documents relating to Magic in the Reign of Queen Elizabeth', *Archaeologia* 40 (1866), pp. 389–97, at pp. 395–6; D. Willis, *Malevolent Nurture: Witch-hunting and Maternal Power in Early Modern England* (Ithaca, NY: Cornell University Press, 1995), pp. 1–5.
84. T. Cogan, *The Haven of Health* (London, 1636), p. 318. See also N. Wanley, *The Wonders of the Little World* (London, 1673), p. 60.

CHAPTER 4 'A TRAITOROUS HEART TO THE QUEEN':
EFFIGIES AND WITCH-HUNTS, 1578–1603

1. Bernardino Mendoza to Gabriel de Zayas, 8 September 1578, *Simancas*, vol. 2, 524.
2. Z. Dovey, *An Elizabethan Progress: The Queen's Journey into East Anglia, 1578* (Stroud: Sutton, 1996), pp. 61–2.
3. Mendoza to Zayas, 8 September 1578, *Simancas*, vol. 2, 524.
4. M. Reynolds, *Godly Reformers and their Opponents in Early Modern England: Religion in Norwich, c. 1560–1643* (Woodbridge: Boydell, 2005), pp. 56–7.
5. On East Anglia's Catholic gentry in Elizabeth's reign see J. Rowe and F. Young, 'East Anglian Catholics in the Reign of Elizabeth, 1559–1603' in F. Young (ed.), *Catholic East Anglia: A History of the Catholic Faith in Norfolk, Suffolk, Cambridgeshire and Peterborough* (Leominster: Gracewing, 2016), pp. 37–60.
6. Scot (1665 [1584]), p. 145.
7. Cambridge University Library MS Add. 3544, fol. 82 (see Foreman (2015), pp. 82–3): *Si volueris viro vel mulieri nocere recipe de terra recentis mortui: & libram & semis de cera virginea & fac inde Imagine[m] ad longitudine[m] palme manus, terra ab umbellico sup[er]ius cera quide[m] inferius: & scribatur in vertice capitis: Dathyn: Maby: Chayl: in fronte imaginis no[m]en pro quo fit opus, circa turga hec nomina scribatur: Xethenata: Martha: Xatenosate: Sathan: in pectore scribe: Strayl: Chayl: in umbellico scribe Xathagundus: in planta pedis dextre: Baxtrala: hiis ita partis habeas de vesto alicuius mortui & liga quodvis membru[m] volueris auferre: invocando no[m]ina supradicta in ymagine dicendo quod facis huius ymagini contingat & ipsi: N: & N: factis tribus dilictis & trib[u]s crepusculis pungatur ymago cum fuerit hora: [Saturni] cum acu & punge in quodvis membro volueris invocando supradicta & dicendo quod facis huic ymagini contingat & ipsi: N & N: sepeleatur ymago in quocu[n]q[ue] loco volueris: & enim sanare eum volueris, acum & vestem delve & lava me[m]brum*

cum lacte dulce & statim sanabitur. nota quod ista ymago debet fieri in hora: [Saturni]: [Luna] existente in [Capricornu]: vel in [Virgo].
8. Cambridge University Library MS Add. 3544, fol. 83 (Foreman (2015), pp. 83–4): *fac ymagine[m] ad similitudine[m] hominis vel fere de cera virginea & fac o[m]nia de turpa natura, in quolibet digito & quolibet articulo fige stuppas lineas postea p[r]ofera ea[m] quasi infante[m] p[er] no[m]en suu[m] & punge eam in quo membro volueris ea[m] aggravare, postea illas stuppas in illo membro flexas fexas califacias me[m]bru[m] illius pro quo ymago e[st] supputata sed cave ne me[m]bru[m] periet neq[ue] ascenssurat.*
9. Parry (2011), pp. 92–102.
10. According to Parry (2011), p. 132, Dee set out from Mortlake on 15 August having been summoned by Leicester to help persuade Elizabeth to intervene in the Netherlands. There is no direct evidence of this, and it is contradicted by Dee's own account of having received several letters in one morning about the wax images, which were not sent to the Council until 15 August. The earliest he could have received a letter about the images was the morning of 20 August; if Dee set off at around noon that day, the earliest he could have arrived in Norwich was early evening on 22 August. The distance from Mortlake to Norwich by road was around 125 miles, and in wet conditions Dee would not have been able to travel much faster than three miles an hour (see the analysis of Tudor travel times in I. Mortimer, *The Time Traveller's Guide to Elizabethan England* (London: Vintage, 2013), p. 201); therefore it would have taken Dee a little over 40 hours to reach Norwich even if he was riding post (changing horses at every inn) and riding through the night.
11. Mendoza to Zayas, 8 September 1578, *Simancas*, vol. 2, 524.
12. *Acts of the Privy Council*, vol. 10, p. 309.
13. J. Dee, 'John Dee's Account of his Life and Studies for half an hundred Years' in *Johannis, confratris & monachi Glastoniensis, chronica sive historia de rebus Glastoniensibus*, ed. T. Hearne (Oxford, 1726), vol. 2, pp. 497–551, at pp. 521–2.
14. Dovey (1996), pp. 88–9.
15. BL MS Sloane 3846, fol. 95r. See also the spell on fol. 98r 'To help one that is bewitched'. Parry (2011), p. 301n. suggests these as possible models for the 'proceedings' enacted by Dee.
16. Young (2013), pp. 39–40.
17. S. Bowd, 'John Dee and the Seven in Lancashire: Possession, Exorcism, and Apocalypse in Elizabethan England', *Northern History* 47 (2010), 233–46.
18. R. J. Roberts and A. G. Watson (eds), *John Dee's Library Catalogue* (London: Bibliographical Society, 1990), D14.
19. On Menghi see G. Romeo, *Inquisitori, esorcisti e streghe nell'Italia della Controriforma* (Florence: Sansoni, 2003), pp. 114–44; Young (2016), pp. 107–9.
20. H. A. Kelly, *The Devil at Baptism: Ritual, Theology and Drama* (Ithaca, NY: Cornell University Press, 1985), pp. 112–15.

21. G. Menghi, *Flagellum daemonum* (Bologna, 1577), pp. 259–61: *Benedicat te creatura ignis, qui creauit te; qui famulo suo Moysi apparauit in igne flammae rubi; qui in columna ignis per noctis tenebras suum populum antecessit in desertum; qui iudicaturus orbem, te iudicis faciem praeire iubebit; qui te sue iustitie instrumentum in Spiritus contumaces delegit; vt qui tres pueros maiestatis sue cultores in te seruauit illesos, etiam per te excruciet, & explodat omnes Spiritus apostaticos.*
22. H. C. Agrippa (trans. R. Turner), *Henry Cornelius Agrippa His Fourth Book of Occult Philosophy* (London, 1655), p. 25.
23. Menghi (1577), p. 167: ... *strictissime coactus recedat de hac creatura Dei N. statim, non rediturus ad eam, sine laesione ipsius corporis, & omnium nocumento.*
24. Ibid. p. 170.
25. Ibid. pp. 174–82.
26. *Acts of the Privy Council*, vol. 10, pp. 322, 326.
27. Parry (2011), p. 133.
28. Dee (1726), pp. 521–2.
29. Parry (2011), p. 135.
30. P. Elmer, *Witchcraft, Witch-Hunting and the State in Early Modern England* (Oxford: Oxford University Press, 2015), pp. 28–9.
31. P. Collinson, 'Pulling the Strings: Religion and Politics in the Progress of 1578', in J. E. Archer, E. Goldring, and S. Knight (eds), *The Progresses, Pageants and Entertainments of Queen Elizabeth I* (Oxford: Oxford University Press, 2007), pp. 122–41, at pp. 132–3.
32. P. Lake, 'A Tale of Two Episcopal Surveys: The Strange Fates of Edmund Grindal and Cuthbert Mayne revisited', *Transactions of the Royal Historical Society* 18 (2008) pp. 129–63, at p. 149; Dovey (1996), p. 54.
33. Collinson (2007), p. 133.
34. Van Patten (1983), p. 25.
35. *Acts of the Privy Council*, vol. 11, pp. 36–7.
36. *Acts of the Privy Council*, vol. 10, pp. 310–13.
37. Parry (2011), pp. 48–9.
38. Ibid. pp. 63–8.
39. Ibid. pp. 134–5.
40. Thomas Wilson to Leicester and Warwick, 13 November 1578, BL MS Harley 286, fol. 37r.
41. Scot (1665 [1584]), p. 285.
42. Ibid. p. 286.
43. Parry (2011), pp. 136–7.
44. J. Bodin, *De la Démonomanie des Sorcières* (Paris, 1580), Preface: 'Il est encores nouvellement advenu d'un Prestre Sorcier d'Angleterre, et Curé d'un village, qui s'appelle Istincton, demye lieuë pres de Londres, qui a esté trouvé saisi au mois de Septembre, mil cinq cens septante huict, de trois images de cire coniurées, pour faire mourir la Royne d'Angleterre, et deux autres proches à sa personne'.

Notes to Pages 134–144

45. M. Casaubon, *Of Credulity and Incredulity in Things Natural, Civil and Divine* (London, 1668), p. 93.
46. Elmer (2015), p. 30.
47. [R. Verstegan], *The Copy of a Letter, lately written by a Spanishe gentleman* (London, 1589), p. 5.
48. Ibid. p. 8.
49. See Young (2013), pp. 134–44.
50. Scot (1665 [1584]), pp. 285–6.
51. Ibid. p. 122.
52. Ibid. p. 285.
53. Parry (2011), p. 136.
54. Elmer (2015), p. 29.
55. *Acts of the Privy Council*, vol. 12, pp. 251–2.
56. Ewen (1933), p. 449.
57. Elmer (2015), p. 29.
58. Ibid. p. 30.
59. *CSPD Elizabeth*, Addenda 1580–1625, p. 120.
60. Ewen (1933), p. 449.
61. BL, MS Lansdowne 99, fols 244v–257r.
62. Ibid. fol. 257r.
63. Parry (2011), pp. 140–1.
64. BL, MS Lansdowne 99, fols 244v–r.
65. Ibid. fols 245v–247r.
66. Ibid. fol. 248v.
67. *CSPD Elizabeth*, 1591–1594, pp. 17–18.
68. The National Archives, Kew, C 65/172, no. 2.
69. Owen Oglethorpe and Roderick Warcop to Lord Burghley, 19 August 1585 in *Salisbury MSS*, vol. 3, p. 106.
70. *The Manuscripts of Lord Kenyon*, Historical Manuscripts Commission, Fourteenth Report (London: HMSO, 1894), p. 607.
71. A. Walsham, '"Frantick Hacket": Prophecy, Sorcery, Insanity, and the Elizabethan Puritan Movement', *The Historical Journal* 41 (1998), pp. 27–66.
72. Parry (2011), pp. 219–21.
73. R. Cosin, *Conspiracie for Pretended Reformation; viz. Presbyteriall Discipline* (London, 1592), Sigs. b2r–v.
74. [R. Parsons], *Elizabethae, Angliae Reginae Haeresim Calvinianam Propugnantis, Saevissimum in Catholicos sui Regni edictum ... cum Responsione* (Rome, 1592), p. 36: *quam modo ita notam et publicam suis in aedibus habere dicitur, Astronomo quodam necromantico praeceptore; ut juventutis nobilioris non exiguae turmae, tam Moysis legem veterem, quam novam Christi Domini, ingeniosis quibusdam facetiis ac dicteriis eludere, ac in circulis suis irridere didicerint.*
75. E. A. Strathmann, 'John Dee as Ralegh's "Conjurer"', *Huntington Library Quarterly* 10 (1947), pp. 365–72.

76. *CSPD Elizabeth*, 1591–1594, pp. 17–18.
77. Ibid. pp. 17–18.
78. Ewen (1933), p. 450.
79. F. Edwards, 'Sir Robert Cecil, Edward Squier and the Poisoned Pommel', *Recusant History* 25 (2001), pp. 377–414, at pp. 393–5.
80. Ibid. p. 404.
81. Willis (1995), p. 4.
82. On the dating of *Henry VI Part Two* and the other history plays see N. Grene, *Shakespeare's Serial History Plays* (Cambridge: Cambridge University Press, 2002), pp. 7–30, R. Warren (ed.), *Henry VI, Part Two* (Oxford: Oxford University Press, 2002), pp. 60–74.
83. W. Shakespeare, *The First Part of the Contention of the Two Famous Houses of York and Lancaster with the Death of the Good Duke Humphrey* (London, 1594), Sig. Cr.
84. Warren (2002), pp. 182–3.
85. The celebrated Spanish demonologist Martin Delrio's interest in demonology was initially stimulated by editing the text of Seneca's *Medea* (see J. Machielsen, *Martin Delrio: Demonology and Scholarship in the Counter-Reformation* (Oxford: Oxford University Press, 2015), pp. 137–59).
86. Kieckhefer (2000), p. xi.
87. 'Asmath' is the name printed in the First Folio, read as 'Asnath' by the editors of the Oxford Shakespeare and Arden Shakespeare. For a discussion of the spirit's name see M. Gibson and J. A. Esra (eds), *Shakespeare's Demonology: A Dictionary* (London: Arden Shakespeare, 2014), pp. 17–18. Roger Warren (2002), p. 144 suggests that 'Asmode', an abbreviated form of the biblical demon Asmodeus, is the correct reading.
88. On the reception of Tasso in England see C. P. Brand, *Torquato Tasso: a study of the poet and of his contribution to English literature* (Cambridge: Cambridge University Press, 1965), p. 226–76.

CHAPTER 5 'A BREACH IN NATURE': MAGIC AS A POLITICAL CRIME IN EARLY STUART ENGLAND, 1603–42

1. Warnicke (1991), pp. 240–1.
2. R. Parsons, *A Discussion of the Answere of M. William Barlow, D. of Divinity, to the Booke intituled: The Iudgment of a Catholike Englishman living in Banishment for his Religion* (St Omer, 1612), pp. 218–19.
3. Maxwell-Stuart (2001), p. 36.
4. Ibid. pp. 48–9.
5. Ibid. pp. 90–1.
6. *Newes from Scotland* (London, 1591), pp. 16–17.
7. Maxwell-Stuart (2001), pp. 144–7.
8. Ibid. p. 154.
9. *Newes from Scotland* (1591), p. 16.

10. Ibid. p. 14.
11. Ibid. p. 15.
12. Maxwell-Stuart (2001), p. 156.
13. *Newes from Scotland* (1591), p. 29.
14. James VI, *Daemonologie* (Edinburgh, 1597), p. 78.
15. For a discussion of the probability of Bothwell's guilt see Maxwell-Stuart (2001), pp. 171–80.
16. Ibid. pp. 201–2.
17. James VI and I (1597), pp. 45–6.
18. Ibid. p. 32.
19. Ibid. p. 79.
20. James VI and I, *Basilicon Doron* in *Political Writings*, ed. J. P. Somerville (Cambridge: Cambridge University Press, 1994), p. 23.
21. James VI and I, *The Trew Law of Free Monarchies* in *Political Writings*, ed. J. P. Somerville (Cambridge: Cambridge University Press, 1994), p. 77.
22. Maxwell-Stuart (2014), p. 198.
23. R. Booth, 'Standing within the Prospect of Belief: *Macbeth*, King James, and Witchcraft', in J. Newton and J. Bath (eds), *Witchcraft and the Act of 1604* (Leiden: Brill, 2008), pp. 47–68, at p. 51.
24. P. G. Maxwell-Stuart, 'King James's Experience of Witches, and the English Witchcraft Act of 1604' in J. Newton and J. Bath (eds), *Witchcraft and the Act of 1604* (Leiden: Brill, 2008), pp. 31–46, at pp. 38–9.
25. Ibid. pp. 40–1.
26. P. C. Almond, *Demonic Possession in Early Modern England: Contemporary Texts and their Cultural Contexts* (Cambridge: Cambridge University Press, 2004), pp. 287–8.
27. Maxwell-Stuart (2008), pp. 42–44.
28. Maxwell-Stuart (2014), pp. 200–1.
29. Rosen (1991), pp. 57–8.
30. Parry (2011), pp. 265–7.
31. *Salisbury MSS*, vol. 17, pp. 22–4.
32. D. Purkiss, *The Witch in History: Early Modern and Twentieth-Century Representations* (London: Routledge, 1996), pp. 156–8.
33. Young (2013), pp. 149–51.
34. On the case of Anne Gunter see J. Sharpe, *The Bewitching of Anne Gunter: A Horrible and True Story of Deception, Witchcraft, and the King of England* (New York: Routledge, 2000).
35. On Darrell and Protestant exorcism see T. S. Freeman, 'Demons, Deviance and Defiance: John Darrell and the Politics of Exorcism in Late Elizabethan England' in P. Lake and M. Questier (eds), *Conformity and Orthodoxy in the English Church, c. 1560–1660* (Woodbridge: Boydell, 2000), pp. 34–63; M. Gibson, *Possession, Puritanism and Print: Darrell, Harsnett, Shakespeare and the Elizabethan Exorcism Controversy* (London: Pickering and Chatto, 2006).

36. G. Bray (ed.), *The Anglican Canons, 1529–1947* (Woodbridge: Boydell, 1998), pp. 362–5.
37. *The Arraignment and Execution of the Late Traitors* (London, 1606), p. 50. On the portrayal of the Gunpowder Plot as diabolical treason see Johnstone (2006), pp. 189–93.
38. Maxwell-Stuart (2014), p. 225.
39. M. Kennedy, 'How stately home owner planned to protect a royal visitor from witches', The *Guardian* (5 November 2014), p. 11.
40. E. F. Gay, 'The Midland Revolt and the Inquisitions of Depopulation of 1607', *Transactions of the Royal Historical Society*, New Series 18 (1904), pp. 195–244, at p. 217.
41. R. Lockyer, 'Lake, Sir Thomas' in *ODNB*, vol. 32, pp. 247–9.
42. Francis Bacon to George Calvert, 5 February 1619, in J. Spedding (ed.), *The Life and Letters of Francis Bacon* (London: Longmans, 1857–74), vol. 7 [14], p. 76.
43. Francis Bacon to King James, 10 February 1619, ibid. vol. 7 [14], p. 77.
44. John Chamberlain to Dudley Carleton, 26 February 1619, in ibid. vol. 7 [14], pp. 79–80. On the Peacock case see also *CSPD James I, 1619–1623*, p. 125.
45. J. Cook, *Dr Simon Forman: A Most Notorious Physician* (London: Chatto and Windus, 2001), pp. 199–205.
46. Steible (2003), p. 3.
47. G. J. Guenther, *Magical Imaginations: Instrumental Aesthetics in the English Renaissance* (Toronto: University of Toronto Press, 2012), p. 100.
48. Ibid. p. 94.
49. V. Hart, *Art and Magic in the Court of the Stuarts* (London: Routledge, 1994), p. 10.
50. Maxwell-Stuart (2014), pp. 208–9.
51. Hart (1994), pp. 9–10.
52. Underdown (1996), pp. 34–5; Johnstone (2006), p. 197. For an exhaustive account of the conspiracy theories surrounding James' death see Bellany and Cogswell (2015).
53. Bellany and Cogswell (2015), p. 185.
54. J. Rushworth, *Historical Collections* (London, 1659–1701), vol. 1, p. 391.
55. *A Briefe Description of the Notorious Life of Iohn Lambe, otherwise called Doctor Lambe* (Amsterdam, 1628), pp. 4–6.
56. Ibid. p. 12.
57. A. McConnell, 'Lambe, John' in *ODNB*, vol. 32, pp. 296–7. On Lambe see also C.-R. Millar, 'Witchcraft and Deviant Sexuality: A Case Study of Dr Lambe' in M. Harmes, L. Henderson, B. Harmes and A. Antonio (eds), *The British World: Religion, Memory, Society, Culture* (Toowoomba: University of Southern Queensland, 2012), pp. 51–62.
58. Anne Bodenham was one of the few cunning-women to be tried for witchcraft (Davies (2007), pp. 71–2).

59. E. Bowden, *Doctor Lambe Reviv'd, or, Witchcraft condemn'd in Anne Bodenham a servant of his* (London, 1653), p. 32.
60. Ibid. pp. 26–7.
61. Bellany and Cogswell (2015), p. 186.
62. Ibid. p. 326.
63. *Calendar of State Papers, Domestic series: Charles I, 1639–40,* ed. W. D. Hamilton (London: HMSO, 1877), p. 269.

CHAPTER 6   THE DECLINE OF MAGIC AS A POLITICAL CRIME, 1642–1700

1. Quoted in Elmer (2015), p. 104.
2. On the case of Mother Lakeland see Gaskill (2005), pp. 173–8.
3. Quoted in ibid. p. 166.
4. M. Stoyle, *Soldiers and Strangers: An Ethnic History of the English Civil War* (New Haven, CT: Yale University Press, 2005), pp. 139–40.
5. Ibid. p. 142.
6. I am indebted to Inga Jones for this suggestion.
7. Gaskill (2005), p. 149.
8. R. Weisman, *Witchcraft, Magic and Religion in 17th-century Massachusetts* (Amherst, MA: University of Massachusetts Press, 1984), p. 159.
9. On the Lowes case see Gaskill (2005), pp. 138–44.
10. Johnstone (2006), p. 243.
11. Ibid. p. 245.
12. L. E. Ingelhart, *Press Freedoms: A Descriptive Calendar of Concepts, Interpretations, Events and Court Actions from 4000 B.C. to the Present* (Westport, CT: Greenwood Press, 1987), pp. 51–4.
13. Davies (2009), p. 52.
14. H. C. Agrippa, *Henrici Cor. Agrippæ ... de occulta philosophia lib. III.; item spurius liber de caeremoniis magicis, qui quartus Agrippæ habetur* (Lyons, 1560).
15. R. Turner, 'The Preface to the Unprejudiced Reader' in H. C. Agrippa (trans. R. Turner), *Henry Cornelius Agrippa His Fourth Book of Occult Philosophy* (London, 1655).
16. Ibid. p. 68.
17. Davies (2007), pp. 119–45.
18. *The English Devil: or, Cromwel and his Monstrous Witch discover'd at White-Hall* (London, 1660), pp. 6–7.
19. Ibid.
20. H. Townshend (ed. J. W. Willis Bund), *The Diary of Henry Townshend* (Worcester: Worcestershire Historical Society, 1920), vol. 1, p. 40.
21. Ewen (1933), p. 459.
22. L. W. Mollenauer, *Strange Revelations: Magic, Poison and Sacrilege in Louis XIV's France* (University Park, PA: Pennsylvania State University Press, 2007), p. 150 n. 192.

23. Copenhaver (2015), pp. 345–9.
24. J.C. Petitfils, *L'affaire des poisons* (Paris: Perrin, 2010), p. 131.
25. Ibid. pp. 206–7.
26. Quoted in Mollenauer (2007), p. 65.
27. Sir Henry Savile to Secretary of State Henry Coventry, 25 January 1680, quoted in Mollenauer (2007), p. 148 n. 153.
28. Mollenauer (2007), p. 37.
29. Petitfils (2010), p. 168.
30. Mollenauer (2007), p. 15.
31. Ibid. p. 158n.175.
32. Sir Henry Savile to Secretary of State Henry Coventry, 16 April 1679, quoted in Mollenauer (2007), p. 142n.65.
33. See Petitfils (2010), pp. 179–83.
34. Quoted in Petitfils (2010), p. 183.
35. The beginning of the canon of the mass, the unchanging part of the ritual that does not alter according to the liturgical seasons.
36. A dry mass or *missa sicca* was properly a mass said without the consecration of the elements (for instance at sea owing to the danger of spilling the chalice). Guibourg's use of this term suggests that he intended to parody the mass rather than say an actual mass in which he attempted to consecrate the poisonous mixture.
37. Quoted in Petitfils (2010), pp. 310–11.
38. Petitfils (2010), p. 183.
39. Quoted in ibid., pp. 184–5.
40. Ibid. pp. 308–9.
41. De la Reynie seems to have doubted that the man really was a nobleman, describing him as 'l'étranger prétendu milord anglais' ('the foreigner claiming to be an English nobleman'), ibid. p. 311.
42. J. P. Kenyon, *The Popish Plot* (London: Penguin, 1974), p. 60.
43. Petitfils (2010), p. 88.
44. Young (2013), pp. 220–2.
45. Paton (2012), p. 242.
46. Young (2013), pp. 189–92.
47. Ibid. pp. 26–32.
48. Some English Catholics were, however, involved in magic (see ibid. pp. 157–62).
49. On this shift see ibid. p. 146.
50. G. Burnet, *Bishop Burnet's History of his own Time* (London, 1724), vol. 1, pp. 608–10.
51. *Historical Manuscripts Commission, 3rd Report* (London: HMSO, 1872), p. 41.
52. On Luxembourg's involvement see Petitfils (2010), pp. 133–45.
53. J. Sergeant, *A Letter from a Trooper in Flanders to his Comrade shewing that Luxemburg is a Witch, and deals with the Devil* (London, 1695).

54. J. Sergeant, *An Historical Romance of the Wars between the mighty Giant Gallieno, and the great Knight Nasonius* (Dublin, 1694), pp. 22–6. On Sergeant's use of witchcraft in his satire see Young (2013), pp. 167–8.
55. For discussions of the decline of elite witchcraft belief in eighteenth-century England see I. Bostridge, *Witchcraft and its Transformations c. 1650–c. 1750* (Oxford: Oxford University Press, 1997); O. Davies, *Witchcraft, Magic and Culture 1736–1951* (Manchester: Manchester University Press, 1999); B. Levack, 'The Decline and End of Witchcraft Prosecutions', in M. Gijswit-Hofstra and R. Porter (eds), *Witchcraft and Magic in Europe: The Eighteenth and Nineteenth Centuries* (London: Athlone Press, 1999), pp. 1–94; R. Porter, 'Witchcraft and Magic in Enlightenment, Romantic and Liberal Thought' in M. Gijswit-Hofstra and R. Porter (eds), *Witchcraft and Magic in Europe: The Eighteenth and Nineteenth Centuries* (London: Athlone Press, 1999), pp. 191–254; Young (2013), pp. 163–88; Davies (2015), pp. 521–46.
56. P. K. Monod, *Jacobitism and the English People, 1688–1788* (Cambridge: Cambridge University Press, 1989), p. 233.
57. [H. Walpole] *A Description of the Villa of Mr. Horace Walpole ... at Strawberry-Hill near Twickenham, Middlesex* (Strawberry Hill, 1784), pp. 41–2.
58. Kittredge (1928), pp. 90–1.
59. F. Barrett, *The Magus; or, Celestial Intelligencer, Book II, Part I* (London, 1801), pp. 19–20.
60. W. Godwin, *Lives of the Necromancers, or, an account of the most eminent persons in successive ages who have claimed for themselves, or to whom has been imputed by others, the exercise of magical power* (London: F. J. Mason, 1834), pp. 269–73.
61. Ibid. pp. 272–3.
62. On the case of Helen Duncan see J. Hazelgrove, *Spiritualism and British Society between the Wars* (Manchester: Manchester University Press, 2000), pp. 212–22.
63. M. Murray, *The Divine King of England* (London: Faber and Faber, 1954), p. 18.
64. Ibid. p. 186.
65. M. Howard, *Children of Cain: A Study of Modern Traditional Witches* (Richmond Vista, PA: Three Hands Press, 2011), p. 96.
66. Luhrmann (1989), pp. 206–19.
67. R. Petitpierre, *Exorcising Devils* (London: Robert Hale, 1976), p. 131.
68. Hutton (1999), p. 251.
69. 'Witches cast "mass spell" against Donald Trump', BBC News, 25 February 2017, http://www.bbc.co.uk/news/world-us-canada-39090334, retrieved 25 February 2017.

Bibliography

MANUSCRIPTS

The British Library, London
MS Add. 35830
MS Add. 48023
MS Add. 70984
MS Harley 286
MS Lansdowne 87
MS Lansdowne 99
MS Sloane 312
MS Sloane 3846

Cambridge University Library, Cambridge
MS Add. 3544
MSS EDR (Ely Diocesan Records) B/2/5; G/I/5
MS Dd.xi.45

Gonville and Caius College, Cambridge
MS 53/30

The National Archives, Kew
C 65/172, no. 2

PRIMARY SOURCES

Acts of the Privy Council of England (London: HMSO, 1890–1974), 45 vols.

Agrippa, H. C., *Henrici Cor. Agrippæ ... de occulta philosophia lib. III.; item spurius liber de ceremoniis magicis, qui quartus Agrippæ habetur* (Lyons, 1560).
——, (trans. R. Turner), *Henry Cornelius Agrippa His Fourth Book of Occult Philosophy* (London, 1655).
Aquinas, T. (ed. P. Caramello), *S. Thomae Aquinatis Summa Theologiae* (Turin: Marietti, 1962–3).
The Arraignment and Execution of the Late Traitors (London, 1606).
Bale, J. (ed. J. Payne Collier), *King Johan: A Play in Two Acts* (London: Camden Society, 1838), 2 vols.
Barrett, F., *The Magus; or, Celestial Intelligencer, Book II, Part I* (London, 1801).
Bodin, J., *De la démonomanie des sorcières* (Paris, 1580).
Bowden, E., *Doctor Lambe Reviv'd, or, Witchcraft condemn'd in Anne Bodenham a servant of his* (London, 1653).
Bray, G. (ed.), *The Anglican Canons, 1529–1947* (Woodbridge: Boydell, 1998).
A Briefe Description of the Notorious Life of John Lambe, otherwise called Doctor Lambe (Amsterdam, 1628).
Burnet, G., *Bishop Burnet's History of his own Time* (London, 1724), 2 vols.
Calendar of Letters and State Papers relating to English Affairs: preserved principally in the Archives of Simancas, ed. M. A. S. Hume (London: HMSO, 1892–99), 4 vols.
Calendar of the Manuscripts of the Most Hon. the Marquis of Salisbury (London: HMSO, 1883–1973), 24 vols.
Calendar of Patent Rolls preserved in the Public Record Office: Elizabeth I (London: HMSO, 1891–1964), 35 vols.
Calendar of State Papers: Domestic Series, of the reigns of Edward VI, Mary, Elizabeth and James I, 1547–[1625], ed. R. Lemon and M. A. E. Green (London: HMSO, 1856–72), 12 vols.
Calendar of State Papers, Domestic Series: Charles I, 1639–40, ed. W. D. Hamilton (London: HMSO, 1877).
Calendar of State Papers, Foreign Series, of the Reign of Elizabeth, ed. A. J. Crosby (London: HMSO, 1863–1950), 16 vols.
Camden, W., *Annals, or, The historie of the most renovvned and victorious princesse Elizabeth, late Queen of England* (London, 1635).
Casaubon, M., *Of Credulity and Incredulity in Things Natural, Civil and Divine* (London, 1668).
Cobbett's Complete Collection of State Trials (London, 1809), 34 vols.
Cogan, T., *The Haven of Health* (London, 1636).
Collyer, J. (ed.), *The Criminal Statutes of England* (London: S. Sweet, 1832).
A Copie of a Letter lately sent by a Gentleman, Student in the Lawes of the Realme, to a Frende of his concernyng. D. Story (London, 1571).
Correspondance politique de MM. de Castillon et de Marillac, ambassadeurs de France en Angleterre (1537–1542), ed. J. Kaulek (Paris: Germer Baillière, 1885).
The Correspondence of Reginald Pole, ed. T. F. Mayer and C. B. Walters (Aldershot: Ashgate, 2008), 4 vols.

Bibliography 233

Cosin, R., *Conspiracie for Pretended Reformation; viz. Presbyteriall Discipline* (London, 1592).

Coxe, F., *A Short Treatise declaringe the detestable wickednesse, of magicall sciences, as Necromancie. Conjurations of spirites, Curiouse Astrologie and suche lyke* (London, 1561).

Dee, J., 'John Dee's Account of his Life and Studies for half an hundred Years' in *Johannis, confratris & monachi Glastoniensis, chronica sive historia de rebus Glastoniensibus*, ed. T. Hearne (Oxford, 1726), vol. 2, pp. 497–551.

An English Chronicle of the Reigns of Richard II, Henry IV, Henry V, and Henry VI written before the year 1471, ed. J. S. Davies (London: Camden Society, 1856).

The English Devil: or, Cromwel and his Monstrous Witch discover'd at White-Hall (London, 1660).

Foreman, P. (trans. F. Young), *The Cambridge Book of Magic: A Tudor Necromancer's Manual* (Cambridge: Texts in Early Modern Magic, 2015).

Foxe, J., *The first volume of the ecclesiasticall history contayning the actes and monumentes of thynges passed in euery kynges tyme in this realme, especially in the Church of England* (London, 1570).

Gesta Herwardi incliti exulis et militis in Geoffroy Gaimar, *Lestorie des Engles*, ed. T. D. Hardy and C. T. Martin (London: HMSO, 1888), vol. 1, pp. 339–404.

Gibbons, A. (ed.), *Ely Episcopal Records: A Calendar and Concise View of the Episcopal Records Preserved in the Muniment Room of the Palace at Ely* (Lincoln: J. Williamson, 1891).

Hawkins, W., *A Treatise of the Pleas of the Crown* (London, 1716).

Historical Manuscripts Commission, 3rd Report (London: HMSO, 1872).

Historical Manuscripts Commission, 5th Report (London: HMSO, 1876).

James VI and I, *Daemonologie* (Edinburgh, 1597).

——, *Political Writings*, ed. J. P. Somerville (Cambridge: Cambridge University Press, 1994).

The Lawes against Witches and Conjuration (London, 1645).

Leslie, J., *A Treatise of Treasons against Q. Elizabeth, and the Crown of England* (London, 1572).

Letters and Papers Illustrative of the Reigns of Richard III and Henry VII, ed. J. Gairdner (London: Longman, 1863), 2 vols.

Letters and Papers, Foreign and Domestic, of the Reign of Henry VIII, ed. J. Brewer, J. Gairdner and R. Brodie (1892–1932), 35 vols.

Liber Eliensis, ed. E. O. Blake, Camden Third Series 92 (London: Royal Historical Society, 1962).

The Life and Letters of Thomas Cromwell (Oxford: Oxford University Press, 1902), 2 vols.

The Manuscripts of Lord Kenyon, Historical Manuscripts Commission, Fourteenth Report (London: HMSO, 1894).

Menghi, G., *Flagellum daemonum* (Bologna, 1577).

More, T., *The History of King Richard III*, ed. R. S. Sylvester, in *The Complete Works of St. Thomas More* (New Haven, CT: Yale University Press, 1961–88), 15 vols.

[Morwen, J.], *An Apologie to the Causes of the Brinnynge of Paule's Church* (London, 1561).

Norden, J., *Speculum Britanniae* (London, 1593).

Parsons, R., *An Epistle of the Persecution of Catholickes in England* (Douai [Rouen], 1582).

——, *Elizabethae, Angliae Reginae Haeresim Calvinianam Propugnantis, Saevissimum in Catholicos sui Regni edictum ... cum Responsione* (Rome, 1592).

——, *A Discussion of the Answere of M. William Barlow, D. of Divinity, to the Booke intituled: The Iudgment of a Catholike Englishman living in Banishment for his Religion* (St Omer, 1612).

Peck, F., *Desiderata Curiosa* (London, 1779), 2 vols.

Reformatio Legum Ecclesiasticarum (London, 1641).

Relations Politiques des Pays-Bas et de l'Angleterre sous le règne de Philippe II, ed. J. M. B. C. Kervyn de Lettenhove (Brussels: F. Hayez, 1882–1900), 11 vols.

Rushworth, J., *Historical Collections* (London, 1659–1701), 8 vols.

Sander, N., *De origine et progressu schismatis Anglicani* (Cologne, 1585).

Scot, R., *The Discoverie of Witchcraft* (London, 1665).

Sergeant, J., *An Historical Romance of the Wars between the mighty Giant Gallieno, and the great Knight Nasonius* (Dublin, 1694).

——, *A Letter from a Trooper in Flanders to his Comrade shewing that Luxemburg is a Witch, and deals with the Devil* (London, 1695).

Shakespeare, W., *The First Part of the Contention of the Two Famous Houses of York and Lancaster with the Death of the Good Duke Humphrey* (London, 1594).

——, *William Shakespeare: The Complete Works*, ed. S. Wells, G. Taylor, J. Jowett, and W. Montgomery (Oxford: Clarendon Press, 1986).

Spedding, J. (ed.), *The Life and Letters of Francis Bacon* (Longmans: London, 1857–74), 14 vols.

The St Albans Chronicle: The Chronica Maiora *of Thomas Walsingham*, ed. J. Taylor (Oxford: Clarendon, 2003), 2 vols.

Stowe, J., *The Annales of England* (London, 1592).

Townshend, H. (ed. J. W. Willis Bund), *The Diary of Henry Townshend* (Worcester: Worcestershire Historical Society, 1920), 2 vols.

Underhill, E., *The Autobiography of Edward Underhill*, in *Narratives of the Days of the Reformation* (London: Camden Society, 1859).

[Verstegan, R.], *The Copy of a Letter, lately written by a Spanishe gentleman* (London, 1589).

[Walpole, H.], *A Description of the Villa of Mr. Horace Walpole ... at Strawberry-Hill near Twickenham, Middlesex* (Strawberry Hill, 1784).

Wanley, N., *The Wonders of the Little World* (London, 1673).

Whitelock, D. (ed.), *English Historical Documents, c. 500–1042* (London: Eyre and Spottiswoode, 1953).

[Wright, W.], *Newes from Scotland* (London, 1591).

Young, F. (ed.), *A Medieval Book of Magical Stones: The Peterborough Lapidary* (Cambridge: Texts in Early Modern Magic, 2016).

SECONDARY WORKS

Almond, P. C., *Demonic Possession in Early Modern England: Contemporary Texts and their Cultural Contexts* (Cambridge: Cambridge University Press, 2004).
Ashton, D. J., 'Hungerford, Walter' in *ODNB*, vol. 28, pp. 827-8.
Bailey, G. and Peoples, J., *Essentials of Cultural Anthropology*, 3rd edn (Stamford, CT: Wadsworth, 2013).
Bailey, M. D., 'Diabolic Magic' in D. J. Collins (ed.), *The Cambridge History of Magic and Witchcraft in the West: From Antiquity to the Present* (Cambridge: Cambridge University Press, 2015), pp. 361-92.
Baldwin Smith, L., *Treason in Tudor England*, 2nd edn (London: Pimlico, 2006).
Beard, M., North, J. and Price, S., *Religions of Rome* (Cambridge: Cambridge University Press, 1998), 2 vols.
Beccatelli, R., *The Life of Cardinal Reginald Pole* (London, 1766).
Bellamy, J. G., *The Tudor Law of Treason: An Introduction* (London: Routledge and Kegan Paul, 1979).
Bellany, A. and Cogswell, T., *The Murder of King James I* (New Haven, CT: Yale University Press, 2015).
Booth, R., 'Standing within the Prospect of Belief: *Macbeth*, King James, and Witchcraft', in J. Newton and J. Bath (eds), *Witchcraft and the Act of 1604* (Leiden: Brill, 2008), pp. 47-6.
Bostridge, I., *Witchcraft and its Transformations c. 1650-c. 1750* (Oxford: Oxford University Press, 1997).
Boureau, A. (trans. T. L. Fagan), *Satan the Heretic: The Birth of Demonology in the Medieval West* (Chicago, IL: University of Chicago Press, 2006).
Bowd, S., 'John Dee and the Seven in Lancashire: Possession, Exorcism, and Apocalypse in Elizabethan England', *Northern History* 47 (2010), 233-46.
Brand, C. P., *Torquato Tasso: a study of the poet and of his contribution to English literature* (Cambridge: Cambridge University Press, 1965).
Butler, E. M., *Ritual Magic* (Cambridge: Cambridge University Press, 1949).
Carey, H. M., *Courting Disaster: Astrology at the English Court and University in the Later Middle Ages* (Basingstoke: MacMillan, 1992).
Chave-Mahir, F., *L'Exorcisme des Possédés dans l'Eglise d'Occident (Xe–XIVe siècle)* (Turnhout: Brepols, 2011).
Clark, S., *Thinking with Demons: The Idea of Witchcraft in Early Modern Europe* (Oxford: Clarendon, 1997).
Collins, D. J., 'Introduction' in D. J. Collins (ed.), *The Cambridge History of Magic and Witchcraft in the West: From Antiquity to the Present* (Cambridge: Cambridge University Press, 2015), pp. 1-14.
———, 'Learned Magic' in D. J. Collins (ed.), *The Cambridge History of Magic and Witchcraft in the West: From Antiquity to the Present* (Cambridge: Cambridge University Press, 2015), pp. 332-60.

Collinson, P., 'Pulling the Strings: Religion and Politics in the Progress of 1578', in J. E. Archer, E. Goldring and S. Knight (eds), *The Progresses, Pageants and Entertainments of Queen Elizabeth I* (Oxford: Oxford University Press, 2007), pp. 122–41.

Cook, J., *Dr Simon Forman: A Most Notorious Physician* (Chatto and Windus: London, 2001).

Cooper, T. (revised D. D. Rees), 'Sayer, Robert [*name in religion* Gregory] (1560–1602)' in *ODNB*, vol. 49, p. 161.

Copenhaver, B., *Magic in Western Culture: From Antiquity to the Enlightenment* (Cambridge: Cambridge University Press, 2015).

Cressy, D., *Dangerous Talk: Scandalous, Seditious and Treasonable Speech in Pre-Modern England* (Oxford: Oxford University Press, 2010).

Cronin, H. S., 'The Twelve Conclusions of the Lollards', *English Historical Review* 22 (1907), pp. 292–304.

Cross, C., 'Hastings, Henry, third earl of Huntingdon' in *ODNB*, vol. 25, pp. 756–9.

Davies, A., 'Witches in Anglo-Saxon England: Five Case Histories' in D. G. Scragg (ed.), *Superstition and Popular Medicine in Anglo-Saxon England* (Manchester: Manchester University Press, 1989), pp. 41–56.

Davies, O., *Witchcraft, Magic and Culture 1736–1951* (Manchester: Manchester University Press, 1999).

——, *Popular Magic: Cunning-folk in English History*, 2nd edn (London: Continuum, 2007).

——, *Grimoires: A History of Magic Books* (Oxford: Oxford University Press, 2009).

——, 'Magic in Common and Legal Perspectives' in D. J. Collins (ed.), *The Cambridge History of Magic and Witchcraft in the West: From Antiquity to the Present* (Cambridge: Cambridge University Press, 2015), pp. 521–46.

De la Bédoyere, G., *Gods with Thunderbolts: Religion in Roman Britain* (Stroud: Tempus, 2007).

Devine, M., 'Treasonous Catholic Magic and the 1563 Witchcraft Legislation: The English State's Response to Catholic Conjuring in the Early Years of Elizabeth I's Reign' in M. Harmes and V. Bladen (eds), *Supernatural and Secular Power in Early Modern England* (Farnham: Ashgate, 2015), pp. 67–94.

Dodds, M. H., *The Pilgrimage of Grace 1536–1537 and the Exeter Conspiracy 1538* (Cambridge: Cambridge University Press, 1915), 2 vols.

Doherty, P., *Isabella and the Strange Death of Edward II* (London: Constable, 2003).

Dover Wilson, J., 'A Note on *Richard III*: The Bishop of Ely's Strawberries', *Modern Language Review* 52 (1957), pp. 563–4.

Dovey, Z., *An Elizabethan Progress: The Queen's Journey into East Anglia, 1578* (Stroud: Sutton, 1996).

Duffy, E., *The Stripping of the Altars: Traditional Religion in England, 1400–1580* (New Haven, CT: Yale University Press, 1992).

Bibliography

Edwards, F., 'Sir Robert Cecil, Edward Squier and the Poisoned Pommel', *Recusant History* 25 (2001), pp. 377–414.

Elmer, P., *Witchcraft, Witch-Hunting and the State in Early Modern England* (Oxford: Oxford University Press, 2015).

Elton, G. R., *Policy and Police: The Enforcement of the Reformation in the Age of Thomas Cromwell* (Cambridge: Cambridge University Press, 1972).

Evans-Pritchard, E. E., *Witchcraft, Magic and Oracles among the Azande* (Oxford: Clarendon Press, 1937).

Ewen, C. L., *Witchcraft and Demonianism* (London: Heath Cranton, 1933).

Freeman, J., 'Sorcery at court and manor: Margery Jourdemayne, the witch of Eye next Westminster', *Journal of Medieval History* 30 (2004), pp. 343–57.

Freeman, T. S., 'Demons, Deviance and Defiance: John Darrell and the Politics of Exorcism in Late Elizabethan England' in P. Lake and M. Questier (eds), *Conformity and Orthodoxy in the English Church, c. 1560–1660* (Woodbridge: Boydell, 2000), pp. 34–63.

Gaskill, M., *Witchfinders: A Seventeenth-Century Tragedy* (London: John Murray, 2005).

———, 'Witchcraft and Evidence in Early Modern England', *Past and Present* 198 (2008), pp. 33–70.

Gay, E. F., 'The Midland Revolt and the Inquisitions of Depopulation of 1607', *Transactions of the Royal Historical Society*, New Series 18 (1904), pp. 195–244.

Gibson, M., *Possession, Puritanism and Print: Darrell, Harsnett, Shakespeare and the Elizabethan Exorcism Controversy* (London: Pickering and Chatto, 2006).

Gibson, M. and Esra J. A. (eds), *Shakespeare's Demonology: A Dictionary* (London: Arden Shakespeare, 2014).

Godwin, W., *Lives of the Necromancers, or, an account of the most eminent persons in successive ages who have claimed for themselves, or to whom has been imputed by others, the exercise of magical power* (London: F. J. Mason, 1834).

Grene, N., *Shakespeare's Serial History Plays* (Cambridge: Cambridge University Press, 2002).

Griffiths, R. A., 'The trial of Eleanor Cobham: an episode in the fall of Duke Humphrey of Gloucester', in R. A. Griffiths (ed.), *King and Country: England and Wales in the Fifteenth Century* (London: Hambledon, 1991), pp. 233–52.

Guenther, G. J., *Magical Imaginations: Instrumental Aesthetics in the English Renaissance* (Toronto: University of Toronto Press, 2012).

Harris, C. L., 'Eleanor [née Eleanor Cobham], duchess of Gloucester' in *ODNB*, vol. 18, pp. 27–8.

Hart, V., *Art and Magic in the Court of the Stuarts* (London: Routledge, 1994).

Hart, W. H., 'Observations on some Documents relating to Magic in the Reign of Queen Elizabeth', *Archaeologia* 40 (1866), pp. 389–97.

Hazelgrove, J., *Spiritualism and British Society between the Wars* (Manchester: Manchester University Press, 2000).

Heal, F., *Reformation in Britain and Ireland* (Oxford: Oxford University Press, 2003).

Hicks, M., 'George, duke of Clarence' in *ODNB*, vol. 21, pp. 792–5.

Hough, C., *'An Ald Reht': Essays on Anglo-Saxon Law* (Newcastle-upon-Tyne: Cambridge Scholars Publishing, 2014).

Howard, M., *Children of Cain: A Study of Modern Traditional Witches* (Richmond Vista, PA: Three Hands Press, 2011).

Hughes, J., *The Religious Life of Richard III: Piety and Prayer in the North of England* (Stroud: Sutton, 1997).

Hutton, R., *The Pagan Religions of the Ancient British Isles: Their Nature and Legacy*, 2nd edn (Oxford: Blackwell, 1993).

——, *The Triumph of the Moon: A History of Modern Pagan Witchcraft* (Oxford: Oxford University Press, 1999).

Ingelhart, L. E., *Press Freedoms: A Descriptive Calendar of Concepts, Interpretations, Events and Court Actions from 4000 B.C. to the Present* (Westport, CT: Greenwood Press, 1987).

Johnstone, N., *The Devil and Demonism in Early Modern England* (Cambridge: Cambridge University Press, 2006).

Jones, M., 'Joan [Joan of Navarre]' in *ODNB*, vol. 30, pp. 139–42.

Jones, N., 'Defining Superstitions: Treasonous Catholics and the Act against Witchcraft of 1563', in C. Carlton (ed.), *State, Sovereigns and Society in Early Modern England: Essays in Honour of A. J. Slavin* (Stroud: Sutton, 1998), pp. 187–204.

Jones, W. R., 'Political Uses of Sorcery in Medieval Europe', *The Historian* 34 (1972), pp. 670–87.

Kelke, W. H., 'Master John Schorne', *Records of Buckinghamshire* 2 (1869), pp. 60–74.

Kelly, H. A., 'English Kings and the Fear of Sorcery', *Mediaeval Studies* 39 (1977), pp. 206–38.

——, *The Devil at Baptism: Ritual, Theology and Drama* (Ithaca, NY: Cornell University Press, 1985).

——, 'Canon Law and Chaucer on Licit and Illicit Magic', in R. M. Karras, J. Kaye and E. A. Matter (eds), *Law and the Illicit in Medieval Europe* (Philadelphia, PA: University of Pennsylvania Press, 2008), pp. 210–21.

Kennedy, M., 'How stately home owner planned to protect a royal visitor from witches', *The Guardian* (5 November 2014), p. 11.

Kenyon, J. P., *The Popish Plot* (London: Penguin, 1974).

Kieckhefer, R., *European Witch Trials: Their Foundation in Popular and Learned Culture, 1300–1500* (Berkeley, CA: University of California Press, 1976).

——, *Forbidden Rites: A Necromancer's Manual of the Fifteenth Century* (Stroud: Sutton, 1997).

——, *Magic in the Middle Ages*, 2nd edn (Cambridge: Cambridge University Press, 2000).

King, E. J., *The Seals of the Order of St John of Jerusalem* (London: Taylor and Francis, 1932).

Kittredge, G. L., *Witchcraft in Old and New England* (Cambridge, MA: Harvard University Press, 1928).
Klaassen, F., 'English Manuscripts of Magic, 1300–1500: A Preliminary Survey' in C. Fanger (ed.), *Conjuring Spirits: Texts and Traditions of Medieval Ritual Magic* (Stroud: Sutton, 1998), pp. 3–31.
——, 'Medieval Ritual Magic in the Renaissance', *Aries* 3 (2003), pp. 166–99.
——, 'Learning and Masculinity in Manuscripts of Ritual Magic of the Later Middle Ages and Renaissance', *Sixteenth Century Journal* 38 (2007), pp. 49–76.
——, 'Ritual Invocation and Early Modern Science: The Skrying Experiments of Humphrey Gilbert' in C. Fanger (ed.) *Invoking Angels: Theurgic Ideas and Practices, Thirteenth to Sixteenth Centuries* (University Park, PA: Pennsylvania State University Press, 2010), pp. 341–66.
——, *The Transformations of Magic: Illicit Learned Magic in the Later Middle Ages and Renaissance* (University Park, PA: Pennsylvania State University Press, 2013).
Knighton, C. S., 'Westminster Abbey Restored' in E. Duffy and D. Loades (eds), *The Church of Mary Tudor* (Farnham: Ashgate, 2006), pp. 77–123.
Kreider, A., *English Chantries: The Road to Dissolution* (Cambridge, MA: Harvard University Press, 1979).
Lake, P., 'A Tale of Two Episcopal Surveys: The Strange Fates of Edmund Grindal and Cuthbert Mayne revisited', *Transactions of the Royal Historical Society* 18 (2008), pp. 129–63.
Larner, C., *Witchcraft and Religion: The Politics of Popular Belief* (Oxford: Blackwell, 1984).
Leland, J., 'Witchcraft and the Woodvilles: a standard medieval smear?' in D. L. Biggs, S. D. Michalove and A. Compton Reeves (eds), *Reputation and Representation in Fifteenth-Century Europe* (Brill: Leiden, 2004), pp. 267–88.
Levack, B., 'The Decline and End of Witchcraft Prosecutions', in M. Gijswit-Hofstra and R. Porter (eds), *Witchcraft and Magic in Europe: The Eighteenth and Nineteenth Centuries* (London: Athlone Press, 1999), pp. 1–94.
Lidaka, J., '*The Book of Angels, Rings, Characters and Images of the Planets*: Attributed to Osbern Bokenham' in C. Fanger (ed.), *Conjuring Spirits: Texts and Traditions of Medieval Ritual Magic* (Stroud: Sutton, 1998), pp. 32–75.
Lock, J., 'Story, John' in *ODNB*, vol. 52, pp. 955–8.
Lockyer, R., 'Lake, Sir Thomas' in *ODNB*, vol. 32, pp. 247–9.
Luhrmann, T. M., *Persuasions of the Witch's Craft: Ritual Magic in Contemporary England* (Oxford: Blackwell, 1989).
Lynch, J. H. and Adamo, P. C., *The Medieval Church: A Brief History*, 2nd edn (London: Routledge, 2014).
MacFarlane, A., *Witchcraft in Tudor and Stuart England: A Regional and Comparative Study* (London: Routledge and Kegan Paul, 1970).
Machielsen, J., *Martin Delrio: Demonology and Scholarship in the Counter-Reformation* (Oxford: Oxford University Press, 2015).

Malinowski, B., 'Magic, Science and Religion' in B. Malinowski, *Magic, Science and Religion and Other Essays* (Glencoe, IL: Free Press, 1948), pp. 1–71.
Maxwell-Stuart, P. G., *Satan's Conspiracy: Magic and Witchcraft in Sixteenth-Century Scotland* (East Linton: Tuckwell Press, 2001).
———, 'King James's Experience of Witches, and the English Witchcraft Act of 1604' in J. Newton and J. Bath (eds), *Witchcraft and the Act of 1604* (Leiden: Brill, 2008), pp. 31–46.
———, *The British Witch: The Biography* (Stroud: Amberley, 2014).
Mayer, T. F., *Reginald Pole: Prince and Prophet* (Cambridge: Cambridge University Press, 2000).
McConnell, A., 'Lambe, John' in *ODNB*, vol. 32, pp. 296–7.
Merrifield, R., *The Archaeology of Ritual and Magic* (London: Batsford, 1987).
Millar, C. R., 'Witchcraft and Deviant Sexuality: A Case Study of Dr Lambe' in M. Harmes, L. Henderson, B. Harmes and A. Antonio (eds), *The British World: Religion, Memory, Society, Culture* (Toowoomba: University of Southern Queensland, 2012), pp. 51–62.
———, 'Sleeping with Devils: The Sexual Witch in Seventeenth-century England' in M. Harmes and V. Bladen (eds), *Supernatural and Secular Power in Early Modern England* (Farnham: Ashgate, 2015), pp. 207–31.
Mollenauer, L. W., *Strange Revelations: Magic, Poison and Sacrilege in Louis XIV's France* (University Park, PA: Pennsylvania State University Press, 2007).
Monod, P. K., *Jacobitism and the English People, 1688–1788* (Cambridge: Cambridge University Press, 1989).
Mortimer, I., *The Time Traveller's Guide to Elizabethan England* (London: Vintage, 2013).
Murray, M., *The Divine King of England* (London: Faber and Faber, 1954).
Murray, T. B., *A Notice of Ely Chapel, Holborn* (London: John Parker, 1840).
Oxley, J. E., *The Reformation in Essex: To the Death of Mary* (Manchester: Manchester University Press, 1965).
Page, S., *Magic in the Cloister: Pious Motives, Illicit Interests, and Occult Approaches to the Medieval Universe* (University Park, PA: Pennsylvania State University Press, 2013).
Parish, H., 'Magic and Priestcraft: Reformers and Reformation' in D. J. Collins (ed.), *The Cambridge History of Magic and Witchcraft in the West: From Antiquity to the Present* (Cambridge: Cambridge University Press, 2015), pp. 393–425.
Parry, G., *The Arch-Conjurer of England: John Dee* (New Haven, CT: Yale University Press, 2011).
Paton, D., 'Witchcraft, Poison, Law, and Atlantic Slavery', *William and Mary Quarterly* 69 (2012), pp. 235–64.
Petitfils, J.-C., *L'affaire des poisons* (Paris: Perrin, 2010).
Petitpierre, R., *Exorcising Devils* (London: Robert Hale, 1976).
Pierce, H., 'Pole, Arthur' in *ODNB*, vol. 44, pp. 691–2.
Porter, R., 'Witchcraft and Magic in Enlightenment, Romantic and Liberal Thought' in M. Gijswit-Hofstra and R. Porter (eds), *Witchcraft and Magic in*

Europe: *The Eighteenth and Nineteenth Centuries* (London: Athlone Press, 1999), pp. 191–254.

Purkiss, D., *The Witch in History: Early Modern and Twentieth-Century Representations* (London: Routledge, 1996).

Reynolds, M., *Godly Reformers and their Opponents in Early Modern England: Religion in Norwich, c. 1560–1643* (Woodbridge: Boydell, 2005).

Rider, C., 'Common Magic' in D. J. Collins (ed.), *The Cambridge History of Magic and Witchcraft in the West: From Antiquity to the Present* (Cambridge: Cambridge University Press, 2015), pp. 303–31.

Roberts, R. J. and Watson, A. G. (eds), *John Dee's Library Catalogue* (London: Bibliographical Society, 1990).

Romeo, G., *Inquisitori, esorcisti e streghe nell'Italia della Controriforma* (Florence: Sansoni, 2003).

Rosen, B. (ed.), *Witchcraft in England, 1558–1618* (Amherst, MA: University of Massachusetts Press, 1991).

Rowe, J. and Young, F., 'East Anglian Catholics in the Reign of Elizabeth, 1559–1603' in F. Young (ed.), *Catholic East Anglia: A History of the Catholic Faith in Norfolk, Suffolk, Cambridgeshire and Peterborough* (Leominster: Gracewing, 2016), pp. 37–60.

Ryrie, A., *The Sorcerer's Tale: Faith and Fraud in Tudor England* (Oxford: Oxford University Press, 2008).

Sharpe, J., *The Bewitching of Anne Gunter: A Horrible and True Story of Deception, Witchcraft, and the King of England* (New York: Routledge, 2000).

Simpson, W. S., 'Master John Schorne', *Records of Buckinghamshire* 3 (1870), pp. 354–69.

Srivastava, V. K., 'Ethnographic Notebook: Modern Witchcraft and Occultism in Cambridge', *The Cambridge Journal of Anthropology* 13 (1988), pp. 50–71.

Steible, M., 'Jane Shore and the Politics of Cursing', *Studies in English Literature, 1500–1900* 43 (2003), pp. 1–17.

Stoyle, A., *Soldiers and Strangers: An Ethnic History of the English Civil War* (New Haven, CT: Yale University Press, 2005).

Strathmann, E. A., 'John Dee as Ralegh's "Conjurer"', *Huntington Library Quarterly* 10 (1947), pp. 365–72.

Thomas, K., *Religion and the Decline of Magic*, 4th edn (London: Penguin, 1991).

Underdown, D., *A Freeborn People: Politics and the Nation in Seventeenth-Century England* (Oxford: Oxford University Press, 1996).

Van Patten, J. K., 'Magic, Prophecy, and the Law of Treason in Reformation England', *The American Journal of Legal History* 27 (1983), pp. 1–32.

Voigts, L. E., 'The "Sloane Group": Related Scientific and Medical Manuscripts from the Fifteenth Century in the Sloane Collection', *British Library Journal* 16 (1990), pp. 26–57.

Walsham, A., '"Frantick Hacket": Prophecy, Sorcery, Insanity, and the Elizabethan Puritan Movement', *The Historical Journal* 41 (1998), pp. 27–66.

——, *Providence in Early Modern England* (Oxford: Oxford University Press, 2001).

Warnicke, R. M., 'Sexual Heresy at the Court of Henry VIII', *The Historical Journal* 30 (1987), pp. 247–68.

———, *The Rise and Fall of Anne Boleyn: Family Politics at the Court of Henry VIII*, 3rd edn (Cambridge: Cambridge University Press, 1991).

———, *The Marrying of Anne of Cleves: Royal Protocol in Tudor England* (Cambridge: Cambridge University Press, 2000).

Warren, R. (ed.), *Henry VI, Part Two* (Oxford: Oxford University Press, 2002).

Weisman, R., *Witchcraft, Magic and Religion in 17th-century Massachusetts* (Amherst, MA: University of Massachusetts Press, 1984).

Willis, D., *Malevolent Nurture: Witch-hunting and Maternal Power in Early Modern England* (Ithaca, NY: Cornell University Press, 1995).

Young, F., *English Catholics and the Supernatural, 1553–1829* (Farnham: Ashgate, 2013).

———, 'Early Modern English Catholic Piety in a Fifteenth-Century Book of Hours: Cambridge University Library MS Additional 10079', *Transactions of the Cambridge Bibliographical Society* 15 (2015), pp. 541–59.

———, *A History of Exorcism in Catholic Christianity* (London: Palgrave MacMillan, 2016).

WEB SOURCES

'Witches cast "mass spell" against Donald Trump', BBC News, 25 February 2017, http://www.bbc.co.uk/news/world-us-canada-39090334, accessed 25 February 2017.

Index

abortion, 63, 188, 190, 194
Adeane, John, 115
Aeneid, The, 40-1
Agrippa, Heinrich Cornelius, 10, 128, 203
Ailsworth, Northants, 28
Alba, duke of, 112, 114
alchemy, 10, 11, 56, 67, 105, 113, 115, 139, 140, 145, 146, 170
Alexander VI, pope, 51
almanacks, 163 *see also* astrology
Anabaptists, 81-2, 143
Anderson, Edmund, 162
Anderson, McKolme, 159
angels, 20, 40, 42, 92, 125, 127, 143, 163-4
Anglicanism *see* Church of England
Anglo-Dutch Wars, 187, 192-3
Anjou, duke of, 120, 133
Anne of Denmark, queen of England, 155-6, 172
Antwerp, 111
Antwerp, Lionel of, 47
apothecaries, 52, 146, 198
apples, 102-3
Appleyard, John, 140
Aquinas, Thomas, 42, 67
Arabic magic, 20, 28, 29, 36
Aragon, Catherine of, queen of England, 57, 59
Arc, Joan of, 35, 44, 147, 196
Armada, Spanish, 134
Arthur, king, 123, 201
Arundel, earl of, 145
Ashmole, Elias, 105, 125

astrology, 10, 11, 34, 36, 40, 44, 46, 49, 51-2, 53, 67, 84, 92, 101, 103, 105, 141, 169, 174
calculations, 12, 36-8, 50, 53, 87, 113, 163
horoscopes, questionary, 36-8, 46, 49, 51, 82, 99, 100, 132, 141
judicial, 82
see also magic, astral
atheism, 144, 193
Atholl, countess of, 155
Augustus, emperor, 36-7
Austria, Margaret of, 99
Awder, William, 142-3, 169

Babraham, Cambs, 25
Bacon, Francis, 168
Bacon, Roger, 67
Baillie, Robert, 180
Bale, John, bishop of Ossory, 70
Bancroft, Richard, archbishop of Canterbury, 165
baptism, 40, 82, 92, 122
Barker, Robert, 25
Barrett, Francis, 198-9
Barwick, Humphrey, 100-1
Barton, Elizabeth, 61-3, 186
Barton, William, 63
Bath, Somerset, 1
Bayezid II, sultan, 51
Beaton, David, archbishop of St Andrews, 154
Beauchamp, John, 45
Beaufort, Edmund, 2nd duke of Somerset, 59
Beaufort, Henry, cardinal, 36, 39, 43

Beaufort, Margaret, 50, 51, 171
Beaulieu, Palace of, Essex, 96
Becket, St Thomas, 64
Beckwith, William, 138
Bell, Ralph, 69
Belleau, Catherine, 194
Benger, Thomas, 82, 83
Bergen-op-Zoom, 112
Bible, 59, 81, 91, 94, 127, 140, 197
   Authorised Version, 2, 95, 217n.14
   Geneva Bible, 2, 95, 217n.14
   Vulgate, 114, 217n.14
Bible and key, 63–4, 78
   see also divination
Bilson, Leonard, 97, 99, 101–2, 104
Blake, Thomas, 48
Blower, Henry, 131, 134
Bockenham, William, 40
Bodenham, Anne, 175, 226n.58
Bodin, Jean, 134
Boleyn, Anne, queen of England, 57, 61, 71–3, 83, 87, 153
Bolingbroke, Roger, 36–8, 39, 40, 42, 43, 44, 45, 46, 49, 51, 106, 147–9
Bologna, university of, 40
Bonner, Edmund, bishop of London, 84, 91–2, 95, 101, 106, 112
Borley, Suff, 96
Bostock, Lancelot, 111
Bosworth, battle of, 50
Bourne, John, 83
Bowes, Robert, 159
Bracon Ash, Norf, 119
Brandeston, Suff, 182
Branktre, Richard, 63
Bridgewater, Somerset, 104
Brigge, Mabel, 68–9, 111
Brinvilliers, marquise de, 190
Brodford, Wilts, 63
Browne, Gabriel, 176
Browning, John, 137
Brownists, 142
Brussels, 114
Bucke, Isabel, 68
Buggery, Statute of, 75, 76, 95, 108, 215n.48 see also homosexuality
Bull, Charles, 195
Bungay, Suff, 106
Burchard of Worms, 24
Burdett, Thomas, 48, 49
Burgate, Agnes, 35
Burgh, Thomas, 3rd baron Burgh, 157
burial, 29–30, 41, 73, 121, 122, 123, 133

Burnet, Gilbert, bishop of Salisbury, 195
burning, penalty of, 5, 26, 34, 45, 59, 60, 67, 69, 94, 131, 138, 181
Butler, Eleanor, 49
Bury, Charlotte, 198
Bury St Edmunds, Suffolk, 129, 181
Byngham, Richard, 100
Byrd, William, 63, 75

Cade, Jack, 46–7
Caerleon, Lewis of, 50
Calton, Edmund, 145
Calvert, George, 168
Calvinism, 93, 116, 142
Cambridge, 44, 50, 67
   university of, 82, 92
Camden, William, 101
canon law, 23, 24, 26, 39, 49, 61, 79, 80, 112, 165
Canterbury, Kent, 19
Caroline of Brunswick, queen of Great Britain, 198, 199
Carr, Robert, viscount Rochester, 169
Cary, Henry, 1st baron Hunsdon, 145
Carye, Christopher, 83
Casaubon, Meric, 134
Catesby, Isabel, 92
Catharism, 23, 75
Catherine of Braganza, queen of England, 20, 187
Catholicism, 10, 18, 57, 58–9, 60, 64, 70, 72, 80–1, 82, 84, 87, 88–90, 91, 92, 93–4, 96, 98, 100, 101, 104, 106, 107, 108, 110, 112, 113, 115–16, 117–18, 120, 124, 125, 126, 129–32, 134, 135, 138, 142, 143, 144, 146, 151, 153–4, 155, 164–5, 166, 167, 173, 176, 179, 180, 186, 192, 193–5, 196, 197, 228n.48
Catlyn, Robert, 102
Cecil, Robert, 1st earl of Salisbury, 154, 159, 167
Cecil, Thomas, 1st earl of Exeter, 168
Cecil, William, 1st baron Burghley, 96, 100, 101, 102, 104, 108, 113, 114, 115, 132, 137, 142, 143, 145, 154, 157
Cecil, William, 16th baron Ros, 167–8
censorship, 183
cerecloth, 41
Cessac, comte de, 189
Chamberlain, John, 169
Chambre Ardente, 188

Index

chantry priests, 69–70, 111
Chapuys, Eustace, 71
Charles I, king of England, 6, 173, 174, 176, 177, 181, 182, 185, 186, 200, 203
Charles II, king of England, 180, 183, 186, 187, 188, 189, 190, 192, 194, 195, 196
Charles V, emperor, 57, 68, 81
charming, 15, 16, 71, 94, 102, 107, 108, 109, 136, 145, 162, 164, 176, 191, 195–6
Chaucer, Geoffrey, 26
cheese, 102, 104, 167
Chelmsford, Essex, 110
Chichele, Henry, archbishop of Canterbury, 39, 43
church courts *see* canon law
Church of England, 58, 59, 60, 79, 87–8, 89, 95, 96, 118, 126, 134, 142, 144, 195
circles, magical, 27, 53, 79, 94, 104, 123, 144, 156, 174
Civil War, English, 6, 21, 177, 180–1, 186, 203
Clarence, George duke of, 48–9, 66, 72, 97
Clene, Dr, 65
clergy, benefit of, 141
Cleves, Anne of, queen of England, 73, 74, 76
Cobham, Eleanor, duchess of Gloucester, 5, 35–8, 43–4, 45, 46, 50, 53, 62, 72, 147–9, 151
Cochrane, Robert, 201
Cockoyter, John, 100
Coggeshall, Essex, 63
Coke, Edward, 45, 168, 169
Colchester, Essex, 50
Common Prayer, Book of, 111, 188, 195
Commonwealth *see* Interregnum
conjuration *see* exorcism; magic, ritual
Cordell, William, 124
Cornwall, 13, 97
corpses, 122, 156, 162, 184
Cosin, Richard, 143
Cosyn, Edward, 100, 101
de Cotton, Bartholomew, 26
counterfeiting, 56, 160
counter-magic, 13, 124–5, 128, 181
Counter-Reformation, 60, 92, 106, 214n.22
counter-witchcraft *see* counter-magic
Covenanters, 176
Coventry, Warks, 27, 30

Cowpar, Henry, 78
Cox, Richard, bishop of Ely, 93–4
Coxe, Francis, 90–1, 99, 103–5, 110
Coxe, John, 95–6, 97, 98, 99, 102, 103, 104, 110
Crane, Nicholas, 63
Cranmer, Thomas, archbishop of Canterbury, 59
Croft, Christopher, 195
Cromwell, Oliver, lord protector, 181, 183, 185–6
Cromwell, Thomas, earl of Essex, 58, 69, 61–2, 64, 65, 66, 67, 71, 73–6
crosses, 76, 77–8
cunning-folk, 14, 45, 63, 64, 72, 75, 78, 132, 133, 174, 175, 184 *see also* magic, popular
cursing, 1, 45, 57, 111, 114, 126, 128, 153, 171–2

Darcy, Brian, 137
Darrell, John, 165
Dartford, Kent, 47
Daunger, John, 47
Dedham, Suff, 137
de la Pole, William, 1st duke of Suffolk, 148–9
de Vere, John, 16th earl of Oxford, 96
de Vere, Robert, duke of Ireland, 33
Dee, John, 6, 82–4, 85, 92, 123–9, 131–2, 139, 140, 143, 144, 163, 197, 201, 221n.10
Delrio, Martin, 224n.85
Delves, John, 111
demonic magic *see* magic, ritual
demonology, 24, 72, 126, 134, 160, 224n.85
demons, 2, 12, 13, 20, 23, 24, 30, 31, 37, 42, 79, 83–4, 87, 99, 107, 110, 126–8, 150, 154, 166, 174
Denmark, 155, 158, 170
Deshayes, Catherine, 190, 192
Deshayes, Marie Marguerite, 192
Desmond, earl of, 139
Despenser, Hugh, earl of Winchester, 27, 31
Device, Jennet, 164
devil, the *see* Satan
devil worship, 13, 25
Dewse, Mrs, 117
Digby, Everard, 166
dissenters, 97, 138, 142, 188
see also Puritanism
dissolution of the monasteries, 58, 62, 70, 85, 95, 96

divination, 3, 34, 36, 63-4, 80 *see also* astrology; Bible and key; sieve and shears
divine right of kings, 17, 18, 160, 188, 200
dove, blood of, 103
Dover, Treaty of, 192
drama, 70-1, 147-50, 151, 162, 170-2
Draper, Hugh, 99
Dudley, John, 1st duke of Northumberland, 59, 81
Dudley, Robert, earl of Leicester, 99, 113, 120, 123, 129, 132-4, 135, 137-8, 140, 145, 221n.10
Duncan, Geillis, 155, 157
Duncan, Helen, 200
Dundee, Scotland, 159
dung, 73, 119, 150
Durham, 113

ecclesiastical courts *see* canon law
Edgar, king of England, 28
Edinburgh, Scotland, 158
  Holyrood Park, 211n.53
Edward I, king of England, 26
Edward II, king of England, 27, 31, 105
Edward III, king of England, 33, 46, 47, 102
Edward IV, king of England, 47, 48, 49, 97
Edward V, king of England, 48, 49
Edward VI, king of England, 59, 60, 70, 73, 77, 78-9, 80, 81, 84, 85, 89, 96, 97, 137
effigy magic, 12, 13, 20, 28, 29, 30, 32, 40, 48, 56, 73, 78, 87, 105, 115-16, 121, 123, 124-5, 126, 131, 153, 156, 160, 166, 184, 198, 199
Eglisham, George, 174, 176
Elizabeth I, queen of England, 6, 7, 17, 21, 72, 82-3, 84, 85, 92, 95, 96, 98, 99, 108, 110, 113, 114, 118, 132, 133, 136, 137, 141, 143, 145, 151
  accession, 89-91, 96, 132
  childlessness, 97, 153
  death, 146
  illness, 17, 101, 120-1
  image cult, 115-16
  progress of 1578, 119-20, 123, 129-31
  religious policy, 86-9, 93-4, 106, 142, 144
Elkes, Thomas, 133, 134, 135, 137
Elm, Cambs, 163

Ely, Cambs, 23-4
Englefield, Francis, 83
Erasmus, Desiderius, 81, 216n.68
Erastianism, 95
Essex, 96, 111, 137
Euston, Suffolk, 129-31
excommunication, 25, 80, 88, 130
Exeter, Devon, 35
exorcism, 19, 25, 65, 67, 104-5, 125-8, 143, 148, 149, 165, 194, 195, 201, 214n.22

fairies, 39
Fakenham, Suffolk, 99
Falmouth, Cornwall, 187
familiars, 15, 110, 181
Family of Love, 142
Farleigh, Somerset, 74, 75
fasting, 68-9, 104, 111, 127, 165
Fawkes, Guido, 165, 166
Ferrars, George, 83
Fian, John, 155, 156
figures, magical, 12, 32, 43, 79, 107, 119, 127, 128, 141
Fisher, John, bishop of Rochester, 58, 61
Flanders *see* Low Countries
Fleet prison, 65, 80, 146
Fontanges, duchesse de, 189
forgery, 89, 117, 132, 140, 168
  see also counterfeiting
Forman, Simon, 169
Fortescue, Anthony, 91, 92, 98, 100, 101
Foxe, John, 60, 112, 132, 214n.31
France, 14, 23, 34, 35, 46, 58, 71, 75, 88, 89, 100, 154, 179, 189, 192, 193, 194, 196, 212n.79
Francis I, king of France, 190
fraud, 17, 18, 56, 78, 83, 93, 133, 135, 165, 186, 200
Frazer, James, 7, 201
Frear, Dr, 97
friars, 19, 31, 33, 52, 66-7, 212n.79
  Carmelite, 66, 70
  Dominican, 33-4, 66, 67, 214n.23
  Franciscan, 26, 34, 66, 67, 126, 214n.22, 23
Furies, 148
Fyloll, Jasper, 67

Gardiner, Stephen, bishop of Winchester, 71, 97
Gardner, Gerald, 200
Gaule, John, 18

Index

Gaunt, John of, duke of Lancaster, 34, 36, 46, 47
geomancy, 36
George IV, king of Great Britain, 198
Giffard, George, 162
Glover, Mary, 162
Godfrey, Edmund Berry, 194
Godwin, William, 199
Göldi, Anna, 11
Gospellers, 81–2, 91, 96, 107, 111, 144
Goswill, Robert, 63
Graham, Richard, 157
Gratian, 24
Gravesend, Kent, 95, 101
Gray, William, bishop of Ely, 25
Great Fire of London, 106, 108
Great Milton, Oxfordshire, 82
Great Yarmouth, Norfolk, 112
Greek Fire *see* wildfire
Green, Bartlet, 84
Grey, Jane, 59, 80
Grierson, Robert, 155, 156
grimoires, 41, 65, 183, 198, 199
Grindal, Edmund, archbishop of Canterbury, 101, 102, 109
Guibourg, Etienne, 190–1, 192, 228n.36
Guichard, bishop of Troyes, 212n.79
Guise, duke of, 100
Guise, Mary of, 154
Gunpowder Plot, 108, 165, 166, 226n.37
Gunter, Anne, 165

Hacket, William, 143, 144, 167, 176
Hallay, Bartholomew, 38
Hamilton, James, earl of Arran, 154
Hanmer, Thomas, 138
Harding, Thomas, 131, 133, 134, 135
Harnington, Worcs, 100
Harriot, Thomas, 144
Hastings, Edward, baron Loughborough, 97, 98–9, 100, 139
Hastings, George, 138, 139–40
Hastings, Henry, 3rd earl of Huntingdon, 97, 139
Hastings, Walter, 139
Hastings, William, baron Hastings, 49
Hawe, Andrew, 143
Hawkins, William, 15
hebona, 170
Hecate, 171
Henry, Prince of Wales, 159, 173
Henry I, king of England, 28

Henry IV, king of England, 25, 32–3, 34, 46
Henry V, king of England, 34–5, 36, 46, 67
Henry VI, king of England, 35, 36, 37, 38, 39, 45, 46–7, 48, 51, 149–50
Henry VII, king of England, 50, 51–2, 57, 96, 158
Henry VIII, king of England 3, 5, 6, 21, 53, 56, 57–9, 60, 61, 62, 64, 65, 66, 68, 69, 70, 71–4, 76, 77, 78, 80, 82, 84, 85, 87, 88, 97, 109, 111, 118, 154, 173, 186
Hepburn, James, earl of Bothwell, 155, 156
herbalism, 20
Herbert, Henry, 1st earl of Pembroke, 113
Hereford, 44
heresy, 9, 23, 25–6, 37, 42, 44, 45, 53, 57, 60, 75, 76, 81, 131, 209n.7
Hereward the Wake, 23–4
Hertfordshire, 83, 142
Heywood, Thomas, 162
Hinchinbrook, Hunts, 163
Hody, John, 44
Hogekyn, Robert, 65
Holden, Thomas, 187–8
Holderness *see* Yorkshire
Holland, Anne, 98
Holme, John, 44, 147–8
Holme, Yorkshire, 69
Holmpton, Yorks, 69
holy water, 103, 126, 128
homosexuality, 63, 75 *see also* Buggery, Statute of
Hopkin, Arnold, 65
Hopkins, Matthew (East Anglia), 4, 18, 182
horoscopes *see* astrology
Horsey, William, archdeacon of London, 51–2
hosts, consecrated, 19, 42 *see also* mass
Howard, Frances, countess of Essex, 169
Howard, Michael, 203
Howard, Thomas, 3rd duke of Norfolk, 68, 69, 80
Howard, Thomas, 4th duke of Norfolk, 113, 120
Hrabanus Maurus, 24
Hugh of St Victor, 24
Huguenots, 194
Hum, John *see* Holme, John

Humphrey, duke of Gloucester, 35–6, 43, 51
Hungerford, Walter, 74–6, 77, 138, 149
Huntley, Mother, 74
Hussey, Elizabeth, 74

Ibn Bishr, Sahl, 28
iconoclasm, 130–1
idolatry, 2, 25, 77, 93, 95, 102, 105, 130–1
images, religious, 130–1
impotence, 41, 71, 72, 74
incest, 71, 72, 73, 160, 161, 169
Inglewood, John, 33
Inold, William, 64
inquisitors, 9, 51, 94
Interregnum, 183
invisibility, cloak of, 66
Ipswich, Suff, 33, 57, 137, 181, 182
Ireland, 70, 88, 99, 139, 161, 181, 197
Ireton, Henry, 185
Isidore of Seville, 24
Ivo of Chartres, 24

Jacobitism, 196, 197
James II, king of England, 186, 187–8, 194, 196
James V, king of Scots, 154, 155
James VI and I, king of England, 6, 17, 18, 21, 114, 150, 172, 182, 186
  English reign, 161–2, 165, 166–7, 168, 169–70, 172–4, 175–6, 179, 180, 194, 195
  Scottish reign, 154, 155–61
Jenks, Rowland, 116–18, 175
Jewel, John, bishop of Salisbury, 93
John, king of England, 70–1
John XXII, pope, 14, 31, 209n.7
Johnson, Nicholas, 137
Jolly, William, 96
Jones, Richard, 66
Jonson, Ben, 172
Jourdemayne, Margery, 5, 39, 43, 44–5, 46, 138, 147, 148, 149
Julius III, pope, 92

Kele, Thomas, 91, 95, 98
Kemp, John, archbishop of York, 36, 43
Kendal, John, 51, 52, 213n.97
Kenninghall, Norf, 120
Kent, 46, 61, 96
Kers, John, 157
Kidderminster, Worcs, 187
Kimberley, Norfolk, 124

Kinnevsley, William, 144–5
Kittredge, George, 4, 201
Knole, Kent, 166
Knox, John, 142
Kylden, Stephen, 137

Lake, Thomas, 167–70, 173
Lakeland, Mary, 5, 181
Lambe, John, 174–5
Lancashire, 125, 164
Lancaster, 164
Lancaster, Duchy of, 145
Lancaster, John of, duke of Bedford, 35, 47
Langley, Edmund of, 47
Lateran IV, Council, 23, 24
Laud, William, archbishop of Canterbury, 180
Lee, John, 115
Leeds Castle, Kent, 34, 43
Leicestershire, 167
Leith, Scotland, 156, 182
lèse majesté 2, 17, 56, 202
Leslie, John, bishop of Ross, 116
Levellers, 186
libertinism, 189, 193
Lilburn, John, 186
Lincolnshire, 62, 69, 197
Lincolnshire Rising, 75
literacy, 8, 15, 17, 19, 26, 143
lithomancy, 20
Littledean, Gloucs, 115
Lokkar, John, 68, 69
Lollardy, 25, 81, 142
London, 28, 39, 43, 44, 45, 47, 63, 73, 82, 83, 98, 110, 115, 120, 123, 129, 131, 140, 161, 162, 173, 174, 175, 177, 180, 194, 201
  Blackfriars, 67
  Cheapside, 38, 99, 143
  Clerkenwell, 52, 100
  Fulham Palace, 84
  Greenwich, 36
  Hampton Court, 79, 82, 83
  Holborn, 174
  Hornsey Park, 38–9
  Islington, 119
  St James's Palace, 83
  Lambeth, 92, 100, 101
  Lincoln's Inn Fields, 119, 124
  London Bridge, 28, 44
  Mortlake, 123, 126, 221n.10
  Pallenswick, 33
  Richmond Palace, 123, 129
  St Paul's Cathedral, 105–8

Index

St Paul's Cross, 39, 46, 106
Smithfield, 44
Southwark, 100, 137
Tower of London, 26, 35, 38, 44, 50, 58, 66, 79, 80, 99, 101, 113, 124, 129, 131, 134, 140, 144, 161, 168, 169
Twickenham, 197
Tyburn, 44
Westminster, 28, 36, 99, 100, 106
  Abbey, 38, 96, 97
  Palace of, 48, 165, 175
  St Stephen's Chapel, 37, 43
London, Lord Mayor of, 79, 119, 124, 128
Looe, Cornwall, 187, 188
Lostwithiel, battle of, 181
Louis XIV, king of France, 179, 188, 189, 190, 192, 193–4, 195
Louvain, 82, 92
Love, William, abbot of Coggeshall, 63–4
Low Countries, 88, 95, 99, 100, 112, 114, 115, 116, 120, 123, 133, 221n.10
Lowes, John, 14, 182
Lugge, Richard, 115
Lutheranism, 57, 59, 19, 142
Luxembourg, duc de, 196
Lyons, France, 183

Magdalene, John, 32
magic
  astral, 28–9, 30, 121, 125, 126–7, 128, 129, 171 *see also* astrology
  definitions of, 8–12
  learned, 10, 46, 72, 183
  love, 10, 33, 45, 46, 49, 65, 71, 72, 76, 77, 78, 96, 102–3, 108, 109, 121, 133, 135, 188, 191
  natural, 10, 11, 17, 19–20, 105, 160, 170, 171, 172, 183, 198–9
  popular, 16, 78, 94, 105, 155, 184
  ritual, 4, 6, 9, 10, 12, 14, 20, 25, 27, 28, 33, 34, 35, 37, 38, 39–40, 43, 46, 48, 49, 50, 53, 64, 65, 67, 69, 99, 101, 102, 104, 109, 111, 121–3, 125, 127, 130, 144, 146, 149, 160, 161, 162, 163–4, 172, 179, 180, 181, 184, 186, 193, 194, 195, 198, 199, 201, 203
  sympathetic, 12, 20, 28, 40, 56, 76, 125, 127, 155
  see also divination; treasure-hunting, magical; *veneficium*

Mainwaring, Mary, lady Cotton, 102, 218n.38
Maldon, Essex, 137
maleficalia see witchcraft, instruments of
malefice, 13, 71, 77, 78, 94, 108, 110, 162, 180, 186 *see also* witchcraft
Malinowski, Bronislaw, 10
Malleus maleficarum, 118
Man, John, 103
Man, Robert, 99
Mancini, Hortense, 189
Mancini, Olympe, comtesse de Soissons, 189
Mandelson, Peter, 203
Mantell, Robert, 137
Mar, Violat, 155
Maranicho, Stefano, 51
Mareschall, Robert le, 27, 30, 39
Marillac, Charles de, 75
Marlowe, Christopher, 19, 149, 162
Marner, Robert, 33
Marshall, Thomas, 69
Marshalsea prison, 102, 110
Marston Moor, battle of, 181
Martin, Roger, 216n.68
Mary I, queen of England, 21, 57, 59–60, 80–5, 90, 91, 92, 93, 95, 96, 97, 99, 106, 111, 112, 120, 125, 131, 144
Mary II, queen of England, 196
Mary, Queen of Scots, 87, 88, 100, 113, 114, 120, 154–5, 156
mass, 12, 19, 38, 39, 42, 43, 59, 64, 68, 69–70, 81, 82, 96, 98, 99, 100, 102, 103, 106, 113, 189, 190, 191, 192, 193, 194, 195, 228n.35, 36
Massachusetts, 181–2
Maudlin, Dr, 75
Maxwell, John, earl of Morton, 155
Maydland, Dr, 67
Mayhow, James, 65
Mazarin, cardinal, 189
Medea, 149
de Medici, Catherine, 100
medicine, 36, 40, 97, 163, 170, 176
melancholy, 43
Mendoza, Bernardino, 119, 120, 123, 124, 130
Menghi, Girolamo, 126–7, 128
Mesmer, Franz Anton, 199
MI5, 201
Middlesex *see* London
Minucius Felix, 90
misogyny, 94

misprision of treason, 56, 69
moles, 26, 103
monks, 9, 19–20, 32, 40, 63, 66, 67, 70, 71, 95–6, 97, 102, 103
monsters, 19
Montespan, Madame de, 188, 190, 191
Montgomery, François, 190
More, Thomas, 58
Morigny, John of, 9
Mortlock, Elizabeth, 16
Morton, John, bishop of Ely, 49, 50
Morton, William, 163
Morwen, John, 106, 107, 118
Murphyn, Vincent, 132–3, 134, 139–40, 163
Murray, Margaret, 200–1

Nandyk, Thomas, 50
Naples, 159, 172
Naseby, battle of, 181
Navarre, Joan of, 34, 35, 36, 67, 100
Navy, Royal, 187
necromancy *see* magic, ritual
Nectanebus, 33
Neoplatonism, 115, 172, 199
Netherlands *see* Low Countries
Neville, Richard, earl of Warwick, 66
Neville, William, 65–6
New World, 60, 123, 214n.23
newssheets, 181, 182
Newtonianism, 179, 197
Norfolk, 119–20, 129, 131, 163
North Berwick, Scotland, 150, 157, 182
North Nibley, Gloucestershire, 115
Northamptonshire, 47, 143, 167
Northern Earls, Rebellion, 113, 120
Norton, Thomas, 91
Norwich, Norfolk, 40, 120, 123, 124
Nostradamus, 91
Nottingham, 177
Nottingham, John of, 27–30, 31, 39, 105

Oates, Titus, 194
Ockley, Surrey, 78
Œillets, Claude de Vin des, 191
Oglethorpe, Owen, 142
ointment, 51, 52
Orléans, France, 52
d'Orléans, Marie Louise, 189
Osborne, Ruth, 197
Overbury, Thomas, 169
Owen, Henry, 93

Oxford, 44, 48, 93, 116–17, 165
 university of, 37, 67, 73, 92, 97, 99, 112, 165

pact, Satanic, 14–15, 79, 182, 191
 see also witchcraft
Paget, Thomas, 3rd baron Paget
Pampisford, Cambs, 16
Paris, France, 35, 83, 188, 189, 190, 191, 192, 193, 194
Parker, William, 112
Parliament, 25, 32, 33, 49, 50, 56, 60, 62, 74, 76, 77, 78, 79, 80, 81, 82, 85, 87, 95, 108, 109, 110, 140, 162, 165, 173, 174, 176, 180, 194
 Scottish, 155
Parliamentarians, 177, 180, 181, 182, 183, 185, 196
Parma, duke of, 115
Parsons, Robert, 89–90, 107, 116, 117, 118, 144, 153–4
Peacham, Thomas, 169
Peacock, Mr, 168–9, 176
Pecham, John, archbishop of Canterbury, 24
peine forte et dure, 45, 114
Peldon, Essex, 137
penance, 25, 43, 44, 61, 80
Pendle, Lancashire, 164
Percy, John, 173
Percy, Thomas, 7th earl of Northumberland, 98, 100, 113, 138
Perrers, Alice, 33
Perth, Scotland, 161
Petitpierre, Robert, 201–2
Pevensey, Sussex, 34
petty treason, 5, 44, 77, 181
Phillip II, king of Spain, 60, 81, 82, 83, 84, 88, 89, 99
physiognomy, 72
Picatrix see magic, astral
Pilgrimage of Grace, 58, 62, 65, 68, 69, 75
pillory, 99, 100, 102, 104, 107, 108, 116, 117, 163
Pirton, Herts, 143
Pius V, pope, 88
Pliny the Elder, 20
poisoning *see veneficium*
poisons, affair of the, 14, 21, 179, 188–93
Pole, Arthur, 97, 98, 100, 101, 109, 110, 113, 139
Pole, Edmund, 100
Pole, Margaret, countess of Salisbury, 97

Index

Pole, Reginald, cardinal, 59, 60, 91, 92, 97, 98
Popish Plot, 144, 179, 193–4, 195
possession, demonic, 125, 126, 127, 128, 162, 165 *see also* exorcism
Pothay, Richard, 145
Poynings, Nicholas, 115
Poyntell, Rudolf, 99
prayer, 15, 34, 42, 68, 79, 81, 82, 90, 110, 111, 118, 125, 127, 128, 144, 163, 164, 165, 196
preaching, 33, 39, 64, 66, 89, 93, 142, 143, 165, 194
pregnancy, 81, 82, 94
Prestall, John, 87, 91–3, 95, 98, 100, 101, 108, 109, 110, 112–15, 118, 132–3, 134, 139, 140, 144–5, 163, 216n.9
Prestonpans, Scotland, 155, 156
Prideaux, Thomas, 83
priests, missionary, 88
Printing Act (1649), 183
Priuli, Alvise, 92
Privy Council, 32, 35, 36, 37, 38, 39, 47, 48, 74, 80, 83, 84, 91, 93, 96, 108, 109, 115, 119, 120, 123, 124, 126, 127, 128, 129, 131, 132, 133, 137, 138, 139, 140, 149, 176, 194, 200
prophecy, 3, 5, 7, 44, 61–3, 66, 67, 74, 78, 80, 84, 90, 91, 92, 94, 109, 111, 113, 132, 139, 141, 143, 163, 167, 169, 171, 176, 185, 186
Protestantism, 18, 58–9, 60, 81, 87, 88, 90, 91, 92, 93, 94, 95, 99, 102, 106, 107, 116, 117, 120, 123, 125, 127, 129, 130, 132, 133, 135, 142, 143, 144, 150, 153, 154, 155, 164, 165, 173, 180, 181, 186, 193, 194, 195, 196, 203, 214n.31
see also dissenters; Gospellers; Puritanism
providence, 5, 90, 106–7, 118, 158, 182
purgatory, 59, 69–70
Puritanism, 18, 89, 137, 142, 151, 165, 173, 176, 177, 180, 181

de la Quadra, Alvaro, 98, 99, 100
Quick, Juliana, 45

Raleigh, Walter, 144
Ramridge, John, 97
Randall, William, 137
Randolph, John, 34–6, 51, 67

rebellion, 1, 2, 3, 18, 36, 46–7, 50, 58, 60, 62, 69, 75, 76, 88, 95, 98, 113, 120, 123, 156, 161, 163, 166, 182, 186, 196, 197, 202
recusants, 88, 124, 129, 143
see also Catholicism
Reformation, 8, 10, 17, 18, 56, 71, 72, 106, 107, 111, 142, 149, 164, 173
Edwardine, 59, 60, 81, 89
Elizabethan, 87–9, 93
Henrician, 7, 21, 58–9, 60, 69
Restoration of the monarchy, 21, 185, 186, 188, 189, 193
Restraint of Appeals, Statute in, 58
Reynie, Gabriel de la, 188, 190, 192, 194, 228n.41
Reynoldes, John ('Captain Pouch'), 167, 196
Rich, Robert, 2nd baron Rich, 137
Richard II, king of England 32–3, 46
Richard III, king of England, 5, 49–50, 97
Richardson, William, 64
rings, magical, 33, 65, 66, 184
Ripon, Yorks, 138
ritual protection marks, 166
Roche, Mother, 75
Rochester, Kent, 65, 115
Roman Catholicism *see* Catholicism
Rome, Italy, 36, 40, 51, 52, 57, 58, 62, 67, 92
Rookwood, Edward, 129–30
Rotas Square, 103
Royalists, 181, 182, 185
Rupert of the Rhine, prince, 181, 196
Ruthven, John, earl of Gowrie, 161, 196
Rye, Sussex, 64

sacrifice, 93, 104, 184
animal, 102, 103, 104–5, 156
human, 90, 190, 191, 200
sacrilege, 20, 189, 190, 192, 193, 194
St Albans, Hertfordshire, 32
Saint-Cloud, France, 193
St Donats, Wales, 110
Saint-Germain-en-Laye, France, 193
St Ives, Cambridgeshire, 163
St John, Lord, 102
St Loe, William, 103, 107, 109
St Osyth, Essex, 137
Salisbury, Wiltshire, 97, 175
Salisbury, John of, 24
Samford, Thomas, 33
Samlesbury, Lancashire, 164
Sampford, John, abbot of Coggeshall, 63

sanctuary, 38, 62, 141
Sander, Nicholas, 72
Satan, 13, 14–15, 18, 23, 25, 27, 42, 47, 64, 65, 91, 94, 102, 103, 104, 106, 110, 111, 122, 126, 130, 150, 155, 156, 157, 158, 160, 161, 163, 166, 175, 181, 182, 184, 187, 190, 196, 198
Satanism *see* devil worship
Savile, Henry, 189, 190
Sayer, Robert, 96
Schorne, John, 65
scoring above the breath *see* counter-magic
Scot, Reginald, 17, 18, 121, 133, 135–7, 142, 151, 159
Scotland, 2–3, 4, 6, 89, 113–14, 150, 154–61, 164, 165, 167, 176, 180, 182, 197, 203, 211n.53
Scott, James, 1st duke of Monmouth, 195–6
scrying, 65, 143, 197
Sedgemoor, battle of, 196
sedition, 2, 17, 56, 74, 101, 116, 117, 202
seditious words and rumours, act for suppressing, 6, 81, 140–1, 171
Sergeant, John, 196–7
Seton, David, 155
Seville, Spain, 146
Seymour, Jane, queen of England, 73
Shakespeare, William, 21, 146, 166
 Hamlet, 170–1
 Henry VI Part Two, 138, 147–50, 151, 170
 Macbeth, 147, 170, 171
 Richard II, 147
 Richard III, 147, 171
 The Tempest, 172
Shelley, Jane, 146
Sherman, John, 97
ships, sinking of, 156, 172, 182, 187, 188
Shore, Jane, 49, 147, 171
sieve and shears, 78 *see also* divination
Sittingbourne, Kent, 65
smallpox, 101, 109, 163
Smith, Richard, 63
Sole Bay, battle of, 187
Solomon, 20, 66, 210n.17
Somerset, 74
Somersham, Cambridgeshire, 163
sorcery *see* magic
Southminster, Essex, 137
Southwell, Thomas, 37, 38, 39, 40, 42, 43, 44, 46, 49, 51, 148

Southworth, Christopher, 164
de Sowe, Richard, 27, 30
Sowerbutts, Grace, 164
Spain, 23, 30, 57, 60, 81, 88, 89, 100, 112, 114, 123, 134, 145, 167
Spencer, Anthony, 100
Spiritualism, 200
Squier, Edward, 146
Stacy, John, 48
Stafford, Henry, duke of Buckingham, 50
Stafford, Humphrey, 149
Star Chamber, Court of, 61, 84, 101, 104, 109, 168
Starkey, Nicholas, 125
Stearne, John, 182
Stewart, Francis, earl of Bothwell, 156, 157–8, 159, 160, 161, 169, 172
Stewart, Henry, Lord Darnley, 155
Stewart, James, 1st earl of Moray, 114, 155
Stoke Poges, Buckinghamshire, 100
stolen property, magical detection of, 69, 76, 77, 78, 80
Story, John, 111–16
Stowe, John, 117
Stradling, Thomas, 110
de Stratton, Adam, 26–7
Stuart, Charles Edward, 197
Stuart, Henrietta Anne, 189, 193
Suffolk, 129, 137, 187, 216n.68
suffumigation, 41, 128
supremacy, act of, 58, 59, 75, 85, 95, 97, 106, 138
Swineshead, Lincolnshire, 70, 71
Switzerland, 11

Taillebois, Ivo, 23
Tanner, John, 27
Tasso, Torquato, 150
Ten Commandments, 25, 26, 45, 111
Tewkesbury, battle of, 48
Thatcher, Margaret, 203
theatre *see* drama
Thetford, Norfolk, 131
Theobalds, Hertfordshire, 172
Thompson, Agnes, 155, 156
Throckmorton, Nicholas, 99
Thweng, John, 51
toads, 26, 70, 156–7
Topcliffe, Richard, 129, 130
torture, 84, 131, 133, 146, 155, 158, 168, 169, 188, 191–2, 197
Townshend, Henry, 187
Towton, battle of, 47

Index

Tranent, Scotland, 155
treason, definition of, 2, 5–7, 16–20, 76, 81, 112, 116, 138, 176
  constructive, 10, 32, 56, 80, 202
  Statute of (1351), 31–5, 37, 82, 109, 116, 118, 141, 199
  Statute of (1534), 58, 62, 78–9
  see also petty treason
treasure-hunting, magical, 16, 25, 76, 77, 78, 94, 108, 109
Trent, Council of, 110
Trinian, saint, 69
Trojan revenge, 40–1, 121, 123, 148, 184
Trump, Donald, 204
Tudor, Edmund, 50
Turner, Anne, 169
Turner, Robert, 183
Tyndale, William, 59
Tyndall, Gervase, 67

Ucca, Wulfstan, 28
Uniformity, Act of, 95, 96, 100

Vallière, duchesse de la, 191
Valois, Catherine of, queen of England, 34
Vaughan, Fulk, 73
Vaughan, Thomas, 145
veneficium, 10–11, 25, 33, 146–7, 170, 171, 176, 189, 194, 195, 198, 203
Vermigli, Pietro Martire, 93
Verstegan, Richard, 134–5
vices, 70, 75, 76
Vignolles, Bernard de, 51, 146
Villiers, George, 1st duke of Buckingham, 168, 170, 173–4, 175, 176, 177, 180
Villiers, Mary, countess of Buckingham, 168, 170, 174
Vincennes, France, 35
Voisin, La *see* Deshayes, Catherine

Wade, William, 66
Wake, Thomas, 47
Wakefield, battle of, 47
Wakeman, George, 194
Waldegrave, Edward, 96, 110, 217n.20
Wales, 31, 100, 110, 181
Walpole, Henry, 197, 198
Walpole, Horace, 197–8
Walpole, Richard, 146, 198
Walsingham, Francis, 32
Walsingham, Thomas, 111

Warcop, Roderick, 142
Wareham, William, archbishop of Canterbury, 61
Wars of the Roses, 46–51, 66, 87, 97
Warwick, Edward of, 66
Warwickshire, 47, 48, 167
Waterhouse, Agnes, 110, 111, 164
Welwick, Yorks, 68
Wentworth, Thomas, earl of Strafford, 176–7
Westmoreland, earl of, 113, 139
Weyer, Johann, 126, 160
Wharton, Thomas, 96, 110, 217n.20
White, Ronald, 201
Whitgift, William, archbishop of Canterbury, 143, 144
Wicca, 200, 204
wildfire, 115, 145
William I, king of England 23–4
William II, king of England, 200
William III, king of England, 196–7
William the Silent, prince of Orange, 120
Williamson, Joseph, 187
Wilson, Thomas, 124, 129, 132
Wiltshire, 74, 138
Winchester, Hampshire, 81, 115
Windsor, Thomas, 6th baron Windsor, 174
Windsor, Berkshire, 51, 137
Winwood, Ralph, 167
Wisbech, Cambridgeshire, 163
Wisdom, Gregory, 80
witch's mark, 15, 72, 155
witchcraft, 4–5, 6, 8, 9, 11, 12–16, 35, 39, 44–5, 49, 50, 55, 62, 64, 70, 71, 72, 73, 81, 83, 119, 125, 126, 133, 135, 136, 138, 141, 145, 147, 148, 149, 150, 153, 154, 155–9, 160, 161, 166, 170, 171, 172, 174, 175, 179, 180, 181–2, 185–6, 187, 188, 194, 195, 196, 198, 199, 200, 202
  instruments of, 28, 107, 126, 127, 128
  metaphor for treason, 2, 95, 182, 186, 197, 202
  Sabbath, 13
'witchcraft' acts
  of 1542, 76–8, 79, 109
  of 1559 (unsuccessful bill), 93–5
  of 1563, 108–11, 118, 149
  of 1563 (Scottish), 155
  of 1604, 110, 162–5, 186, 197, 203
  of 1735, 197, 200

witchcraft studies, 4
witch-hunting, 5, 18, 118, 129, 137, 151, 164–5, 180, 188
Withers, Fabian, 100
Witton, William, 51
Wodham, William, 44
Wolsey, Thomas, cardinal, 57, 65, 66, 214n.17
Wood, Hugh, 75
Woodham Mortimer, Essex, 137
Woodstock Palace, Oxon, 82
Woodville, Elizabeth, queen of England, 47, 48, 49–50

Worcester, 174–5, 187
Wright, John, 100
Wright, William, 158
Wriothesley, Thomas, 73
Wymondham, Norf, 124

York, 5, 44, 50, 138
York, Richard duke of, 47
Yorkists, 53, 60, 62, 66
Yorkshire, 62, 66, 68, 69, 87
Young, Richard, 145

Zwingli, Huldrych, 59